STRANGE STARS

DAVID **BOWIE**, **POP** MUSIC,
AND THE **DECADE SCI-FI**
EXPLODED

JASON HELLER

🏠 MELVILLE HOUSE
BROOKLYN
LONDON

To the memory of David G. Hartwell,

who first encouraged this book

And for Lyn, my mom,

who showed me music is life

CONTENTS

INTRODUCTION

THE AIR WAS HOT AND CHARGED WITH ELECTRICITY AS I THREADED my way through the crowd at Mile High Stadium. It was August 12, 1987. I was fifteen. And I was there to see David Bowie.

I'd camped out for tickets a few weeks before that. Those were the pre-Internet days, when taking such drastic action was not just the best way to secure good seats at a concert, but the ideal method by which to flaunt your fandom. After standing in line for half a day, I snagged a coveted seventh-row ticket. All I had to do then was wait for August 12 to arrive—easier said than done, especially for a fidgety, high-strung teen.

I can't remember a world without David Bowie in it. My mom had given birth to me when she was still in high school; in fact, August 12, 1987, was her thirty-first birthday. She was a child of the rock 'n' roll age, and being a free-spirited ex-hippie, she flooded our household with music. It was mostly the radio—and rock radio in the '70s and '80s could not play Bowie enough. As popular as he'd become, though, he retained an overwhelming mystique. My mom also loved Lynyrd Skynyrd and Tom Petty, dressed-down rock stars you could easily imagine bumping into at the supermarket. The thought of seeing Bowie at Safeway seemed absurd. He wasn't from here. He wasn't of Earth.

Being like any other reasonable kid who had reached his teens, I rejected the music my mom listened to. Bowie, however, was the exception. Sure, his music belonged to the generation before me. But he'd also reinvented himself in the early '80s as a creature of that decade, one who was both an honored forefather and a vital contemporary of all the new wave artists I loved. One of those bands, Duran Duran, was opening for Bowie that night at Mile High Stadium. They were at the height of their popularity, and I was excited beyond belief to see them. But the gravity belonged to Bowie.

There was another reason why Bowie appealed to me, apart from his ability to remain cutting-edge over twenty years into his career as a recording artist. More than any other singer or band I knew of, he embodied something else I loved, something that, by the age of fifteen, had become stamped onto my psyche as an inextricable part of my identity: science fiction.

I saw *Star Wars* during its first run in the summer of 1977. My grandmother managed a tiny single-screen movie theater in a strip mall in Englewood, Florida, and it was there that one of the defining moments of my life occurred. It's almost embarrassing today to speak so glowingly about seeing *Star Wars*. The experience has been shared so many times, by so many people, it's become rote. That doesn't soften the impact that movie had on me: it filled my entire body, it seemed, with its images and movements and ideas and sounds. I reveled, even at that young age, in its contradictions. It was futuristic, yet it happened in the past. The technology was advanced, yet it was grimy. I had grown up watching reruns of *Star Trek* with my grandfather, but this was nothing like that shiny, gleaming, immaculate tableau. *Star Wars* felt lived-in. As such, it was a place kids could imagine living in. And becoming so much more than they already were.

One of the first records I remember owning was Meco's *Star Wars Theme/Cantina Band*. Being 1977, disco was huge, and I heard those hypnotic beats on the radio just as much as Southern rock. The fact that the orchestral music from *Star Wars* had been turned into disco struck me as profound. I wasn't aware of who made that music or how they did it. But I was shown the eye-opening idea that movies and music were able to have a conversation, and that songs could be a vehicle for science fiction. By the end of the '70s, my ear glued to the radio, I'd begun cataloging such songs in my head: "Rocket Man" by Elton John, "Iron Man" by Black Sabbath, "Space Cowboy" by Steve Miller Band, and a particularly enthralling tune about a wayward astronaut named Major Tom.

IN 1969, DAVID BOWIE RELEASED his sci-fi anthem, "Space Oddity." In 1980, he released its sequel, "Ashes to Ashes." Both starred Major Tom, a spaceman who'd become trapped in his ship, adrift in nothingness, never to touch Earth again. These two songs also neatly bookended the '70s, the decade when sci-fi music came of age.

Bowie had not been the first to sing about space travel. Throughout the '50s and '60s, scores of novelty songs depicted comedic visits from aliens—and although his music was instrumental, the jazz bandleader Sun Ra imbued his albums with cosmic titles, ideas, and sounds. But it wasn't until the late '60s that popular music began taking sci-fi seriously. Granted, it was a time when sci-fi began taking itself more seriously; the age of pulp had faded, and a raft of revolutionary new films and novels were reimagining what sci-fi could do and be. Stanley Kubrick's *2001: A Space Odyssey* and Samuel R. Delany's *Nova*, both from 1968, were among the works that brought fresh depth, nuance, and sophistication to sci-fi. Emboldened, musicians with latent sci-fi tendencies began to follow suit: the Byrds, Jimi Hendrix, Jefferson Airplane, Pink Floyd.

It was "Space Oddity," though, that launched sci-fi music in earnest. Released to coincide with and capitalize on the Apollo 11 moon landing—while also hinting at the title of Kubrick's movie from the year before—the song didn't just contain sci-fi lyrics. Sonically, it was a reflection of sci-fi, full of futuristic tones and the innovative manipulation of studio gadgetry.

"Space Oddity" set off a chain reaction. The '70s began with a wave of progressive rock bands—from hit-makers like Yes to obscure acts like Magma—working sci-fi into their music. Other genres of music followed, each incorporating the motifs of aliens, robots, space exploration, artificial intelligence, and dystopianism in different ways: Krautrock, glam, heavy metal, funk, disco, post-punk. A wholly original school of electronic music emerged. Artists developed and assimilated new technology in the effort to make music sound more like tomorrow: synthesizers, voice modulators, drum machines, samplers. Running parallel to this music were dramatic developments—and setbacks—in the space program, as well as a proliferation of books, films, and eventually video games that changed the face of sci-fi forever.

Star Wars is the first movie that springs to mind when thinking about '70s sci-fi, and Bowie is the first musician. Both are touchstones of the decade's pop culture. As I grew older and became more immersed in sci-fi of all media, though, I began to realize how isolated sci-fi music was. Literature and cinema were taken as serious sci-fi and discussed openly as such; sci-fi music, on the other hand, was still seen as sort of a novelty. After I grew to adulthood and got into music journalism, that out-of-hand dismissal began to frustrate me. The Hugo Awards, sci-fi's highest accolade, honored books, films, and television every year; only on the rarest of occasions did they acknowledge the contribution to the sci-fi canon made by music. When the openly sci-fi songs of artists like Bowie did pop up in the sci-fi discourse, the conversation swiftly pivoted to something else—as if a thorough analysis of sci-fi's influence on music was either tangential or trivial.

I should have been used to it. I grew up before the geek revolution of the twenty-first century, during the '70s and '80s when sci-fi was largely snubbed and dismissed by critics. Good sci-fi, rare as it was, succeeded in spite of being sci-fi: that was the unspoken premise underlying mainstream criticism of the genre. That prejudice carried over to sci-fi music. There were welcome exceptions: Paul Williams, Lester Bangs, Simon Reynolds, and Kodwo Eshun are among the small circle of critics and thinkers over the years who embraced the overlap between sci-fi and popular music. Still, I was at a loss for something that fit all the pieces together—that told the tale of how sci-fi music came to be.

I dreamed up the idea for *Strange Stars* in 2015. Two years earlier, I'd contributed an essay about the influence of sci-fi writer J. G. Ballard on the post-punk scene of the late '70s and early '80s to *Adventure Rocketship!*, a literary journal published by British editor Jonathan Wright. The entire journal was filled with interviews and essays about sci-fi musicians as varied as Mick Farren, Boney M., Parliament, and Be-Bop Deluxe. It was a patchwork, as all good journals are. But rather than slaking my desire for the story of sci-fi music, it whetted it.

Strange Stars was already underway when Bowie died in January of 2016 of liver cancer. There had been no forewarning; Bowie, up until the end, maintained his mystique. I'd never felt the passing of a celebrity with such a sense of loss. It was intensified by the release of *Blackstar*, his final album, which came out two days before his death. Not only was it an incredibly powerful album, it was a return to sci-fi—something Bowie had dipped into only occasionally since the heyday of sci-fi music in the '70s. *Strange Stars* was written in the shadow of his absence, in the void he left.

The story is about more than Bowie, though. His relationship with sci-fi throughout the '70s was a complicated one, and its convoluted path threads throughout the larger tale of that decade's sci-fi music. His story crosses over with those of Hawkwind and T. Rex and Kraftwerk and Devo and the Human League and any number of other artists of the '70s who speculated about the reality of the present or probed the possibilities of the future. Some of them were cult heroes who persisted in singing about outer space when it was obvious career suicide; others were platinum-selling opportunists who jumped on the sci-fi bandwagon the minute it became profitable. Both, to me, are valid and important to the discussion—not only of sci-fi music but of how '70s pop culture forged a special interface with the future. That story begins and ends with two songs about an astronaut named Major Tom: "Space Oddity" and "Ashes to Ashes"—how they came about, what they meant, who they inspired, and why so much happened in the decade between them.

AS THE APPLAUSE DIED AND the crowd of thousands dispersed through the gates of Mile High Stadium, I tried to wrap my head around what I'd just witnessed. Later I'd learn that Bowie's Glass Spider Tour of 1987 was generally considered by critics to be a flop, a bloated and excessive spectacle barely able to disguise the shortcomings of an aging rock star in decline. The magazine *Smash Hits* summed it up pointedly: "If Dame David Bowie is such a bleeding chameleon, why, pray, can't he change into something more exciting than the skin of an aging rock plodder?"

That's not what I saw that night. I saw David Bowie descend sixty feet from a giant spider while lounging in an office chair, casually reciting the ominous opening lines of his song "Glass Spider." I saw a tornado of catsuits, astronaut costumes, and gold lamé. I saw him perform a song from his 1974 sci-fi masterpiece *Diamond Dogs*: "Big Brother," which had originally been intended for a combination album-and-stage adaptation of George Orwell's *Nineteen Eighty-Four*. I saw, in short, a songwriter who loved the wonder and fear and fun and transformation of science fiction—and who, against all odds, had passed that love along to millions. In doing so, he compelled a decade's worth of fellow travelers to explore the farthest reaches of music along with him.

STRANGE STARS

THE STARS LOOK VERY DIFFERENT TODAY: *THE END OF THE '60s*

THE SCREEN BEFORE DAVID BOWIE WAS BLACK. SO WAS THE THEATER.
It was hard to tell where the movie ended and the room began. Against that blackness, images appeared. Astronauts danced a slow-motion, zero-gravity ballet across the cosmic void. A spaceship drifted. A computer spoke with a cold, polite intelligence. And most stupefying of all, a monolith—rectangular and lightless—loomed in the dark, baffling, beckoning.

Stanley Kubrick's *2001: A Space Odyssey* opened in London in May of 1968. At the time, Bowie lived in a modest flat in London's South Kensington. It was a neighborhood full of nightclubs and upscale shops, not far from one of his favorite King's Road boutiques, the aptly named Dandie. There the ambitious, struggling young musician would try on bright, paisley shirts and run the risk of bumping into some of the shop's far more famous clientele, including a flamboyant American expatriate named Jimi Hendrix—a guitar wizard who was known to sing about, among other things, outer space. He wasn't alone. Everyone from the Byrds to the Rolling Stones to Pink Floyd had suddenly started singing about aliens and spaceships. It was as if they were collectively anticipating the United States' imminent Apollo 11 mission, scheduled to land humans on the Moon the following summer.

Bowie didn't wait long to watch *2001*. In 1968, it was the hip thing to do. That summer, Ray Davies, the leader of the Kinks—a group that the Manish Boys, one of Bowie's early bands, had toured with in 1964 when Bowie was still known as Davie Jones—raved about the majestic, big-budget picture. *The Hollywood Reporter* wrote, "[*2001* forces] the question whether our progress in space will merely amplify the depersonalizing congestion, the news and opinion by manipulation, the rote attitudes hopefully left at the launching pad."

It was a challenging film, making the sci-fi cinema that preceded it seem hokey by comparison. To some, drugs were part of the appeal. "I was out of my gourd," Bowie said of his *2001* experience. "I was very stoned when I went to see it, several times, and it was really a revelation to me." In particular, he was transfixed by the imagery of the monolith and its lonely, haunting voyage through eternity.

He and his friend Tony Visconti—a record producer and fellow musician who had moved to London from Brooklyn—partook of marijuana tincture and watched *2001* over and over. For Bowie, who had spent the last few months training as a mime with famed choreographer Lindsay Kemp, the film's vast stretches of elegant silence must have held a special resonance. But Kubrick's latest triumph wasn't simply the next psychedelic craze to Bowie. It called to him. Sci-fi was in his blood.

THE BOOK'S COVER GRABBED THE young David Robert Jones. Illustrated in lurid yellow and green, it depicted a man and woman entering a shadowy forest. Behind them, a spaceship shaped like a giant light bulb perched on the surface of some strange planet. In the sky, alien octopi bobbed like sentient balloons, peering down at the humans with a mix of curiosity and hunger. Written by sci-fi legend Robert A. Heinlein, *Starman Jones* was published in 1953, when Jones was six. It was one of the boy's favorites. He was awed by the fact that the story's astronautical protagonist shared his last name. And who knew? Maybe one day, he might become his own kind of Starman Jones.

Jones's working-class family had just moved to the London suburb of Bromley. His childhood was steeped in sci-fi. In addition to Heinlein, he devoured the work of Ray Bradbury, Theodore Sturgeon, and Isaac Asimov, along with many of the increasingly popular British sci-fi magazines of the '50s and '60s, including *New Worlds* and *Impulse*. Their stories of spaceships from strange planets and technology gone awry countered the doldrums of postwar England.

The BBC's popular Quatermass serials in the '50s helped instill in him a sense of dread about the future. Each installment depicted the stoic rocket scientist Bernard Quatermass beating back the threat of alien invasion, an ever-present specter. Bowie admitted that as a boy he would watch the harrowing adventures "from behind the sofa when my parents thought I had gone to bed. After each episode I would tiptoe back to my bedroom, rigid with fear."

As a teenager, Jones was captivated by the cryptic, spacetime-traversing mythology of a show strongly influenced by Quatermass called *Doctor Who*. The program debuted in 1963. In it, the main character—known only as the Doctor—periodically died and was reborn in a new incarnation that barely resembled the one that came before—an act of metamorphosis that Bowie would employ, again and again, to equally mythic effect throughout his career.

When *2001* came out, the twenty-one-year-old Bowie was still groping toward stardom. He'd played in various bands, including the King Bees, the Manish Boys, and the Lower Third, that made little impact. His unsuccessful solo debut, 1967's *David Bowie*, was a mishmash of styles that confused more listeners than it converted. But it did mark a telling milestone: Bowie's first recorded foray into sci-fi. One of its most bewildering tracks was "We Are Hungry Men." Amid a culture that favored the peace-and-love ideal, the song was anything but sunny.

Musically, it's jaunty and lighthearted, propelled by upbeat acoustic guitars and peals of brass. But the lyrics created a harsh cognitive dissonance The song opens with a frantic, spoken-word setup, voiced by producer Gus Dudgeon, that paints a frightful portrait of a future in which the world's population has soared. From there, things degenerate into fascism, reproductive oppression, and oxygen rationing. It all culminates in a shocking verse in which Bowie, sounding as robotic and despotic as one of the villainous Daleks from *Doctor Who*, exclaims, "I have prepared a document / Legalizing mass abortion / We will turn a blind eye to infanticide!" Ultimately, the whole situation devolves into cannibalism. It's not a far cry from *Make Room! Make Room!*, a dystopian novel by the American author Harry Harrison. The book was serialized in one of Bowie's favorite sci-fi magazines, *Impulse*, in the summer of 1966, before it eventually served as the basis of the 1973 cult sci-fi film *Soylent Green*—with its infamous, Charlton Heston–uttered catchphrase, "Soylent Green is people!"

Bowie recorded "We Are Hungry Men" in November of 1966; the UK serialization of *Make Room! Make Room!* concluded one month before that. Whether the similarities between the story and Bowie's song were a case of direct influence or simply an incredible coincidence, one thing was clear: as humankind hurtled toward putting its first footprint on an extraterrestrial body, Bowie was ready to colonize sci-fi.

✸ **THE TOP-FLOOR FLAT IN THE** house on Redington Road in Hampstead overflowed. Young men and women, equally long of hair, carried musical equipment in and out of the communal residence at all hours of the day and night. The flat overlooked the 790-acre Hampstead Heath, an ancient park full of woodlands and teeming with history. It also happened to be one of the highest points in London, a fact surely not lost on the flat's enthusiastic drug-takers. The Summer of Love, 1967, was in full swing, and London was far from immune to its libertine, bohemian excess. Old mores and lingering repressions were falling away, replaced with a new kind of hedonistic freedom that included sex, drugs, and rock 'n' roll. Although it didn't factor into the stereotype, it also included sci-fi.

Wild-haired and possessing of a wide, wickedly mischievous grin, Alex Harvey, aged thirty-two, was a little older than most of the other hippies who came and went at the Redington house. But he and his new wife, Trudy, fit in perfectly. The place was a haven for musicians, and the Glasgow-born Harvey had been working the London club scene for years as a singer with a reputation for onstage ferocity. Unknown to most of his fans, he also had a quiet side. He read avidly—and much of what he read was sci-fi. Luckily, one of the musicians who hung out at the house shared Alex's love of spectacular stories about aliens and spaceships.

"We knew him around the time he was working with the mime artist Lindsay Kemp," Trudy Harvey said of David Bowie. "He stayed with us for a while, and then just on and off." During Bowie's frequent flops at the Harveys' house, he and Alex would get deep into conversation about outer space and sci-fi. The elder musician also turned Bowie on to an author who would play a large part in Bowie's fusion of sci-fi and music: "Alex recommended that David read Arthur C. Clarke's *Childhood's End*. It was absolutely that atmosphere of flying saucers." One of the flat's other residents, a singer named Lesley Duncan, organized sessions where her roommates and friends would smoke dope, meditate, and gaze out over the vast expanse of Hampstead Heath earnestly hoping to spot the glimmer of a UFO flitting above the primeval woodland.

Childhood's End fed into their quest. Published in 1953, the book posits the arrival of an alien species called the Overlords. Rather than conquering Earth by force, they insinuate themselves into civilization through a series of benign acts; eventually, as humanity realizes how much of its identity its losing, children begin to be born with telepathic powers, heralding a new stage in human evolution.

Clarke's novel was a sensation upon publication, and in the mid-'60s, Stanley Kubrick made an effort to adapt it to the silver screen. That effort fell through—but it led to another collaboration with Clarke, one based on his 1951 short story "The Sentinel," which revolved around a geometric artifact left on the Moon by an alien race long ago. As this new project solidified, its titled was changed. "The Sentinel" became *2001: A Space Odyssey*.

Bowie's fixation on that film involved more than just its trip-augmenting mystery. He was setting himself adrift in a universe created by a sci-fi author he'd already come to admire, and whose alternately awe-inspiring and terrifying visions of humankind's future had begun to shape the young songwriter's view of the world. And of worlds beyond. At some point that summer—with a sci-fi song in the form of "We Are Hungry Men" under his belt, the work of Clarke and Heinlein embedded in his brain, and barraged by constant news of NASA's rapidly accelerating Apollo program—something dawned on Bowie. Maybe he should write a song about space.

IN THE LATE '60S, SPACE was everywhere. It beamed forth from television sets via every episode of *Star Trek*, a series that debuted in 1966 to transform pop culture's vision of space exploration. Created by Gene Roddenberry and written in part by sci-fi authors such as Harlan Ellison and Theodore Sturgeon, the show delved into the United States' hopes and fears about the future and the present. The Cold War tensions between the United States and Russia were encoded in the antipathy between the Earth-based United Federation of Planets and the hostile, alien Klingon Empire. At the same time, it projected the aspirations of the late President John F. Kennedy—who famously vowed in a 1961 speech before Congress to send men to the Moon before the close of the decade—into the uncertainty of tomorrow.

One of *Star Trek*'s boldest statements was entirely implicit: that in the twenty-third century, human beings actually still exist, an increasingly remote possibility to those living through the turmoil of the mid-twentieth. Roddenberry's optimism marked a shift. Up to that point, sci-fi film and television had largely focused on humanity's nobility and virtue—with certain notable exceptions, such as Rod Serling's haunting *The Twilight Zone* and 1968's nightmarish depiction of a subjugated humanity, *Planet of the Apes*. In sci-fi literature, a darker picture was taking shape.

Dystopian fiction had been around for more than a century, a natural outgrowth of the Industrial Era and its rapid infusion of technology into society. But thanks to sci-fi authors, complex and nuanced new ways of speculating about a grim tomorrow were emerging. In 1966, Frank Herbert's *Dune* won the Hugo Award, sci-fi's highest honor, for Best Novel. It eventually became a phenomenon, with millions of copies of the book and the series it spawned in print. The story takes place thousands of years from now, after humankind has spread throughout the galaxy. Yet a new kind of feudalism has taken hold, a regression to the dynastic brutality of the Middle Ages—one whose existence hinges on a single commodity, the spice-like substance known as melange, which was produced by giant sandworms and allowed for the navigation of spaceships between worlds.

From there, dystopia got even weirder. The Hugo winner for Best Novel in 1967 was *The Moon Is a Harsh Mistress* by Robert A. Heinlein, the author Bowie loved so much in his boyhood. But where Heinlein established his career in the '40s and '50s with his juveniles—as his novels for young readers were called—he'd evolved into an entirely different kind of writer by the late '60s. Dripping with libertarian philosophy and skepticism about monogamy and government, *The Moon Is a Harsh Mistress* offered a future in which the Moon has been converted into a penal colony. Revolution ensued—and it paralleled the revolution that was taking place in sci-fi itself. Old ideas about social conformity, propriety, and optimism were being questioned and subverted, and the ensuing freedom opened up liberating as well as frightening new territory. Dystopia was no longer a simple equation of collapse or oppression; it became more subtle, more nuanced, and scariest of all, more plausible.

As provocative as Heinlein and Herbert were, 1968's winner of the Hugo for Best Novel took sci-fi even further. Like *Dune*, Roger Zelazny's *Lord of Light* is set in the remote future, after Earthlings have ventured far into space. Instead of reverting to a quasi-feudal state, though, the descendants of humanity have used technology to engineer and augment their bodies and minds—and in doing so, have taken on the identities of ancient Hindu deities. Bordering on godhood, these posthumans reside in a realm called Heaven. But there's more to *Lord of Light*'s radicalism than its blurring of the line between man and god, or between technology and religion. It also made fuzzy the distinction between sci-fi and fantasy, in a way that embodied Arthur C. Clarke's Third Law of Science Fiction, which he'd devised in 1962. That law states, "Any sufficiently advanced technology is indistinguishable from magic." Zelazny took that idea and ran with it.

Where Zelazny tinkered with sci-fi's thematic conventions, his successor for the Best Novel prize, John Brunner, tinkered with its formal conventions. His book *Stand on Zanzibar* won the Hugo in 1969, and it remains one of the most groundbreaking works in the sci-fi canon. Unrelentingly dark, prophetic, and experimental, it's a disjointed and fragmentary work that combines multiple perspectives, clashing tones, and formats of text. It owed as much to the transgressive work of William S. Burroughs—whose contemporaneous novels *Naked Lunch*, *The Soft Machine*, *The Ticket That Exploded*, and *Nova Express* stitched bits of alien-invasion sci-fi into their grotesque, absurdist fabric. Sci-fi had long been a literature about experimentation, yet rarely had that spirit crossed over into the way it was written. With Burroughs, Brunner, and their peers, the elusiveness of quantum reality was applied to the form itself.

The Hugo Award nominations from the late '60s reflected progress in a different way, most of it long overdue. In these years, the African American author Samuel R. Delany and the female authors Ursula K. Le Guin and Anne McCaffrey snared nominations for their work in a field that had been dominated by white men. The influential editor of the sci-fi magazine *Analog*, John W. Campbell, endorsed the segregationist George Wallace for president in 1968; he also objected to Delany's 1968 novel *Nova* being nominated for the Best Novel Hugo on the grounds that Campbell "didn't feel his reader-ship would be able to relate to a black main character." In 1968, five separate episodes of *Star Trek* swept the entire field of nominations for the Hugo for Best Dramatic Presentation; that same year, the show featured one of televi-sion's first interracial kisses, between the white Captain Kirk and the black Lieutenant Uhura. Although it wasn't the very first interracial kiss on TV, as has often been claimed since, it was a milestone, one that caused no small amount of controversy.

Sci-fi got swept up in the larger cultural conversation. Changes were brewing in the world of spaceships and rayguns, much as they were across the whole of the United States and the UK, thanks to the rise of the countercul-ture, civil rights, women's liberation, the Vietnam War, recreational drug use, and, of course, wild innovations in popular music. Homemade, self-published fanzines such as *Crawdaddy* were launched to cover rock music, but they were patterned after the sci-fi fanzines that had already become ubiquitous in the '60s; in fact, *Crawdaddy*'s founder, Paul Williams, had previously published the sci-fi fanzine *Within*. *Crawdaddy* became a home for rock critics such as Sandy Pearlman, who had also begun collaborating with a Long Island–based band called Soft White Underbelly on songs with sci-fi themes—a band that would soon change its name to Blue Öyster Cult. Samuel R. Delany happened to be a regular contributor to *Crawdaddy* too, as was David G. Hartwell, who would go on to be one of the most renowned editors in the science fiction field. In addition to publishing *Crawdaddy*, Williams became one of the most vocal champions of the author Philip K. Dick, whose reality-challenging novels like 1962's *The Man in the High Castle* and 1969's *Do Androids Dream of Electric Sheep?* were laying the groundwork for a revolutionary new style of sci-fi. These associations would become further entangled, and would bear wondrous fruit, in the decade to come.

Across the Atlantic, Michael Moorcock, a young writer and editor in the Ladbroke Grove neighborhood of London, dragged the venerable sci-fi mag-azine *New Worlds*—another Bowie favorite—into the future by stocking its pages with a dizzying array of envelope-pushing writers, among them J. G. Ballard, Thomas M. Disch, M. John Harrison, and Brian Aldiss. They were collectively dubbed the New Wave of Science Fiction, and like John Brunner, they were inspired in part by the ambiguity and deconstructive darkness of William S. Burroughs. Their stories of hopelessness, moral fuzziness, unre-liable science, social speculation, and the ultimately unknowable universe veered sharply from the intrepid adventure stories of sci-fi's previous decades. Musicians moved freely in Moorcock's bohemian social circle, seeing as how Moorcock played music himself—one of those musicians being a long-haired, sci-fi-loving visionary named Dave Brock, who was getting together a new band that was just about to settle on the name Hawkwind.

Brunner, naturally, was lumped in with Moorcock's New Wave insurrection. The book that beat out Delany's *Nova* for the 1969 Hugo, Brunner's *Stand on Zanzibar*, cannily took sci-fi's fluctuating, late-'60s temperature. Set on Earth rather than among the stars—as if to say, "Don't get used to outer space; we won't last there long"—*Stand on Zanzibar* foresaw, among other things, a futuristic Detroit where squatters in abandoned factories held giant parties and danced to a form of electronic music known as zock. "You could hear a zock group playing full blast under a steel roof five hundred feet long," Brunner wrote. "Didn't need lifting—just stand and let the noise wipe you out."

Amid all the turbulent advances in sci-fi in the late '60s, as summed up by the Hugo Awards of the era, there's a small one that's gone mostly unnoticed. In 1969, in the category of Best Dramatic Presentation, the iconic, rocket-shaped Hugo statuette was predictably and deservedly awarded to *2001: A Space Odyssey*—but one of its fellow nominees was in no way so predictable. *Yellow Submarine*, the 1968 animated film depicting cartoon versions of the Beatles and featuring their music, was also nominated for a Hugo for Best Dramatic Presentation. It was the first time the Hugos had acknowledged the existence of popular music, although it wouldn't be the last. It also made sense that the Beatles, the world's foremost ambassadors of pop, psychedelia, and the emerging counterculture, would be the ones to bridge that gap. Not that they were alone. Bowie was there. And so were others.

THE BOY INSISTED ON BEING called Buster. It wasn't his real name, but that didn't matter. He idolized Buster Crabbe, the blond, square-jawed actor who portrayed the interplanetary heroes Flash Gordon and Buck Rogers in Universal Studios serials of the '30s and '40s. The boy named Buster wasn't blond; he was African American, with a branch of Cherokee in his family tree, possessing a toothy grin and eyes that were wise beyond his years. One night, he and his brother, Leon, saw a disc-shaped UFO hovering in their backyard. After that, Buster began filling pages and pages of paper with drawings of spaceships and cosmic phenomena, even as he kept Leon rapt by spinning stories about "ice ages, burning planets, and the creation of the universe."

Jimi Hendrix eventually outgrew the self-bestowed nickname of Buster. But he never outgrew sci-fi. In 1966, after playing the guitar as a sideman for R & B acts such as Curtis Knight, the Isley Brothers, and Little Richard, he'd decided to go solo. Urged by Chas Chandler, the bassist of the successful British Invasion band the Animals, Hendrix moved to London. There he stayed with Chandler, also a sci-fi fan. Chandler began loaning Hendrix books. "The first one Jimi read was [George Stewart's] *Earth Abides*," Chandler said. "It wasn't a Flash Gordon type. It's an end-of-the-world, new-beginning, disaster-type story. He started reading through them all."

Hendrix also devoured a 1957 novel by Philip José Farmer titled *Night of Light*. In it, a planet orbiting a distant sun is inundated in a mysterious radiation that causes reality to distort. At one point in the story, the sunspots visible from an alien planet are described as having a "purplish haze." Backstage before a concert in 1966, Hendrix began filling pages with a story that had appeared in his head. He later whittled down that tangle of poetry and used it as the core of a new song. His original elements of sci-fi—including, among other things, "the history of the wars on Neptune"—were left on the cutting-room floor. But the song's title retained that vivid, two-word phrase that had jumped out at Hendrix while reading Farmer's *Night of Light*. Hendrix called the song "Purple Haze."

"Purple Haze" became Hendrix's breakthrough hit, but it was only the first of many songs he'd write that were influenced by sci-fi. As Chandler remembers, *Earth Abides* is "where [the Hendrix songs] 'Third Stone from the Sun' and 'Up from the Skies' came from." In these two songs, aliens visit Earth, only to be bemused by what they see. Up to that point, sci-fi in popular music had been strictly novelty. The '50s and early '60s abounded with silly sci-fi rock songs like Billy Lee Riley's "Flyin' Saucers Rock and Roll" and Sheb Wooley's "Purple People Eater." Even *Star Trek*'s Leonard Nimoy capitalized on his newfound fame with novelty albums like 1967's *Mr. Spock's Music from Outer Space*. Hendrix, on the other hand, began drawing deeply from the anxieties, aspirations, and imagination of sci-fi.

As Hendrix's star rose in the wake of "Purple Haze," so did his output of sci-fi music. In "The Stars That Play with Laughing Sam's Dice," he depicts a blood-chilling accident in space. In "EXP," Hendrix's drummer, Mitch Mitchell, assumes the role of an interviewer asking questions of an alien visitor played by Hendrix himself. And in "1983 . . . (A Merman I Should Turn to Be)," a nuclear holocaust unleashes "giant pencil- and lipstick-tube-shaped things" that "continue to rain and cause screaming pain" upon the Earth. The devastated narrator uses a machine to transform himself into an amphibian life-form. Using layers of sonic manipulation, studio trickery, and over-dubbed textures, the music itself takes on an eerie, otherworldly air.

Hendrix's death in 1970 at age of twenty-seven meant he'd never live to see the explosion in sci-fi music over the next ten years. He recorded his final sci-fi song, "House Burning Down," for his 1968 album *Electric Ladyland*. Along with its myriad images of Armageddon is a ghostly mention of a "giant boat from space" that has "taken all the dead away." One can but imagine a boy named Buster being on it.

ONE DAY IN THE MID-'50S, a shy, unpopular junior-high student from Santa Barbara was searching the shelves at the local library. A librarian thrust a book into his hand and said, "Here, try one of these. The kids seem to like these." It was Robert A. Heinlein's 1947 novel *Rocket Ship Galileo*, which chronicled the adventures of three teens on a mission to the Moon. From there, the young David Crosby became addicted to sci-fi, latching on to the work of Arthur C. Clarke, Isaac Asimov, Ray Bradbury, and A. E. van Vogt. "Science fiction was so expansive and so unlimited," Crosby said. "Anything could happen, and that was just rich to me. And I lusted after it."

Crosby eventually became less unpopular. In 1964 he cofounded the folk-pop group the Byrds. One of his bandmates, Roger McGuinn, also happened to be a sci-fi fanatic. Together, they became early pioneers of sci-fi music, alongside Hendrix and Bowie. The Byrds' 1966 song "Mr. Spaceman" was the first hint of their interest in writing rock songs with sci-fi themes. Then McGuinn cowrote a song titled "C.T.A.-102," which took its name from a quasar in a recent Soviet report about radio waves that might signal the existence of extraterrestrial intelligence. It came out in 1967 on the band's *Younger Than Yesterday* album, and the middle of the song wandered into a passage of space-age blips that would have sounded at home in a *Star Trek* episode. "On a radio telescope / Science tells us there's hope," sang McGuinn. "Life on other planets might exist." In *Crawdaddy*, Sandy Pearlman singled out *Younger Than Yesterday*'s use of "science fiction," "electronic stuff," and "technological tongues."

Popular music began taking sci-fi seriously. Not long after the release of

"C.T.A-102," the Byrds caught wind of an imminent film adaptation of an Arthur C. Clarke short story. McGuinn and Crosby being Clarke fans, they wanted in on it. The story was "The Sentinel"—and the adaptation would become Kubrick's *2001: A Space Odyssey*. They wrote a song, "Space Odyssey," with the hope it might make it into the soundtrack. The attempt failed, with Kubrick famously going with a classical-based score centering on Richard Strauss's resounding *Also sprach Zarathustra*. The Byrds' "Space Odyssey" did, however, appear on their 1968 album *The Notorious Byrd Brothers*. It was one of the first rock songs to utilize the Moog synthesizer, invented by Robert Moog, a futuristic-sounding device that had fascinated McGuinn when he saw it demonstrated at the Monterey Pop Festival in June of 1967—spectral, droning, and awash in a psychedelic approximation of astral static.

The trickle of sci-fi in popular music became a stream. At the end of 1967, the Rolling Stones released "2000 Light Years from Home" and "2000 Man," songs that dove far into the cosmos, with Mick Jagger emphasizing the loneliness of being adrift in the void that was outer space—a theme not lost on one Stones fan, David Bowie. Also that year, the British band Nirvana released a concept album called *The Story of Simon Simopath*, a whimsical record about a young man on a surreal journey stocked with goddesses and centaurs. It was more fantasy than sci-fi—but it featured spaceships and futuristic computers in the songs "Satellite Jockey" and "1999." In 1968, the Bonzo Dog Doo-Dah Band released the comical song "I'm the Urban Spaceman," with production credited to Apollo C. Vermouth—the collective pseudonym of Paul McCartney and a studio engineer named Gus Dudgeon, who would go on to produce Bowie's "Space Oddity" a year later. At first, "Urban Spaceman" seems like a novelty song. But at its heart, it's a sharp social critique of the smiling, all-too-perfect American astronaut who, by 1968, was already becoming a marketable icon.

"WE'RE ALL DOOMED!" SCREAMED THE cartoon spaceman, his face a mask of terror. He appears, in all his pop-art glory, on a 1967 poster for a basement nightclub on London's Tottenham Court Road. The venue opened late in '66, where it quickly became ground zero for London's psychedelic movement. Proprietors John Hopkins and Joe Boyd needed a name that would succinctly sum up the otherworldliness of the era, so they chose the moniker the UFO Club. The Bonzo Dog Doo-Dah Band played there in '67, as did a handful of others on the experimental fringe of London's rock scene such as the Social Deviants, the Move, and the Crazy World of Arthur Brown—groups whose members would go on to play roles in the sci-fi music of the '70s. In fact, Mick Farren—the unhinged frontman of the Deviants, as the Social Deviants were known on record—had already begun to dip into sci-fi with songs like "Last Man," a skin-crawling depiction of the lonely life of the final person on Earth following the apocalypse. But like the rest of their UFO Club contemporaries, the Deviants were eclipsed by the venue's most startling group: Pink Floyd.

Swirling with lights and thick with the tang of incense, the air inside the UFO Club felt practically alive. A thin young man with curly hair and a far-away gaze played the guitar and sang. Along with the rest of Pink Floyd, Syd Barrett produced sounds that seemed to be relayed from another dimension. The words he poured into his microphone were like nursery rhymes that aliens sang to their children. His songs had titles such as "Interstellar Overdrive" and "Astronomy Domine"; in the latter, Barrett warned that "stars can frighten."

Barrett was quickly becoming a frightening star himself. His beguiling songs were augmented by the latest technology. Like Hendrix, he used a combination of devices and techniques such as the wah-wah, echo boxes, and feedback to turn his guitar into the musical equivalent of a dimensional portal. "Interstellar Overdrive" and "Astronomy Domine" appeared on Pink Floyd's debut album, *The Piper at the Gates of Dawn*. It was released in August of 1967, just as fellow London residents Jimi Hendrix and David Bowie were finding their own paths into sci-fi music. Pink Floyd toured the UK with Hendrix that year—aided by a gravel-voiced young roadie named Ian Kilmister, who went by the nickname Lemmy—and Bowie saw them play at the UFO Club.

Like Bowie, Barrett grew up influenced by sci-fi. He, too, loved *Quatermass*, as well as *Journey into Space*, another BBC sci-fi show from the 1950s, one that focused on a crew of astronauts exploring the vast unknown and encountering alien species along the way—a premise not far from *Star Trek* a decade later. *Quatermass*, *Journey into Space*, and *Doctor Who* were three of the most prominent British programs featuring sound effects, theme songs, and incidental music supplied by a group called the BBC Radiophonic Workshop. Through the groundbreaking use of electronic devices and recording methods, the Workshop presented a new way to hear the future—a domain teeming with beeps, swoops, and pulses of sound, all manipulated through the sorcery of circuitry.

One of the Workshop crew, Maddalena Fagandini, teamed with a promising record producer named George Martin to venture into the pop market in 1962. The result was a single containing the instrumental tracks "Time Beat" and "Waltz in Orbit," released under the collective pseudonym Ray Cathode, a play on the cathode rays used in television sets. A similar approach was taken on a hit single from that year, "Telstar" by the Tornadoes. An instrumental full of twangy guitars and dedicated to the Telstar communications satellite launched that summer, it also sported a space-warping electronic keyboard played by the song's writer and producer, Joe Meek. It wasn't Meek's first space rodeo. Two years earlier, he released a four-song EP under his own name titled, prophetically, *I Hear a New World*. Subtitled "An Outer Space Music Fantasy" and containing songs about alien races on the Moon with names like the Globbots and the Saroos, the record is a whimsical yet unnerving collage of electronic textures and Meek's yearning vocals. "I hear a new world / Calling me / So strange and so real / Haunting me," he sings on the EP, and his words are made even more poignant by the fact that he suffered from acute depression. For the first time in pop music, but far from the last, the emptiness, loneliness, and existential void of outer space became a metaphor for the darkest reaches of the human psyche's inner space.

Unlike most novelty sci-fi songs of the era, "Time Beat," "Waltz in Orbit," and *I Hear a New World* made valiant efforts to approximate what the future of pop in the emerging Space Age might sound like—and the link between these records and the cosmic explorations of Pink Floyd's "Interstellar Overdrive" and "Astronomy Domine" are clear. Barrett had absorbed cosmic reverberations and modulated echoes from space-themed music as a sci-fi-loving youth in the late '50s and early '60s; he also came of age gripping copies of the sci-fi comic book *Dan Dare*, as well as novels like *Childhood's End* by Arthur C. Clarke—who, coincidentally, had served as a science advisor to *Dan Dare*, which prided itself on its technical accuracy—and Frank Herbert's *Dune*.

Additionally, Barrett was smitten with a 1961 book by Robert A. Heinlein that couldn't have been further from the innocence of Bowie's beloved *Starman Jones*; David Crosby's favorite, *Rocket Ship Galileo*; or Heinlein's other juveniles. Titled *Stranger in a Strange Land*, the winner of the 1962 Hugo for

Best Novel involves a Mars-born human who relocates to Earth, innocent of its ways, before becoming embroiled in politics, mysticism, and decadent superstardom.

Barrett—fueled by drugs, rock 'n' roll, and his own swiftly progressing mental illness, widely believed in hindsight to be schizophrenia—used Pink Floyd as a funnel for sci-fi. Through a twist of synchronicity, Pink Floyd recorded *The Piper at the Gates of Dawn* at London's EMI Studios in early 1967, just down the hall from where the Beatles were recording *Sgt. Pepper's Lonely Hearts Club Band*. The Liverpool stars were aided by producer George Martin, who was bringing some of his Ray Cathode innovations to the Beatles' most adventurous recording to date—a year before their Hugo-nominated *Yellow Submarine*. Martin had been working with the Beatles for a few years at that point, but another producer had been offered the job of nurturing the young Fab Four: Joe Meek, who had turned the gig down. Meek, whose deteriorating emotional state would lead to his death in a murder-suicide in 1967, also rejected the opportunity in the mid-'60s to produce David Bowie.

In June of 1968, Pink Floyd's second album, *A Saucerful of Secrets*, hit the shelves. With his own mental state deteriorating, Barrett appears only sporadically, with most of the vocals taken over by bassist Roger Waters—a sci-fi hobbyist in his own right—along with keyboardist Richard Wright and new guitarist David Gilmour. As with *Piper*, there were two explicitly sci-fi songs on *Saucerful*. The first, "Let There Be More Light," is an account of humanity's first contact with aliens. Barrett didn't appear on the track, but he did contribute to "Set the Controls for the Heart of the Sun." Shimmering and atmospheric, the song combined Eastern philosophy with the sci-fi refrain of its title. Barrett was acquainted with Michael Moorcock at the time, and he once told the author that he was particularly a fan of one of his novels, 1965's *The Fireclown*. In it, the main character aims his spaceship, the *Pi-Meson*, to dangerously skirt the edges of the Sun's corona.

By the time *Saucerful* came out, Barrett had left Pink Floyd. A brief solo career ensued, followed by his retirement from the music business and a complete retreat from society. He died of pancreatic cancer in 2006, a reclusive resident of his mother's home who enjoyed painting and gardening. When *Saucerful* came out, though, one historic event had yet to occur—an achievement that would mark a new chapter in Pink Floyd's evolution, not to mention civilization as a whole.

DAVID GILMOUR STOOD IN HIS flat in London and gazed out the window. It was a warm July night, and London throbbed with the bustle of summer. Above the city, the dark sky glimmered. But Gilmour wasn't looking at the city nor at the stars. His eyes were fixed on the Moon. "There are actually people standing up there right now," the twenty-three-year-old thought in amazement as he faced the threshold of a new reality. "It brought it home to me, powerfully, that you could be looking up at the Moon and there would be people standing on it."

The people standing on the Moon that night were Neil Armstrong and Buzz Aldrin. They had just become the first people to set foot on a heavenly body other than Earth. As Barrett's replacement in Pink Floyd, Gilmour had been grappling with the idea of space travel through song, but the reality of humanity's most profound conquest—the bridging of the distance between worlds—impacted him like no song could. Yet just a few hours earlier, Pink Floyd had been given exactly that impossible task: to create the musical equivalent of Armstrong's "one giant leap for mankind."

On the night of July 20, 1969, Pink Floyd convened at a BBC television studio in London. On paper, their commission seemed simple. Pink Floyd, known for their music about outer space, had to improvise a soundtrack to the most profound event in recorded history: humans walking on the Moon.

As the band set up their instruments and equipment, a panel of scientists was being interviewed on the other side of the studio. They were providing the intellectual context to the night's momentous events; Pink Floyd would provide the sonic. The live series was called *Omnibus*, and like most of the BBC's content that week, it was dominated by Moon-landing coverage. The idea was to have Pink Floyd improvise some instrumental music as live footage of the Apollo mission was broadcast. Gilmour admitted the idea was "a bit off the wall," even for an artsy band like Pink Floyd. But the result was spectacular. The five-minute jam—subsequently titled "Moonhead," although it was never released or even performed again—wound up being, according to Gilmour, "a nice, atmospheric, spacey, twelve-bar blues." That's an understatement. "Moonhead" sounds like a ghost trapped in time. Waters's moody, descending bass line—not dissimilar from "Lucifer Sam," a track on *The Piper at the Gates of Dawn*, or Joe Meek's "I Hear a New World," for that matter—captures the awe of the moment. The fact that the live performance was intermittently overlaid with news announcers giving brief updates on the Apollo astronauts' status only heightens the dreamlike feel. "It was fantastic," Gilmour said, "to be thinking that we were in there making up a piece of music, while the astronauts were standing on the Moon."

Pink Floyd helped spearhead sci-fi music. By the summer of 1969, though, the group realized it had to move in a new direction. "It didn't have a significant impact on our later work," Gilmour said of "Moonhead." "I think at the time Roger, our lyricist, was looking more into going inwards, going into the inner space of the human mind and condition. And I think that was sort of the end of our exploration into outer space."

Following "Moonhead," Pink Floyd restricted themselves to a sci-fi song here and there, such as 1969's "Cirrus Minor" and 1972's "Childhood's End." The title of the latter was taken from the Arthur C. Clarke book loved by Barrett, Bowie, and a significant portion of pop's psychedelic royalty. Imagery of outer space and dystopias would pop up in Pink Floyd's *The Dark Side of the Moon* in 1972 and *The Wall* in 1979, but beyond that, Pink Floyd left sci-fi music almost entirely behind. If it had been solely up to them, popular music's flirtation with sci-fi might have died there, just another curious relic of the experimental '60s.

But one other artist was ready to step in and pick up where Pink Floyd left off. And he was waiting in the wings that same night of July 20, 1969, riding the BBC airwaves as the Apollo astronauts were sitting in a tin can, far above the world.

"GROUND CONTROL TO MAJOR TOM / Your circuit's dead, there's something wrong." Those must have been startling words to hear in a song being broadcast during the BBC's coverage of the Apollo moon landing. Pink Floyd's "Moonhead" wasn't exactly cheery and upbeat, but at least it was instrumental, leaving the song open to the interpretation of the listener. With David Bowie's "Space Oddity," though, the lyrics spelled out everything, leaving no room for doubt: An astronaut named Major Tom has gone into space, only to become stranded due to an equipment malfunction. Trapped in that vacuum, he's "sitting in a tin can," drifting "far above the world," imploring Ground Control to "tell my wife I love her very much, she knows."

"Space Oddity" was released as a single on July 11, 1969, five days before the Apollo 11 launch, and nine days before Neil Armstrong became the first man on the Moon. Bowie hadn't intended the release to coincide that way; he'd recorded a demo of the song in January of that year, and the song's pun of a title couldn't have made it more clear that his main inspiration was all those nights in the cinema spent rewatching *2001: A Space Odyssey*. But Bowie's record label rushed the release of "Space Oddity" so that it might capitalize on the Apollo craze.

The tactic only partially worked. "Space Oddity" was miraculously broadcast during the BBC's Apollo coverage despite it's chilling conclusion, which couldn't have been further from the typical cheerleading of the astronauts that was being conducted by the media. No one was more surprised than Bowie. "It was picked up by the British television and used as the background music for the landing itself. I'm sure they really weren't listening to the lyrics at all," he said. "It wasn't a pleasant thing to juxtapose against a moon landing. Of course, I was overjoyed that they did. Obviously, some BBC official said, 'Oh, right then, that space song, Major Tom, blah blah blah, that'll be great.' 'Um, but he gets stranded in space, sir.' Nobody had the heart to tell the producer that."

Even musically, "Space Oddity" was melancholy. It was an odd mix of folk rock and cutting-edge electronics—including the Stylophone, a stylus-operated keyboard, and a more complicated sampling keyboard called the Mellotron. The former was played by Bowie himself, while the latter was played by a promising twenty-year-old named Rick Wakeman, who had only been in a recording studio once before. On one hand, the narrative of Major Tom and his calamity in space read like a straightforward adventure story out of one of Bowie's treasured pulp magazines. On the other hand, the song's complex arrangement, epic effects, and orchestral impact hinted at the boundlessness of space as well as the murky depths of the human consciousness—two vast reservoirs of darkness.

In a short film for "Space Oddity" made in 1969 for *Love Me Till Tuesday*—a promotional movie that wasn't released until 1984—Bowie's face is cold, serene, composed. It might as well be made of plastic, the artificial flesh of some futuristic android. He's wearing a silver spacesuit. Unlike the bulky spacesuits in the widely publicized photos of the ongoing Apollo space missions, however, this astronaut is clad in sleek, formfitting chrome, so as to enhance rather than obscure his lithe physique. With robotic precision, he dons a blue-visored helmet. There's an air of extravagant vanity to this particular space explorer, as well as one of aloofness. His helmet secure, he steps outside his space capsule. He floats. The void beckons, threatening to swallow our hero. He is not humble. His name is no secret. It's emblazoned on the front of his spacesuit in capital letters: MAJOR TOM.

There are no aliens in "Space Oddity"—those beings would factor greatly in some of Bowie's best-known work to come—but a devastating metaphysical awe underpins the song. Faced with the vastness of the cosmos, Major Tom laments in newfound futility, "Planet Earth is blue / And there's nothing I can do." That ennui, bordering on paralysis, humanized astronauts in a way that NASA's promotional sloganeering failed to do. "At the end of the song, Major Tom is completely emotionless and expresses no view at all about where he's at," Bowie said. "He's fragmenting . . . At the end of the song his mind is completely blown—he's everything then." The influence of *2001* looms over "Space Oddity." "I related to the sense of isolation," Bowie said of the film, which had a "seismic impact" on him, "particularly the final, climactic images of the monolith doomed to float eternally in space."

While Bowie never denied the obvious connection between his "Space Oddity" and Kubrick's *A Space Odyssey*, other works may very well have exerted a gravitational pull on the song. The theme of astronauts lost in space was the premise behind 1953's "The Quatermass Experiment," the first serial in the *Quatermass* series that the young Bowie watched in a state of exhilarating fear from behind his parents' sofa. A more immediate influence may have been "Beach Head," an episode of the BBC anthology series *Out of the Unknown*, which aired on January 28, 1969, the same month Bowie worked on his early demo of "Space Oddity." Based on the 1951 sci-fi short story "You'll Never Go Home Again" by Clifford D. Simak, it's a bleak rejoinder to the more heroic, optimistic portrayal of space exploration offered by *Star Trek*, which was fated to go off the air in June of 1969 due to low ratings. In "Beach Head," an astronaut faced with the mortal terror of the unknown universe suffers a gradual breakdown—one not entirely unlike Major Tom's slow descent into numb oblivion. There's also Ray Bradbury's famous short story "Kaleidoscope." Published in 1951 as part of the collection *The Illustrated Man*—whose framing device, a modern-day fantasy involving a man whose full-body tattoos come alive, was clearly borrowed by Bowie for his 1967 song "Karma Man"—"Kaleidoscope" is the horrific account of the crew of a spaceship who are left adrift in their spacesuits after an accident in orbit. Major Tom would have felt right at home.

Many people, the producers of the BBC evidently included, assumed that since "Space Oddity" was about an astronaut, it must be a positive depiction. Bowie offered no such illusion. "The publicity image of a spaceman at work is of an automaton rather than a human being," he said, "and my Major Tom is nothing if not a human being. ['Space Oddity'] came from a feeling of sadness about this aspect of the space thing. It has been dehumanized, so I wrote a song-farce about it, to try and relate science and human emotion. I suppose it's an antidote to space fever, really." Eventually, though, the BBC caught on. After "Space Oddity" was broadcast on July 20, the song wasn't played on BBC radio until after the safe return of the Apollo 11 crew. With astronauts risking their lives on the most dangerous new frontier imaginable, "Space Oddity" was temporarily considered too controversial for airplay. The single didn't hit the charts until six weeks after its release. It took until November to peak at number five in the UK, thanks largely to an appearance on the popular BBC program *Top of the Pops* that featured Bowie miming the song and playing the Stylophone, interspersed with NASA space footage. In the States, "Space Oddity" flopped. Ahead of its time, it wouldn't find a permanent place in the American psyche until the '70s.

"I want it to be the first anthem of the Moon," Bowie said of "Space Oddity." It wasn't an easy process, but eventually "Space Oddity" proved to be Bowie's pivot from pop hopeful to bona fide star, and it remains the most immediately identifiable sci-fi song in rock history. It also marked a bigger pivot for popular culture as a whole. The hippies promoted a bucolic, back-to-the-land, borderline technophobic way of life, often framed in images of the zodiac and cosmic mysticism; meanwhile, military men in crew cuts were planting American flags on alien soil. As noted by sociologist Philip Ennis, "It is probably not hyperbole to assert that the Age of Aquarius ended when man walked on the Moon. Not only was the counterculture's infatuation with astrology given a strong, television-validated antidote of applied astronomy, but millions of kids who had not signed up for either belief system were totally convinced." The social critic Camille Paglia said, "As [Bowie's] psychedelic astronaut, Major Tom, floats helplessly into outer space, we sense that the '60s counterculture has transmuted into a hopelessness about political reform," citing the lyrics "Planet Earth is blue / And there's nothing I can do."

An even less rosy assessment of "Space Oddity" came from *The Observer* in 1969, whose music critic Tony Palmer wrote that the song was a welcome breath of cynicism "at a time when we cling pathetically to every moonman's dribbling joke, when we admire unquestioningly the so-called achievement of our helmeted heroes without wondering why they are there at all." Ironically, Palmer would go on to produce 1979's *The Space Movie*—a documentary celebrating the tenth anniversary of Apollo 11—at the request of NASA.

Anthem or requiem? Celebration or deconstruction? "Space Oddity" was all these things. According to journalist Chris O'Leary, "Bowie once said he considered the fate of Major Tom to be the technocratic American mind coming face-to-face with the unknown and blanking out. His song was a moonshot-year prophecy that we would lose our nerve and sink back into the old world, that we aren't built for transcendence, that the sky is the limit." At the same time, it was embraced as the defining song of the Space Age—one full of beauty, horror, awe, and imagination, and a rethinking of our position in the universe, all the feelings that the best of sci-fi meant to elicit.

With "Space Oddity," Bowie set himself up for even greater sci-fi statements to come. But he had one more to deliver before the '60s were through. Recorded in August and September of 1969, right after the moon landing, and released in November, just as "Space Oddity" was peaking on the British charts, "Cygnet Committee" was his most ambitious song to date. Clocking in at almost ten minutes, it's a melodramatic, melodically meandering song steeped in a profound sadness and disappointment in failed idealism. Years from now, a utopia has collapsed, betrayed by its own ostensibly compassionate ideology. "A love machine lumbers through desolation rows," he sings, "Plowing down man, woman, listening to its command / But not hearing anymore." If "Space Oddity" cryptically augured the demise of the hippie era, "Cygnet Committee" made that point more brutally, encasing it in the blunt messaging of dystopian fiction. The future was barreling down on Bowie— and like the heroes of *Starman Jones* and the other sci-fi novels of his youth, he was either going to conquer or be conquered by it.

THE UNITED STATES WASN'T YET ready for Bowie's space song. A different single sat atop the American pop charts the day that Neil Armstrong set foot on the Moon. It was, however, also a sci-fi song. "In the Year 2525" became a million-selling hit in 1969, written and performed by the Nebraska folk-rock duo Zager and Evans, and its speculative scope made "Space Oddity" pale in comparison. A journey through time rather than space, the song hallucinates what the future might look like between 2525 and 9595, hurtling through the eons as it catalogs the escalating ills of our technological dependence, up to and including genetic engineering.

There's a darkly humorous silver lining to Zager and Evans's predictions: "In the year 2525, if man is still alive," goes the song's opening line. In other words, mankind might mercifully become extinct before all these nightmares come to pass.

Of the sci-fi songs that closed out the '60s, "In the Year 2525" wasn't the only one with a pessimistic view of tomorrow. The 1969 song "21st Century Schizoid Man," by British progressive rock band King Crimson, detailed a future where "Neurosurgeons scream for more / At paranoia's poison door." Guitarist Robert Fripp and bassist-vocalist Greg Lake would wind up having more parts to play in the sci-fi music of the coming decade, but in 1969, "21st Century Schizoid Man" served as a wake-up call for the flower-power generation yearning for utopia. The Los Angeles band Spirit went straight to the source. They based their 1969 song "1984" on the canonical dystopian novel by George Orwell, a book that would also factor heavily into Bowie's sci-fi music of the '70s.

Also in 1969, San Francisco's Steve Miller Band released "Space Cowboy," a propulsive song that rejected Haight-Ashbury's peace-and-love ethos—"And I'm tired of all this talk about love / And the same old story with a new set of words"—only to replace it with the joys of "traveling through space" as a space cowboy, as if returning to the pulp pleasures of '50s sci-fi. Incidentally, it also recalled Gene Roddenberry's original pitch for *Star Trek* as a sci-fi Western, specifically, "*Wagon Train* to the stars."

In England, it didn't take long for two bands to pick up where "Space Oddity" left off. A young group called Smile released a promotional single in 1969, "Earth," that failed to go anywhere, despite its unabashed homage to Major Tom; its narrator is an unnamed astronaut who has been "Cast adrift amongst the stars / I float from sun to sun." An early version of Smile had gone by the name 1984, taken from the Orwell novel; the guitarist of both 1984 and Smile, Brian May, was an avid sci-fi reader who would one day earn a doctorate in astrophysics. He was also destined to be a rock star. Along with Smile's bassist Roger Taylor, he would form Queen in 1970, a band with its own relationship to sci-fi.

The otherworldly sound of the Mellotron that Rick Wakeman played on "Space Oddity" surfaced in a more substantial way at the end of 1969. A London-based keyboardist named Mike Pinder worked for Streetly Electronics, the company that manufactured the Mellotron, which he'd been using to dramatic effect in his band the Moody Blues. The group released the album

To Our Children's Children Children in November, and Pinder's innovative instrument of choice lent a cosmic quality to the record's sumptuous soundscapes; it even simulates the liftoff of a rocket on "Higher and Higher," the album's opening track. Aptly, *To Our Children's Children Children* was directly inspired by the Apollo 11 moon landing. "When Neil Armstrong took that small step for us all, it inspired me to write ['Higher and Higher']," said the Moody Blues' Graeme Edge. If Bowie's "Space Oddity" captured the angst of humanity severing its umbilical cord to Earth, *To Our Children's Children's Children* threw out a rope of wonder for our newly spacefaring species to ascend into the future. Flush with the comingled anticipation, apprehension, and existential turbulence that followed Apollo 11, the Moody Blues came close to crafting popular music's first fully realized sci-fi concept album. But as inspired by space as *To Our Children's Children* was, its lyrics didn't contain enough actual sci-fi to qualify it for that distinction. Within months, though, other bands would succeed where the Moody Blues fell just shy.

"And the stars look very different today," marvels Major Tom as he stares out the porthole of his capsule in "Space Oddity." He's talking, of course, about astronomical stars—the way our view of the universe had shifted since we'd penetrated space and made sci-fi real. But after the success of David Bowie, the Byrds, Jimi Hendrix, and Pink Floyd in the late '60s, stars of the musical kind would start to look, and sound, very different as well.

DANCING ASTRONAUTS OF RENOWN: *1970*

THE FINAL WEEKS OF 1969 WERE HECTIC FOR GEORGE LUCAS. IN November, the twenty-five-year-old filmmaker finished shooting his first feature, *THX 1138*—an expansion of his sci-fi short film *Electronic Labyrinth: THX 1138 4EB*, which he'd made in 1967 while attending the University of Southern California. Although *THX 1138* wouldn't be released until 1971, Lucas was already enjoying some industry buzz. *Electronic Labyrinth* had taken first prize at the 1967–1968 National Student Film Festival, which led to a scholarship from Warner Bros. They saw a rising star in Lucas, and so did a young director named Francis Ford Coppola, who formed the studio American Zoetrope with Lucas in order to produce the feature-length *THX 1138*. Set in the twenty-fifth century, the film imagines a cold, repressive society where sex is outlawed, mood-regulating drugs are mandatory, and police androids enforce draconian law. Lucas filmed *THX 1138* in and around San Francisco— channeling the antiauthoritarian tone that suffused the city during the height of Haight-Ashbury as the tumultuous '60s drew to a close.

On Saturday, December 6, 1969, soon after the filming of *THX 1138* was done, Lucas took a side gig manning a camera at the Altamont Speedway in Tracy, California, not far from his hometown of Modesto. He was a fan of cars, but he wasn't filming a race; instead, almost a third of a million rock fans had converged on the Speedway to take part in the Altamont Free Festival. It was conceived as "Woodstock West," an answer to the momentous outdoor concert that took place in upstate New York, that summer. The Altamont bill featured some of the biggest bands in rock: the Rolling Stones; Santana; Crosby, Stills, Nash & Young; the Flying Burrito Brothers; and Jefferson Airplane, the San Francisco outfit that had organized the concert. Luckily, Lucas liked rock music as much as he liked cars. Unluckily, his camera malfunctioned while he was filming the concert. None of his footage made the final cut of *Gimme Shelter*, the 1970 documentary based on the concert and its tragic climax: the stabbing death of eighteen-year-old attendee Meredith Hunter by one of the Hells Angels hired to provide security at the event.

To many, Altamont represented the end of the idealistic '60s, drenching the psychedelic dream in chaos and blood. In its own way, *THX 1138* also dispensed with the '60s, turning its drugs-and-free-love ethos upside down with a cynical jolt of alarmism. Lucas was still years away from creating the work of science fiction that would revolutionize not just the '70s but popular culture in perpetuity. But at the dawn of the decade, another Altamont participant was writing a saga about a galactic rebellion at war with an evil, oppressive force. That someone was Paul Kantner, one of the founding members of Jefferson Airplane. And the sci-fi album Kantner released in 1970—long before Lucas made *Star Wars*, let alone *The Empire Strikes Back*—was called *Blows Against the Empire*.

SKINNY AND BESPECTACLED, PAUL KANTNER couldn't have felt more out of place at St. Joseph's Military Academy. He was eight years old. His mother had just died of polio. His traveling-salesman father sent his grief-stricken son to St. Joseph's, a Catholic boarding school under the direction of the Sisters of Mercy in Belmont, California, after preventing the boy from attending his mother's funeral. "I was an abandoned child," suddenly surrounded by "nuns and guns," he later said. The twenty miles separating Belmont from Kantner's bustling birthplace of San Francisco might as well have been twenty light-years. There, the bright, inquisitive kid withdrew and grew solitary. His imagination became his oasis. Then one day, in third grade, while left alone in the school library, he discovered something that electrified his young psyche: science fiction.

By the time Kantner turned twenty-four in 1965, he'd become a connoisseur of sci-fi. Among his favorites were the heady novels of Theodore Sturgeon, Kurt Vonnegut, John Wyndham, Robert A. Heinlein, Arthur C. Clarke, and Isaac Asimov, books that defied convention and posited possible futures of the human race. He'd also formed a rock band: Jefferson Airplane. After a pair of hits in 1967, "White Rabbit" and "Somebody to Love," the group became the darlings of the San Francisco scene and icons of the counterculture, thanks largely to lead singer Grace Slick's indomitable voice and presence. Along with his generation, Kantner immersed himself in psychedelics. The first time he played guitar on LSD, he "went off into the cosmos." Instantly, the dizzying sense of infinite possibility—or "alternate quantum universes," as he called them—that science fiction had opened up in his mind as a child became much more navigable. To him, San Francisco's rejection of social reality in favor of a utopian ideal via free love, psychotropics, Eastern philosophy, and antiwar pacifism represented "our new parallel universe." Accordingly, Jefferson Airplane's music was "a reflection of the quantum." Coming from your average stoned hippie, that might have sounded like gibberish—but Kantner's grounding in sci-fi substantiated his connection between the psychedelic and the cosmic.

Still, it took a year after Jefferson Airplane reached a higher altitude of mainstream success before Kantner dared to inject sci-fi into their music. The song was "Crown of Creation," and Kantner was not coy about its source material. Appearing on the 1968 album of the same name, "Crown of Creation" drew directly from *The Chrysalids*, a 1955 novel by the English author John Wyndham that revolves around a community in Labrador long after an apparently nuclear apocalypse has reduced humanity to nineteenth-century levels of technology—a community that has become obsessed with maintaining eugenic purity. Kantner lifted entire lines from the book—one Wyndham quote in particular, "In loyalty to their kind they cannot tolerate our rise; in loyalty to our kind, we cannot tolerate their obstruction," was tweaked only slightly, with Kantner switching the word "rise" to "minds"—but he happily sought permission from Wyndham, which the author granted. "I have thousands of influences in literature and find it a turn-on to leave a little thing like that for people to find," Kantner said, "and then go to the writer who it came from and read it to him."

Another passage from the book furnished Kantner's title for the song, and another piece of the lyrics: "They are the crown of creation, they are ambition fulfilled—they have nowhere more to go," Wyndham wrote. "But life is change, that is how it differs from rocks, change is its very nature." In the book, a group of telepaths must conceal their genetic abnormality from their close-knit society or risk persecution; it's not hard to see why Kantner, at the forefront of the culture clash between the rigid American establishment and the libertine hippie paradigm, saw parallels between *The Chrysalids'* persecuted sensitive-types and his own friends, fans, and band.

Kantner had a musical ally outside his group. In 1963, while living in Venice, California, before the founding of Jefferson Airplane, he played the folk circuit and roomed with David Crosby. They also had a love of science fiction in common. Katner remembered, "We were trying to make a living being folkies. We'd all read *Stranger in a Strange Land* and we kept all our money in a bowl, on the mantelpiece—if you got some you put it in there, and if you needed some you took it out."

By the time "Space Odyssey" was released in 1969, Crosby had left the Byrds, in part over a creative disagreement about a new song he'd written called "Triad." On the surface it was a celebration of a ménage à trois, an arrangement Crosby, in the full swing of free love, was more than happy to promote. But it also reflected Heinlein's own views toward polyamory, which became a recurring theme in his novels starting with the book that Crosby and Kantner used to read together in Venice in 1963: *Stranger in a Strange Land.* Direct references from *Stranger* pop up in Crosby's "Triad," including mentions of "sister lovers" and "water brothers," two terms Heinlein uses in the book. Following his departure from the Byrds, Crosby gave "Triad" to Kantner as a gift—and Jefferson Airplane recorded the song, which appeared on the *Crown of Creation* record.

Kantner and Crosby's collaboration on sci-fi music was far from over. On Crosby's yacht off the coast of Florida in 1968, the former Byrd picked up an acoustic guitar and started jamming with his guests, Kantner and Stephen Stills. Together, the three wrote a song titled "Wooden Ships." Crosby had recently formed the supergroup Crosby, Stills & Nash, and both CSN and Jefferson Airplane released versions of the song in 1969. It remains one of the most haunting sci-fi anthems in the rock canon. Unlike "Crown of Creation" and "Triad," it makes no reference to works of sci-fi literature; instead, it aspires to be one itself. Set in a future ravaged by a nuclear holocaust, it's a conversation about survival and loss in the midst of a horrific new world—a setting that evokes *The Chrysalids*, although the lyrics are too vague and impressionistic to allude to an exact time or place. "[We] imagined ourselves as the few survivors, escaping on a boat to create a new civilization," Crosby said. Along with the triumph of the space program and all it heralded for humanity going forward, 1969 was still mired in the threat of Cold War annihilation—the flip side to the rocket craze of the '60s. Missiles might carry astronauts away into space, but they also might carry warheads to obliterate the world beneath them.

For the Airplane version of "Wooden Ships," Kantner added a prelude, which was printed on the album's lyric sheet but not sung on the recording. That prelude establishes a far more specific and detailed scenario than does CSN's version—an inspired bit of worldbuilding on Kantner's part:

> *Black sails knifing through the pitchblende night*
> *Away from the radioactive landmass madness*
> *From the silver-suited people searching out*
> *Uncontaminated food and shelter on the shores*
> *No glowing metal on our ship of wood only*
> *Free happy crazy people naked in the universe*
> *WE SPEAK EARTH TALK*
> *GO RIDE THE MUSIC*

During the same year that David Bowie's "Space Oddity" offered a futurist melodrama of disillusionment, disorientation, and dysfunction in outer space, two recordings of "Wooden Ships" did the same—only here on Earth. But unlike the bleak detachment of "Space Oddity," "Wooden Ships" glinted with grim hope, similar to the tone found in the work of the legendary sci-fi author Theodore Sturgeon, a hero of Crosby's. So it's no surprise he and Stills hired Sturgeon in 1970 for an ambitious undertaking: they wanted "Wooden Ships" turned into a screenplay. In addition to his stature in the world of sci-fi literature—he'd been publishing stories since 1938 and was widely anthologized and acclaimed—Sturgeon had scripted two episodes of *Star Trek*, 1966's "Shore Leave" and 1967's "Amok Time." He was also a musician himself, who regularly played his guitar and sang at sci-fi conventions, part of a small movement of sci-fi singer-songwriters in the '50s and '60s who established what eventually became known as filk. A subgenre of folk music written around sci-fi and fantasy themes, filk is often played communally at fan conventions.

"I met Ted Sturgeon in 1970," Crosby wrote in his introduction to Sturgeon's short story collection *Baby Is Three*. "He was an unusual guy. He wasn't all cosmic and airy-fairy in how he thought about things. He was actually sort of acerbic and funny and had a great kind of wry wit about stuff. But he could conceive idealism on a level that most other people couldn't get to." Crosby found in his hero a kindred spirit. Work began in earnest on the "Wooden Ships" screenplay. Stanley Kubrick, a hotter commodity than ever since the sensational success of *2001*, was even floated as a possible director for the film adaptation, which might have been a neat bit of vindication for Crosby, seeing as how the Byrds had failed at getting their song "Space Odyssey" onto the soundtrack of *2001*. Said Stills, "It won't be an Arthur C. Clarke screenplay, so it won't have the same cold feeling as *2001*—I hope it will be more like Kubrick's earlier films, with the characters laid out so well." Unfortunately, the project fell through during the scripting process. "It was a nightmare for [Sturgeon]," Crosby said, "because each guy would get him alone and tell him how *he* wanted the script to be . . . We were all such complete egotists by that time, and living so much in our own universes."

When Crosby, Stills, Nash & Young performed "Wooden Ships" at Woodstock on August 18, 1969—the day after Jefferson Airplane played their version—Crosby prefaced the performance with a disclaimer to the crowd: "We're gonna do kind of a science fiction story, if you'll bear with us." He reiterated that in 2008, telling *Rolling Stone* that "Wooden Ships" was "definitely a science fiction song, no question." But as much as hippie ideals, the effects of LSD, and science fiction blended inside the brains of Crosby and Kantner, they seemed to instinctively understand that the world at large wasn't quite yet ready for fully realized sci-fi rock. Even when CSNY's newest member, Neil Young, released his own postapocalyptic opus in 1970, "After the Gold Rush," he granted a great amount of poetic license to its description of the human race leaving its cradle and "flying Mother Nature's silver seed to a new home in the sun," as if to soften the blunt impact of science fiction on a generation still shrouded in utopian mysticism.

"After the Gold Rush" was inspired by a script written by Dean Stockwell for a proposed film called *Gold Rush*. Young agreed to develop some songs for the soundtrack, but the project fell through, leaving Young to recycle "After the Gold Rush" for his album of the same name. Stockwell's original premise for *Gold Rush* was markedly apocalyptic—"It was sort of an end-of-the-world movie"—and Young himself said of the song's doomsday, time-travel, space-ark premise, "There's the future . . . The air is yellow and red, ships are leaving, certain people can go and certain people can't . . . I think it's going to happen."

Kantner wrote and recorded his next sci-fi song with Jefferson Airplane in 1970, "Have You Seen the Saucers?" It marked a turning point. Rather than mysticism and awe, it's flush with anger. Alien visitors have come down to Earth and have grown distraught at the way humanity has abused its planet. It is a message of ecological alarmism and self-criticism that pulls no punches and minces no words. The boy who'd been abandoned to a military school had grown up to adopt his own kind of militancy.

In November of 1970, with the '60s and all that the decade stood for receding in the rearview mirror, Kantner produced a more ambitious piece of sci-fi music that peered relentlessly into the future with greater acuity and curiosity, not to mention greater length. The result was *Blows Against the Empire*. He released the album under the name Paul Kantner and Jefferson Starship, and the contrast with the Jefferson Airplane moniker made a stark statement. With humans visiting the Moon and science fiction plotting a path toward the cosmos, airplanes were contraptions of the past. Starships belonged to tomorrow.

"We are the future / You are the past," Kantner sings on "Mau Mau (Amerikon)," the scathing opening track of *Blows Against the Empire*. He's speaking to a generational shift, but later tracks greatly expand the scope. As the album unfolds—sometimes raw and propulsive, other times delicate and ethereal—a sci-fi story begins to take shape. "The Baby Tree" alludes to both genetic and social engineering. "Sunrise," sung by Jefferson Airplane's frontwoman (and Kantner's romantic partner at the time) Grace Slick, is a dirge condemning the human race's bent for destruction.

It's the album's second side, though, where Kantner's story comes fully into focus. In "Hijack," he outlines a plan—to take over a spaceship and carry humanity away like some kind of space-bound Noah's Ark, and escape the oppression of Earth. There, among the stars, "more than human can we be." Two brief instrumental interludes, "Home" and "XM," are collages of cosmic static and blastoff effects—incidental in and of themselves, but remarkable in their jarring break from the more organic sounds of '60s psychedelia. The heart of Kantner's sci-fi concept, however, lies in "Have You Seen the Stars Tonite?" and "Starship." The former song was cowritten by David Crosby, and it depicts a pensive soul on the deck of the hijacked spaceship, staring out into the universe and pondering life, love, and humanity's place in the grand scheme of existence. Said Crosby of the song's creation, "[Writing sci-fi music] isn't an easy thing to do. It's easier to write about love, because we all experience it, and because it has such a wide spectrum. Whereas wonder for the universe happens to a person only when they get out on a clear night in a place like the high desert, or out on the ocean is where I've seen it. They look up, and all of a sudden it comes on them, and they realize: Wait a minute, I'm standing on the side of a tiny mudball. And they're starstruck. That's the moment I wanted to try to communicate."

For his part, Kantner's evangelic view of human evolution—and space exploration's vital role in that process—comes to a climax in "Starship." The album's closing track, it projects humankind into the far reaches of spacetime, gravity-less and with "a million pounds gone from your heavy mass." Caught up in the escape velocity of his own righteous futurism, he pictures galactic lakes and gardens with "Room for babies and Byzantine dancing astronauts of renown."

Up to that point, the rock establishment hadn't seen anything like *Blows Against the Empire*. It was the first true sci-fi concept album by a major rock band—or at least portions of a major rock band, as it was still billed as a Kantner solo album. Along with Kantner, Slick, and various other members of Jefferson Starship (née Airplane) pitching in, Crosby played on the record, as did Jerry Garcia, Bill Kreutzmann, and Mickey Hart of the Grateful Dead, a band very close with Jefferson Airplane.

Two year earlier, Garcia—a sci-fi fan himself—had led his band to record "Dark Star"; like so many '60s sci-fi songs, it drew parallels between the anticipation and apprehension of humanity's escalating space race with the psychedelic search for meaning and oblivion found in the hippie counterculture. The lyrics—written by the Dead's frequent collaborator Robert Hunter, who, years later, would write a sci-fi novel, as yet unpublished—poetically blended astrophysics with the obscure workings of the subconscious.

Kantner also once again honored his sci-fi roots. As he'd done with John Wyndham, the author who had inspired "Crown of Creation," he contacted a writer who had influenced *Blows Against the Empire*: Robert A. Heinlein. In particular, Heinlein's 1958 novel, *Methuselah's Children*, had served as a partial basis for *Blows*. The book depicts a certain type of spacecraft—a "generation ship," as they're called in science fiction—built to nurture a community of human passengers for centuries. Heinlein genially granted Kantner permission to have his work cited as a loose blueprint for *Blows*, and the author was duly thanked in the liner notes of the album, along with Kurt Vonnegut and Crosby's acquaintance Theodore Sturgeon. The lonely kid in the library of St. Joseph's Military Academy had become more than just an imitator of his heroes. He'd become a fellow traveler.

BLOWS AGAINST THE EMPIRE WAS a daring, pivotal, groundbreaking sci-fi concept album in the canon of popular music. But it can't be called the first. In June of 1970—a full five months before *Blows'* release and minus the fanfare associated with a major rock act like Jefferson Airplane— shopkeepers across Great Britain unassumingly stocked their shelves with an album titled *A Time Before This*. The group who made it called themselves Julian's Treatment. Led by a Dominican-born songwriter named Julian Jay Savarin, the band was not well-known. Nonetheless, *A Time Before This* was an ambitious double album. The first bloom of progressive rock was underway, and a host of bands inspired by Pink Floyd, the Moody Blues, and others were bravely expanding the format of the rock album. Taking cues from the scope and structures of classical music and jazz, this new movement of progressive rock—prog, for short—sought to free itself from the bounds of the single-length pop song. Rather than crafting short, catchy ditties to snare the ear of radio programmers, prog artists wanted their albums to stand as works of art on par with classical compositions and novels. It made perfect sense that musicians of the late '60s and early '70s who also happened to love science fiction would be drawn to prog, where musical and literary ambition collided.

A Time Before This set the bar high for the genre. Listed explicitly as a sequence of twelve chapters that also mirror movements of a suite, the record tells a story of alien contact, galactic turmoil, prophecies, and the slipstreams of time. Savarin's lyrics, delivered by a fellow immigrant, Australian Cathy Pruden, are abstract and atmospheric, yet his song titles hint at specific characters and settings, not to mention a carefully constructed underlying narrative: "Phantom City," "Alda, Dark Lady of the Outer Worlds," "Twin Sun of Centauri." One song, "The Coming of the Mule," alludes to Savarin's grounding in sci-fi literature: the Mule is the name of a character from Isaac Asimov's Foundation series, a sweeping saga of human survival among the stars that won a special Hugo award in 1966 for Best All-Time Series.

"I used to write science fiction stories as a hobby," Savarin told *Melody Maker* in 1970. Throughout the brief article, his name is consistently misspelled as "Savarim," underscoring his dearth of fame. "And then I started writing a book which starts with the colonization of Earth and takes in my ideas of the past, present, and future. When the whole thing is completed it will be in three albums. The lyrics of the song tell the story." Not only was Savarin planning on a trilogy of sci-fi albums, he already had ambitions of adapting the concept behind *A Time Before This* into a trilogy of sci-fi novels. He accomplished this with the 1972 publication of his debut novel *Waiters on the Dance*, the first installment of his Lemmus: A Time Odyssey trilogy. The second and third books, *Beyond the Outer Mirr* and *The Archives of Haven*, followed in 1976 and 1977. Julian's Treatment never released another album, but Savarin issued a solo album in 1973 titled *Waiters on the Dance*, a companion to the novel. None of them made a significant mainstream impact, and *A Time Before This* has gone largely unrecognized, even among fans of sci-fi music, as rock's first true sci-fi concept album.

Even in 1970, Savarin knew his passion of melding sci-fi and music was going to be a hard sell. Like many pioneers, he was also a little too optimistic that he'd soon be vindicated. "Of course the music is strange to the audiences, and I know you can't tell people that you're out to educate them . . . The music hasn't got an instant appeal, and I honestly expect people not to like it at first, but I'm confident that it will be accepted. It is very appealing mentally and is a mental stimulative. It isn't really danceable music, but you can work up a sweat just as well mentally as you can physically."

Savarin suffered the fate of being just slightly ahead of the curve—a trajectory shared by a Frenchman named Christian Vander. In the waning days of 1970, the drummer and composer issued a self-titled album by his band, Magma. One of the most technically adventurous prog outfits at the time, Magma specialized in complex time signatures, abrupt shifts in tone and dynamic, and an approach to rock music that made room for song lengths upward of thirteen minutes. Like Julian's Treatment's *A Time Before This*, Magma's *Magma* was a double album. And like *A Time Before This*, it was a sci-fi concept album.

Unlike Savarin, though, Vander wasn't greatly influenced by the existing canon of science fiction. No Asimov references abounded in Magma. Instead, Vander invented an entire sci-fi cosmology out of whole cloth. Along with it he invented an entire language, dubbed Kobaïan, after the alien world he conceived for the setting of his songs, Kobaïa. In a review of a Magma concert in the '70s, a young Chrissie Hynde, years before she formed the Pretenders, remarked, "The vocalist assumes the stance, seemingly, of an intergalactic interpreter."

The story line of *Magma*—later retitled *Kobaïa*—is a gripping allegory. In it, our civilization has advanced greatly over the centuries. Yet for all its mastery of technology and space travel, its spiritual core has become hollow. Similar to the exodus Paul Kantner depicts in *Blows Against the Empire*, humans depart on a starship in order to found a more enlightened world—in this case, Kobaïa. The story continued over the course of Magma's next few albums, but eventually Vander dropped a huge revelation: Kobaïa wasn't an alien world after all. "We baptized that other world 'Kobaïa.' But, looking back at this today, Kobaïa refers to Earth . . . We were finding that we were actually talking about the story of planet Earth."

It's a twist reminiscent of the 1960 episode of *The Twilight Zone* "I Shot an Arrow into the Air," where astronauts crash-land into a barren asteroid, only to later find out it's the Nevada desert—or more contemporaneously, *Planet of the Apes*, the 1968 movie that, along with *2001: A Space Odyssey*, revived sci-fi as a commercially and critically legitimate cinematic genre at the close of the '60s. *Planet of the Apes'* famous ending—that the ape-ruled planet Charlton Heston lands on is actually Earth, complete with a half-buried Statue of Liberty—was shocking before it became a cliché. But it resonated for a reason. As unsettlingly conveyed in David Bowie's "Space Oddity," the new reality of humans leaving Earth and walking on other heavenly bodies had opened up a kind of existential disorientation. Not only was Earth demoted from being the center of the universe, as Copernicus had once so blasphemously asserted, our home planet was simply one more chunk of space rock, perhaps interchangeable with a myriad others strewn throughout the universe.

But there existed another frontier for mankind to conquer through science fiction. Time travel had been a thematic staple of the genre since H. G. Wells popularized the conceit in his 1895 novel *The Time Machine*, which had been most recently adapted to film in 1960. Picking up, perhaps, on the hurtling-through-the-centuries notion of Zager and Evans' "In the Year 2525," two very different musical acts in 1970 sang of the wonder and peril of time travel. Mick Softley, a psychedelic folk singer, and Stray, a rock band playing in the style that would soon become popularly known as heavy metal, each released a song in 1970 titled, simply, "Time Machine." Despite the difference in sound, the two songs alight on roughly the same basic idea: traveling through time can be pretty trippy, a metaphor for our swiftly accelerating technological culture coupled with the hippie counterculture's yearning for simpler times.

A group that was far more central to the emerging metal scene, Black Sabbath, released a time-travel song of their own in 1970. On their second album, *Paranoid*, the crushing song "Iron Man" is "about a guy who invented a time machine and he goes through time and finds the world is going to end," according to frontman Ozzy Osbourne. "Coming back he turns to iron, and people won't listen to him, they think he's not real. He goes a bit barmy and decides to get his revenge by killing people. He tries to do good but in the end it turns into bad." Another track on *Paranoid*, "Planet Caravan," is a bit less brutal in its sci-fi presentation. Osbourne called the song, with a bit of tongue in cheek, "a smoky, jazz club number about someone going through space and seeing stars and things." Drummer Bill Ward described it more studiously as "a very distant, *2001*-ish track"—once again showing the impact Kubrick's film had on musicians at the time. In his book *On Bowie*, Rob Sheffield goes so far as to ask, "Has any movie inspired rock stars as much as *2001*?" At the advent of the '70s, that question wasn't at all rhetorical, but easily answerable. It's hard not to detect some element of *A Space Odyssey*'s philosophical grandeur in "Starsailor," a song released by the avant-garde folk singer Tim Buckley in 1970. The introduction to the song is a dizzying reverberation of otherworldly voices and effects—like an updated, psychedelic take on Joe Meek's "Outer Space Music Fantasy" from a decade earlier. And the lyrics, penned by Buckley's collaborator Larry Beckett, force a doorway into another reality where "Beyond the suns I speak / And circuits shiver."

Science fiction is treated much less obliquely in "Pioneers Over c.," a 1970 song written by Peter Hammill and released by his group Van Der Graaf

Generator. Hammill contracted the sci-fi virus as a teenager in the '60s. Along with the standard authorial influences such as Heinlein and Harlan Ellison, the young Hammill fell deeply into the works of New Wave writers such as Thomas M. Disch and Michael Moorcock—not to mention the heady, existence-contorting thought experiments of Philip K. Dick. "The '70s, of course, were a great time for science fiction," Hammill said, "and all of us were enthusiasts for it, especially for those writers who were using the form to question matters of reality and philosophy . . . Certainly, the stretches of imagination which were involved appealed to me then." Van Der Graaf Generator could loosely be called a prog band, but Hammill's idiosyncratic style—at times supple, at times confrontational—put his band in a class all its own. And on "Pioneers Over c.," he used the song's twelve-minute expanse to ponder the consequences of the human race leaving Earth, waxing cynical in the face of so much NASA-fied romanticism: "Reddened eyes stared up into the void / One thousand stars to be exploited."

Not all of the emerging sci-fi music used lyrics to make their point. In London, the band UFO used its instrumental song "Unidentified Flying Object" as a vessel for rockets sounds and the vibrational hum of the cosmos. In the coming months and years, this direct attempt at reproducing the experience of space travel, rather than just singing about it, would become known as space rock—and "Unidentified Flying Object" is one of its first and purest expressions.

For his part, the obscure, eccentric electronic musician Bruce Haack used both instrumentation and lyrics to reflect his own creeping ambivalence toward technology and the future—as if the title of his 1970 album, *The Electric Lucifer*, didn't spell that out plainly enough. An electronics expert who built his own devices and used them alongside the Moog synthesizer, he'd previously released sci-fi songs for children, including 1968's bizarre "School for Robots," a sparse track composed of stark electronic rhythms. His vision of artificial intelligence isn't so kid-friendly on the *Electric Lucifer* song "Program Me" and its Kafka-meets-Kubrick plea, "My heart beats electrically / My brain computes, program me." Again, the specter of *2001*—specifically the voice of the malevolent computer HAL—hangs over the song, but it also runs parallel to the 1970 movie *Colossus: The Forbin Project*. Based on D. F. Jones's 1966 novel *Colossus*, it presents a nightmare scenario where a defense computer becomes sentient and pushes the world to the brink of nuclear annihilation. Much of the computer's chilling, inhuman intonation came not from the voice actor—Paul Frees, best known as the man behind the cartoon villain Boris Badenov of *The Rocky and Bullwinkle Show*—but from the device Frees spoke through. Called the vocoder, the electronic, voice-modulation machine was just beginning to be used to its full potential at the start of the '70s—but its ability to conjure a mood of robotic evil would eventually become one of the hallmarks of sci-fi cinema, television, and music.

Electric Lucifer contained another sci-fi song by the name of "Song of the Death Machine"—complete with the comforting lines, "Logic functioning / Reason programming / Kill"—but it paled before a similarly titled track from 1970: "Saviour Machine" by David Bowie. Following the ambitious sci-fi of "Space Oddity" and "Cygnet Committee" on his self-titled 1969 album, he recorded his next full-length, *The Man Who Sold the World*. The title alone seemed to reference a certain work of science fiction, namely Heinlein's 1950 short story collection "The Man Who Sold the Moon," but the album itself wasn't overly concerned with sci-fi—except for "Saviour Machine." In another echo of *2001*, the song envisioned a frightening future in which an advanced supercomputer "hates the species that gave it life," and, like Clarke and Kubrick's HAL, begins to toy with the humans it serves. At a time when the '60s back-to-nature ideal had begun to curdle into a queasy technophobia, the imagery struck a nerve. More prophetic, though, was a line in another of the album's tracks, "After All." At one point in the otherwise sci-fi–free song, Bowie sings, "We're painting our faces and dressing in thoughts from the skies." With "Space Oddity" behind him and an uncertain tomorrow ahead, he was already predicting his own imminent transformation into a stargazing glam-rock messiah.

It's not clear if an American singer-songwriter named Tom Rapp was listening to Bowie at the start of the '70s. But there's no denying the parallels between Major Tom in "Space Oddity" and the unnamed yet equally doomed astronaut in Rapp's 1970 song "Rocket Man"—a folk song released under the name of Rapp's project Pearls Before Swine. It's sung in a hushed, awestruck voice from the point of view of a son whose dad is an astronaut. He watches the night sky, wondering "if a falling star / Was a ship becoming ashes with a rocket man inside." This poignantly morbid sentiment was drawn in part from Rapp's teenage years, when he lived for a time near Cape Canaveral, in sight of NASA's earlier rocket launches. But it also openly adapted the premise, as well as the title, of the Ray Bradbury story "The Rocket Man" from *The Illustrated Man*—a book Bowie loved as well. The song's imagery of a space hero coming home in the form of ashes is something Bowie would also call on years later, at the end of the decade.

More immediately, a sci-fi reader and up-and-coming songwriter named Bernie Taupin took Rapp's "Rocket Man" to heart. In 1970 Taupin began thinking of how he might explore a comparable theme—that is, an astronaut in the future who's not a hero, but simply a hardworking family man—and turn it into a song. He'd begun writing lyrics for a promising singer-pianist from London; in 1970 alone, the singer had released three songs bearing Taupin's sci-fi lyrics. "Taupin was going through a period of reading Michael Moorcock books and things like that," the singer said, "and it all came out through [the 1970 songs] 'Take Me To The Pilot,' 'The Cage,' and 'Bad Side Of The Moon,' which showed the influence he got from reading all those science-fiction books." The singer was born Reginald Kenneth Dwight, but he'd taken the stage name Elton John.

ALONG WITH HIS ADMITTED "FONDNESS for a space story," Paul Kantner had a crusading motivation behind *Blows Against the Empire.* Following the triumphs of Apollos 11 and 12 in 1969, Apollo 13 narrowly escaped tragedy in April of 1970. Technical malfunctions en route to the Moon caused the crew to abort the mission and return to Earth. The ordeal played out on national television as the three astronauts—Jim Lovell, Fred Haise, and Jack Swigert—scrambled to improvise while their capsule's capability slowly ceased to function in the vacuum of space. It was an eerie parallel of the catastrophe Major Tom underwent in David Bowie's "Space Oddity" mere months before.

The Apollo 13 crew heroically survived. But their close call led to a rethinking of the necessity and value of the Apollo program, not to mention space exploration overall. Space exploration declined throughout the '70s, both a frustrating and galvanizing situation for sci-fi fans, writers, and musicians. With the Vietnam War turning into a multibillion-dollar quagmire, the exorbitant funding NASA required was coming under question, especially in light of the fact that the United States' ostensible reason for landing on the Moon—to beat the Soviets—had already been accomplished. In the popular consciousness, awe became mixed with desensitization. "After the first couple of moon shots, Americans were pretty blasé," said Joe Haldeman, a Vietnam vet who would go on to write *The Forever War,* his 1974 sci-fi novel that combined his combat experiences in Southeast Asia with the high-tech subgenre of military space opera. "NBC were showered with complaints when it dared interrupt the Super Bowl to show two clowns walking around on the Moon."

For Kantner, *Blows Against the Empire*—despite its antiauthoritarian tone and copious drug references—was "all promo for the space programs. A lot of people worry about spending money here at home or needing things here at home and see the space thing as wasted effort, or an effort not worthy of the money put into it, because of the needs here at home." One of those nay-sayers was poet Gil Scott-Heron, whose song "Whitey on the Moon"—which also came out in 1970—pointed out the stark contrast between Neil Armstrong's glorious walk on lunar soil and the condition of those living under poverty and inequality in the United States. But in Kantner's view, "A lot of what [the space program] does goes to solve the needs we have here. Like the solar heating thing that's coming into vogue, as we're looking for alternative energy sources, it's directly from the space program. The whole technology was developed within the space program to do that sort of thing . . . Personally I think the whole space program is really a necessity. It's a positive thing. It's natural evolution."

Kantner's obsession with science fiction and real-world technology—along with his and Crosby's direct contact with the likes of Heinlein, Wyndham, and Sturgeon—manifested in an unprecedented way. In August of 1971, *Blows Against the Empire* was nominated for a Hugo Award for Best Dramatic Presentation. The category was almost exclusively devoted to films and TV, and no music album, let alone a rock album, had ever been recognized for science fiction's highest honor.

It didn't win—one could only imagine how Kantner might have felt if that year's Hugo Award presenter, his hero Isaac Asimov, had announced his name—but it was a milestone. The counterculture had infiltrated the sci-fi community at the highest level. Kantner, a rock musician, was listed on that year's Hugo ballot alongside legendary authors such as Harlan Ellison, Larry Niven, and Poul Anderson. At last, popular music was starting to be viewed as a valid medium for speculative stories about space and technology, alongside prose, cinema, and television. It was a fleeting alignment—not until the twenty-first century would the Hugos recognize music again—but it made a game-changing statement as the '70s began forming their own cultural identity: music could be science fiction.

IN SEARCH
OF SPACE:
1971

LIGHTS FLASHED LIKE THE LANDING BEACONS OF A SPACESHIP AS
Michael Moorcock took the stage. That is, if it could be called a stage at all.
The concert wasn't being held in a music venue, but outdoors, under the overpass where the Westway crossed Portobello Road. It was the summer of 1971
in Ladbroke Grove, the West London neighborhood where Moorcock lived
and which had been, for the past few years, the epicenter of England's underground culture. Groups like the Pink Fairies and the Deviants blurred the
lines between realities, occasionally dipping a toe into the fringes of science
fiction. "I had a rotten childhood," said Mick Farren, frontman of the Deviants, before explaining the salvation he found in the interplanetary novels

of the early 1900s sci-fi author Edgar Rice Burroughs. "It made life more bearable to be off in my mind with John Carter on Mars." Years later Farren become a novelist, spinning his love of sci-fi intro prose rather than music.

The crew of lighting technicians supplying the pyrotechnics called themselves Liquid Len and the Lensmen—a reference to E. E. "Doc" Smith's popular *Lensman* series of sci-fi novels. It was only fitting: Moorcock himself was not only an author of science fiction, but the editor of *New Worlds*, one of the most prominent and progressive sci-fi magazines of the '60s and '70s. And the members of the group that performed behind Moorcock—long-haired, luridly dressed, outrageously loud—were beginning to explore the fringes of sci-fi themselves. They'd even adopted their band name from Hawkmoon, a character from Moorcock's books, tweaking it slightly to come up with the moniker Hawkwind.

"In case of sonic attack on your district, follow these rules!" Moorcock bellowed. The members of Hawkwind, rather than playing anything resembling a recognizable rock song, forged jagged waves of electronic noise that hung over their guest vocalist as ominously as the grimy concrete overpass. While not an official member of the band, Moorcock had been writing lyrics for them—which led to an invitation that night to join them onstage. As their technological cacophony escalated, the Lensmen's strobes built in intensity. "Small babies should be placed inside the special cocoons," Moorcock continued, his voice rising in volume and intensity even as it maintained a coldly robotic flatness: "Metal, not organic, limbs should be employed whenever possible." He then delivered the bloodcurdling command, one that resembled the voice of the sinister Daleks from *Doctor Who*: "Do not panic!"—a refrain that would seem eerily familiar when, a few years hence, a young sci-fi writer named Douglas Adams popularized a similar catchphrase. Like many of Hawkwind's songs to come, "Sonic Attack" imagined an alarming yet exhilarating sci-fi future. A future with roots in Moorcock's past.

Michael Moorcock was born in London in 1939. As a baby, he lived through Germany's 1940 and 1941 aerial attacks, which left portions of the city in ruins. He grew up accustomed to destruction and the specter of death from the skies. "I had become used to metamorphosis, of almost constantly changing landscapes," he said, and that deep-seated perception of an impermanent world fueled his writing. At age seventeen he became the editor of the pulp magazine *Tarzan Adventures*. Soon he was writing his own fanciful tales, which tended toward fantasy and science fiction. Even his fantasy characters—like his most famous, Elric, a pale-skinned prince whose amorphous morals were made even more slippery by his reliance on his sentient, parasitic blade Stormbringer—had a tinge of sci-fi to them. Elric, along with many of Moorcock's other creations, were manifestations of a single being called the Eternal Champion, all of whom dwelled in a dizzying cosmos called the Multiverse, which encompassed our own world, along with an infinite number of parallel versions of it. Another manifestation of the Eternal Champion, Jerry Cornelius, even lived in contemporary London—Ladbroke Grove, to be exact—and his stories were more outright sci-fi, in a gonzo sort of way.

The Multiverse is a concept that's become commonplace in speculative literature since then, and it's tied to the sharp shift in humanity's view of reality after the emergence of quantum physics in the early twentieth century. Moorcock embraced the quantum cosmos, as well as the ambiguity that came with it—the underlying idea that reality isn't objective but can change according to the perspective of the observer. Coupled with his childhood memories of bomb-torn Britain, this radical subjectivity fueled a new kind of science fiction.

"The metamorphosis of Blitzed London became the chaotic landscapes of Elric the Albino," Moorcock said. Then he compared Elric to one of jazz's most popular musicians: "As in need of his soul-slurping sword as Chet Baker was in need of junk, he witnessed the death of his Empire, even conspired in it. The adrenaline rushes of aerial bombardment and imminent death informed the Jerry Cornelius stories where London's ruins were re-created and disaster had a celebratory face." When he assumed editorship of the venerable sci-fi magazine *New Worlds* in 1964, Moorcock assembled a stable of like-minded authors such as J. G. Ballard, Thomas M. Disch, M. John Harrison, and Brian Aldiss. In the pages of *New Worlds*, they experimented with ambiguity, pessimism, and at times outright nihilism, an about-face from the intrepid heroes and can-do problem-solving of sci-fi's previous generation. "We tried to create a new literature which expressed our own experience—Ballard of his years in the Japanese civilian camp, Aldiss of the terrors of being a boy-soldier in Malaya—all the great writers who contributed to my journal *New Worlds* were rejecting modernism not from any academic attempt to discover novelty but in order to find forms which actually described what they had witnessed, what they had felt . . . We did not mourn the passing of liberal humanism or indeed our humanity. We sought new ways of expressing them."

But the underpass performance was not Moorcock's first dabbling in music. He'd been in on the ground floor of England's skiffle movement, the country's precursor to rock 'n' roll, and he'd embraced the nascent rock culture, to the point where he began recording demos as a guitarist in the late '50s. Prose had always taken precedent, though, and as *New Worlds* became a literary force later in the '60s—he was even approached by a frustrated Stanley Kubrick to help adapt *2001: A Space Odyssey*, which Moorcock declined out of loyalty to his friend Arthur C. Clarke—his focus on music had receded to a distant second place.

Hawkwind changed that. The band consisted of fellow denizens of Ladbroke Grove—London's equivalent of San Francisco's Haight-Ashbury or New York's Greenwich Village—where hippies lived in squats, anarchist broadsheets were distributed freely, and LSD was as common as milk. The seedy, creatively fertile neighborhood was situated on the other side of Hyde Park from Bowie's far more posh South Kensington. It was in Ladbroke Grove that Jimi Hendrix drew his last breath. Remembered Moorcock, "When Hendrix died [in 1970] about a block from where I lived in Ladbroke Grove, the hub of Britain's 'alternative' culture, it symbolized the beginning of the end." It's telling that he cites Hendrix's death as a watershed. Moorcock noted, "People of my generation were attracted to sci-fi and rock 'n' roll because they had no standing with authority. They were in the margins and out of sight." With Hendrix, though, sci-fi ceased being a novelty in popular music and began being interpreted seriously by musicians.

Despite Moorcock's dire assessment, London's underground rock culture was still alive and kicking in 1971, if in a state of flux—thanks largely to Hawkwind. The collective formed in 1969 around core member Dave Brock, who'd previously spent his days busking with an acoustic guitar on the sidewalks of Ladbroke Grove. Taking the worship of psychedelics and antiauthoritarian stance of the '60s and boiling it down into something less flowery and more militant, Brock and crew made music that did away with any pretense of artistry.

Utilitarian and blunt in a way that wouldn't be seen until the advent of punk half a decade later, Hawkwind caught the eye and ear of Moorcock, just as the imploding '60s were giving way to an inchoate '70s. The first time he saw them play, he remembered, "They were like the mad crew of a long-distance spaceship who had forgotten the purpose of their mission, which had turned to art during the passage of time." He sensed in Hawkwind kindred spirits. The band's saxophonist Nik Turner said, "Moorcock endorsed Hawkwind publicly as the sort of band that his Jerry Cornelius character would listen to." Indeed, Moorcock wrote the band into his next Jerry Cornelius novel, 1971's *A Cure for Cancer*, establishing a music-literature crossover that added a multimedia dimension to Moorcock's Multiverse. The author was not only drawn to Hawkwind's sci-fi vibe and ritualistic, future-druid sound, he was enthralled by their use of technology. Two members of the group, Michael "Dik Mik" Davies and his replacement in 1971, Del Dettmar, used a hodgepodge of electronic devices such as ring modulators, tape-loop echo machines, and a Moog synthesizer to create disorienting, space-age sounds. They turned the band's repetitive, rudimentary rock riffs into the next evolutionary step up—or down, as the case may be—from the BBC Radiophonic Workshop's more refined experiments for the soundtracks of shows like *Doctor Who*.

"When I first saw them," said Moorcock, "they seemed like barbarians who'd got hold of a load of electrical gear. Instead of being self-conscious and pseudo-intellectual, they were actually *of* the electronic age. They weren't impressed by their own gear." As he became further involved with the group as a guest lyricist and occasional performer, his appreciation for Hawkwind's direct, intuitive interface with technology deepened: "We really were trying to find some new way of doing music using the electronics, rather than simply using the electronics as amplification for the acoustics." Brock agreed with Moorcock, saying in less analytical language, "I prefer to be a barbarian with the machines."

Hawkwind's newest recruit in the summer of 1971, singer and lyricist Robert Calvert, was a friend of Moorcock's. While primarily a poet, Calvert harbored his own interest in science fiction. His verse had been published in *New Worlds*, and as far back as his teen years he'd begun picturing some hitherto unimagined fusion of sci-fi and rock 'n' roll. Calvert's first performance with Hawkwind, in May of 1971, began with a reading of a poem of his called "Co-Pilots of Spaceship Earth." That same month, the group recorded a radio session for the BBC that included a new song titled "Master of the Universe"—Hawkwind's first bona fide sci-fi classic. It mirrored the nebulous quantum reality Moorcock had promulgated in his fiction. "I'm charged with cosmic energy / Has the world gone mad, or is it me?"

The infusion of Moorcock and Calvert into Hawkwind's lineup sharpened the band's newfound sci-fi focus. It all solidified in October of 1971, with the release of *In Search of Space*. While not a concept album in the vein of Julian's Treatment's *A Time Before This*, Paul Kantner's *Blows Against the Empire*, or Magma's *Magma* from the year prior, Hawkwind's sophomore album set a new standard in sci-fi music. Not only did certain songs—chief among them "Master of the Universe," "Adjust Me," and "Children of the Sun"—reflect the increasingly urgent sci-fi passions of the band, the overall sound went far beyond acting merely as a vehicle for lyrics about spacetime and androids. *In Search of Space* sounded, as no album did before, like a probe parting the depths of the heavens. Assuming, of course, that probe was propelled by LSD.

Psychedelics fueled Hawkwind's out-of-this-worldview. By 1971, the dreamy idealism of the Summer of Love had disappeared from Ladbroke Grove, and elsewhere, replaced with a hard-edged radicalism. Hawkwind flirted with pagan ritualism and the druidic imagery of Stonehenge, but they didn't reject urban life; instead, their 1973 single "Urban Guerrilla" was so militant in its stance and sound, it presaged punk by three years and was subsequently banned by the BBC. Incubated within the city's decaying infrastructure and the daily acceleration of technology, Hawkwind sought the embrace of Mother Nature beyond Earth herself—and psychotropic revelations in the flood of data coming in about the cosmos, thanks to the space program.

In Search of Space is a document of this. In his review of the record in *Rolling Stone*, Lester Bangs enthused, "This is music for the astral apocalypse," adding, "Hawkwind have the consummate sense of the present decadent state of astropolitics." An advertisement for the album billed Calvert as a "space poet and intergalactic chanter." The back cover of the record warns, TECHNICIANS OF SPACE SHIP EARTH THIS IS YOUR CAPTAIN SPEAKING YOUR CAPTAIN IS DEAD. Amplifying the group's chanted vocals, mechanistic riffs, unearthly electronics, and frantic, escape-velocity rhythms, the album came with a twenty-four-page book titled *The Hawkwind Log*. In it, Calvert—collaborating with graphic designer Barney Bubbles—detailed the band's philosophical trajectory. Hawkwind was not only the band that made the music on *In Search of Space*, it's the name of a crashed spacecraft found at the South Pole by "Captain RN Calvert of the Société Astronomæ (an international guild of creative artists dedicated in eternity to the discovery and demonstration of extra-terrestrial intelligence)." Even more mind-boggling, the *Hawkwind* is a two-dimensional ship. One of the log entries states:

Space/time supply indicators near to zero. Our thoughts are losing depth, soon they will fold into each other, into flatness, into nothing but surface. Our ship will fold like a cardboard file and the noises of our minds compress into a disc of shining black, spinning in eternity . . .

It's something straight out of a New Wave sci-fi novel—especially Moorcock's, which makes sense, considering the cross-pollination of ideas that was happening in Ladbroke Grove. The author's Multiverse Trilogy from the mid-'60s explored fractured, trippy realities and bleak forays into deep space. One of his most audacious *New Worlds* contributors, M. John Harrison, had accompanied Moorcock the first time he saw Hawkwind, and his work developed parallel to the band's—particularly in the form of Harrison's 1973 novel *The Centauri Device*, in which drugs are freighted on spaceships and anarchists roam the galaxy. Moorcock's 1969 novel *The Black Corridor*—cowritten with his wife, Hilary Bailey, although credited to Moorcock alone—was the basis for a Hawkwind song called "Black Corridor," which would end up on the group's hypnotic 1973 live album, the aptly titled *Space Ritual*. Like these works of groundbreaking science fiction, Hawkwind's music wasn't intended as any sort of realistic depiction of what might happen in the future. "It's not predicting what is going to happen," Calvert said. "It's the mythology of the Space Age, in the way that rocketships and interplanetary travel are parallel with the heroic voyages of earlier times."

This all made for the perfect cult band, and that's exactly where Hawkwind found themselves in 1971. But soon after Calvert joined the group that year, bringing a fresh infusion of high-concept sci-fi, another new member balanced the scale with the addition of brute muscularity: Ian "Lemmy" Kilmister, who came aboard as the group's new bassist in September. Hulking and hirsute, Lemmy had become a familiar face around Ladbroke Grove after a stint as a roadie for Jimi Hendrix. He quickly lent his gruff growl to Calvert's lyrics and took up the vocal duties on Hawkwind's newest song, "Silver Machine," which seemed at first glance to be about a spaceship—normally a safe thing to assume with Hawkwind. But Calvert took inspiration from an essay by the French writer Alfred Jarry titled "How to Construct a Time Machine," which Calvert interpreted as being about a bicycle. As Calvert explained:

At that time there were a lot of songs about space travel, and it was the time when NASA was actually, really doing it. They'd put a man on the moon and were planning to put parking lots and hamburger stalls and everything up there. I thought that it was about time to come up with a song that actually sent this all up, which was "Silver Machine." "Silver Machine" was just to say, "I've got a silver bicycle," and nobody got it.

After stints in a mental institution, Calvert was diagnosed as bipolar, leading to his eventual departure from the band. Lemmy's vocals helped push "Silver Machine" into becoming an unlikely hit single in 1972, reaching #3 on the UK charts. *Melody Maker* described Lemmy's intense, gravelly voice as "'look out, the Earth is about to collide with Mars' type singing." Lemmy saw Hawkwind this way: "We were a black fucking nightmare. A post-apocalyptic horror soundtrack." And their mission was only beginning.

A GROUP OF STUDENTS TOOK their seats in the classroom at the University of California, Berkeley, one day in the spring of 1971. They were about to begin a most unusual course. Granted, this was a university campus in the Bay Area in the early '70s; the unusual was commonplace. But something entirely unprecedented was about to happen. As the students settled in, opened their notebooks, and clicked their pens, in walked Sun Ra.

Dressed in a flowing brightly colored caftan—not the dashiki seen often on African Americans at the time, but something that dazzled like the lining of a B-movie astronaut's spacesuit—Ra took command of his class. Its official title was African American Studies 198, but it became better known as the Black Man in the Cosmos. As sci-fi as that sounds, the class was offered alongside UC Berkeley's more traditional courses on subjects such as quantum mechanics, plasma physics, orbit theory, X-ray astronomy, interstellar gas dynamics, artificial intelligence, and aerospace management. Members of the Arkestra, the revolutionary free-jazz ensemble led by Ra, swept through the aisles, collecting recording devices. Ra didn't want his lecture to be taped. Despite that, at least one intrepid student managed to capture the class on audio.

"Music is a language, and my music speaks of everything," he informed the class by way of introduction. What followed was a meandering yet eloquent discursion on various ancient texts, philosophical references, and religious concepts. About a half hour into the lecture, however, his speech took an abrupt turn toward sci-fi:

> This planet is vulnerable to any kind of creature, any kind of being, to come over anytime they want and pretend to be a man or a woman or a child . . . Anything can come on the planet and grab one of your brothers and take him to the Moon, Jupiter, anywhere . . . Some people can come from outer space and take the whole thing over.

Following the lecture, a performance took place. The ensemble played a set of celestially themed, improvised jazz, with Ra taking his place at the keyboard. In recent years he'd started using the Moog synthesizer. He had employed it to innovative, futuristic effect on his album *Space Probe*, which he'd recorded as the '60s shifted into the '70s. It wasn't the first time he'd made music about space. Born Herman Poole Blount in Birmingham, Alabama, in 1914, he'd played in various unremarkable jazz combos before undergoing a transformation in 1936. One day he had a revelation: Surrounded by bright light and the sensation of morphing into a form of energy, he left Earth and traveled to Saturn. There, aliens with "one little antenna on each ear" guided him toward cosmic enlightenment. They also advised him to drop out of college, which he did, ironic in light of the university lectures he'd wind up giving in 1971.

Creating a new identity for himself, complete with glittering robes and headdresses that evoked both Ancient Egypt and pulp science fiction, Sun Ra assembled his Arkestra. Throughout the '50s and '60s, he released a string of albums that tapped into combined sci-fi wonder and space-age hope with the rising tide of African American consciousness and civil rights. These albums were instrumental, but they didn't need lyrics to convey their sci-fi themes: Titles such as *The Nubians of Plutonia*, *We Travel the Space Ways*, and *The Futuristic Sounds of Sun Ra* made it abundantly clear where Sun Ra was coming from. The music telegraphed his cosmic aesthetic; it comprised cutting-edge gadgetry, interstellar pings, washes of textured static, and a methodology derived from the universal freedom espoused by free-jazz contemporaries such as Ornette Coleman and John Coltrane (each of whom dabbled, to a far lesser degree, in sci-fi titles and tones). The term "Afrofuturism" was still decades from being coined, but Sun Ra embodied it—a speculative combination of science fiction and mythology that focuses the histories, tribulations, and hopes of the African diaspora through the technology of tomorrow. Months after Ra's 1971 Berkeley lectures, in nearby Oakland, he began filming a low-budget, independent movie. In a rough sense, it dramatized his own mythic metamorphosis from the Chitlin Circuit organist Herman Poole Blount to the heliocentric messenger Sun Ra. It also served as a call to interplanetary action, a rallying cry for those who would transcend the earthly bedlam of the present and look toward the stars for their salvation. It would be released in 1974 under the title *Space Is the Place*—and it would help spark an explosion in Afrofuturist sci-fi music that would transform the cultural climate.

BY 1971, JAZZ HAD BEGUN to influence certain segments of popular music, most notably prog and funk. But a hard-rock band—whose attack foresaw the intensity of punk years beforehand—had been picking up on Sun Ra's deep-space signals since 1969. The MC5 hailed from the Detroit suburb of Lincoln Park, and their rebellious rabblerousing powered with their debut album, the live record *Kick Out the Jams*. One of its tracks, "Starship," was an eight-minute freeform freak-out that the group cocredited to Sun Ra, due to the fact that they adapted the lyrics from a Ra poem: "Starship, starship, take me / Take me where I wanna go." Science fiction wasn't an overwhelming feature of the MC5's approach—but in 1971, the song "Future/Now," from their final album *High Time*, sketched an alarming scenario not far from David Bowie's emerging apocalyptic prophecies. "Here they plunder, interstellar diplomats," rages lead singer Rob Tyner before warning against the imminent "post-atomic dawn."

But the range of sci-fi rock that spontaneously appeared in 1971 went far beyond the dystopian. *Space Hymns*, an album made by an Englishman named Barrington Frost under the stage name Ramses, surfaced that year, and like Sun Ra's work it twined together the mythology of Ancient Egypt with a dose of interplanetary ecstasy. Musically, though, it couldn't have been more different; haunting and exquisitely sad, *Space Hymns* drips with post-psychedelic eccentricity and an eerie blurring of outer space and emotional turmoil. Just as thought-provoking was the album's sumptuous cover art, which depicted a rocket ship shaped as a cathedral. It was illustrated by a young artist named Roger Dean. His design for a futuristic-looking chair was used in *A Clockwork Orange*, but he was soon to become known for his work in album-cover design. His illustration for the cover of another album that year, *Fragile*, by the British prog band Yes, forged a creative alliance that resulted in great synergy for all involved. Dean's painting for *Fragile* showed a world being circled by a wooden spaceship—"It was literally meant to be a fragile world," he remarked. "I thought about that very literally, painting a fragile world that would eventually break up"—and it established Dean as the foremost visual stylist of '70s sci-fi rock.

Yes were the perfect partners for Dean. Formed in 1968, the band released two albums in 1971, *The Yes Album* and *Fragile*, which cemented their position as one of prog's foremost acts. Buoyed by the weightless vocals of frontman Jon Anderson, the group's intricate songcraft began taking on sci-fi themes. The song "Starship Trooper" off *The Yes Album* was the first Yes track to blatantly exhibit science fiction, even going so far as to share its title with Robert A. Heinlein's popular 1959 sci-fi novel, *Starship Troopers*. But where the book dealt with biting social critique couched in an alien invasion, the song went lofty. Bearing no relation to Heinlein's tale, Anderson's lyrics contain barely any science fiction at all; instead, they use the phrase "Starship Trooper" as a launching-off point to ponder the nature of the universe from a religious standpoint. Explained Anderson, "*Starship Troopers* was a great title of a book by Heinlein. And I just like the idea of Starship Trooper being another guardian angel and Mother Earth . . . So it was as though I was writing about my search for truth and search for an understanding of what God truly is."

Due to the Heinlein reference, Yes became classified as a sci-fi band—even one of prog's foremost practitioners of the genre. In reality, Anderson and company rarely incorporated sci-fi themes into their music. Rather, bits of Roger Dean's cover-art imagery and Anderson's religious awe became part of Yes's broader tapestry, one that incorporated sci-fi ideas like space exploration and ecological collapse (as heard on the group's 1970 song "Survival") as manifestations of spirituality. Curiously, though, both of Yes's keyboardists in 1971 have connections to pop's biggest sci-fi hero of the time: Tony Kaye, who played on *The Yes Album*, would briefly become a member of Bowie's touring band in 1975 and '76, and Kaye's replacement on *Fragile*, Rick Wakeman, was the same Mellotron-wielding keyboardist who played on "Space Oddity" two years prior. Not that Wakeman's involvement in sci-fi music in the '70s was anywhere near over—in 1971, as he performed "Starship Trooper" night after night to Yes's burgeoning fanbase, his greatest expression of sci-fi music was still to come. And, for that matter, so was Jon Anderson's.

The rise of sci-fi album art in the early '70s was already swiftly accelerating in 1971—to the point where it was beginning to influence the actual music on the records it contained, rather than being mere decoration or afterthought. The artist William Neal never became as famous as Roger Dean, whose name remains synonymous with the immersive, alien scenery found on '70s rock albums like Yes's *Fragile*. But Neal's contribution to the canon was vital. In 1971, he was commissioned by the prog group Emerson, Lake & Palmer—who were constantly compared to Yes, and vice versa—to illustrate the cover of their upcoming, as-yet-untitled sophomore album. Neal drew up something arresting: a biomechanical armadillo with tank treads and gun turrets, like something out of a particularly lurid sci-fi pulp. When former King Crimson member Greg Lake, ELP's guitarist and lead singer, saw the artwork, he was still struggling to come up with lyrics for the album. Then inspiration struck.

The group's keyboardist, Keith Emerson, remembered, "One day I walked into the studio after my long drive from Sussex. Greg and [drummer] Carl [Palmer] were looking over the artwork of an artist that had just dropped by. We were all fascinated by his artwork . . . To everyone, it represented what we were doing in that studio. The next day on my drive up from Sussex the imagery of the armadillo kept hitting me. It had to have a name. Something guttural. It had to begin with the letter T and end with a flourish. *Tarka the Otter* may have come into it, but this armadillo needed a science fiction kind of name that represented Charles Darwin's theory of evolution in reverse. Some mutilation of the species caused by radiation . . . *Tarkus!*"

And so the album gained not only a concept, but a title. *Tarkus* became one of ELP's most beloved albums, thanks largely to its outlandish, attention-grabbing, sci-fi cover, as well as its conceptual connection to the music within. For all its highbrow musicianship, *Tarkus* is hardly the stuff of classic sci-fi. Lake's multi-movement composition "Tarkus," which comprises the entire first side of the record, only loosely relates the vague story of a half-machine, half-animal creature that faces extinction before transforming into an amphibious being known, naturally, as Aquatarkus.

Yes and ELP laid the groundwork in 1971 for prog's enduring association with sci-fi. In reality, though, prog was more deeply steeped in the literature of fantasy. Ironically, just as the prog movement was moving forward into the uncharted technological realms of synthesizers, they were falling back on the work of fantasy authors such as J.R.R. Tolkien for creative fuel—books set in the distant past, or some fictionalized version thereof, rather than speculating about the present or future. Yes and ELP were each, in their own way, able to combine science fiction and fantasy, fusing them into a metaphysical, post-hippie meditation on the nature of reality.

The same can be said of Arthur Brown. A veteran of the UFO Club who employed a pre-ELP Carl Palmer in the late '60s, the incendiary singer enjoyed a huge hit with his 1968 single "Fire"—but his theatrical showmanship and gravelly yet operatic voice gravitated toward sci-fi the following year. In 1969 he recorded an album of atmospheric psychedelia titled *Strangelands* (which went unreleased until 1988) that incorporated the first faint stirrings of sci-fi in tracks such as "Planets of the Universe" and "Hold on Cosmos." Brown's fascination with sci-fi's dramatic urgency and big-picture bombast bore fruit in 1971 with his new band Kingdom Come. That year they released *Galactic Zoo Dossier*, an album whose title was not shy in broadcasting its ambition. A kaleidoscope of sounds and concepts, the album created an aggressively inventive world in which a "cosmic chameleon drawn by force" exists, and where a "computer sets dials in my brain." Abounding with paranoiac phantasms, *Galactic Zoo Dossier* ultimately was a quest for liberation and enlightenment amid the dehumanization of technology and the cold void between the stars. The album even featured a rudimentary drum machine, a device utterly alien to recorded popular music in 1971. In a way, the album resembled an avant-garde version of the much more straightforward Hawkwind—Brown even once had violinist Simon House in his band, who would join Hawkwind later in the '70s—but unlike Hawkwind, Brown was crafting his own science fiction rather than drawing from the works of authors or filmmakers. Thankfully, he had many more such stories to tell before the decade ended.

Arthur Brown benefitted greatly from the assistance of a wealthy, famous fan: Pete Townshend of the Who. Townshend first saw Brown perform at the UFO Club in the '60s, and that led to Townshend's associate producer credit on Brown's debut album, 1968's *The Crazy World of Arthur Brown*. Certainly, both Townshend and the Who were heavily invested in the concept-album format—but Brown may have rubbed off on Townshend in another way. Following the massive success of 1969's rock opera *Tommy*, the Who sought to replicate that triumph with a concept album that just so happened to be a work of science fiction. Titled *Lifehouse*, the album, which began as a script, was to be Townshend's profound statement on the dangers of ecological cataclysm, social control through technology, and the redemptive power of music in the face of dystopia. The setting would be an indeterminate future where people wore so-called Lifesuits to protect them from Earth's toxic environment—only, these suits were linked to an oppressive networking system called the Grid.

Townshend sent a treatment of his story to Ray Bradbury, hoping the author might script a film adaptation—one he hoped might be helmed by an exciting young director named Nicolas Roeg. Neither collaboration came to pass. In the midst of trying to realize this sprawling concept, he nearly suffered a nervous breakdown. He abandoned *Lifehouse* in 1971, salvaging bits of it for the decidedly non-sci-fi album *Who's Next*. It remains one of the most legendary unfinished albums in pop history—defeated, in large part, by the maddeningly unlimited possibility of science fiction.

THE YEAR IS 2017. THE United States is a nightmare. A fascist government has taken control of the nation, with the oligarchical ruling class controlling the impoverished masses. In Los Angeles, the population lives in a subterranean network of homes beneath the city proper, which has grown horrendously polluted by unregulated industry. But there's a different kind of underground among the underground: rebels gathers beneath the deserted streets of LA, striving to overthrow the oppressive social order.

Debuting on January 15, 1971, *L.A. 2017* was a made-for-TV movie broadcast under the umbrella of the NBC series *The Name of the Game*. It was an unusual film—not only because it fit only tenuously into *The Name of the Game's* story line, which otherwise took place in the early '70s, but because of its young director. Steven Spielberg, age twenty-four, was not a known quantity, but he was already showing great promise in Hollywood, so he was given the chance to direct this ambitious episode of *The Name of the Game*. Written by veteran author Philip Wylie—whose 1930 sci-fi novel *Gladiator* is widely assumed to have been an influence on the creation of Superman in 1933—*L.A. 2017* was seventy-four minutes long. It was, in effect, Spielberg's first feature-length movie; later, after achieving great success as a sci-fi director, he acknowledged, "That show opened a lot of doors for me."

Being twenty-four in 1971, with youth culture still ascendant, Spielberg couldn't help but work some nods to contemporary music into the movie. At one point, an aging, gray-haired hippie band, a relic from the '60s, performs in a nightclub in that far-off year of 2017, singing of how "better understanding" is "all that we're demanding." They're called the Discards—and their out-spoken message, male/female vocals, and sci-fi context bear a striking resemblance to one band in particular that existed in 1971. It's entirely plausible that Paul Kantner was watching the show that night, wondering if Spielberg might have been parodying him, Grace Slick, and Jefferson Airplane.

Like Kantner's *Blows Against the Empire*, Spielberg's *L.A. 2017* was nominated for a Hugo in the Best Dramatic Presentation category—the first accolade the filmmaker received as a sci-fi visionary. The movie didn't win, as its competition on the 1972 ballot was stiff. Among the 1971 releases up for consideration were George Lucas's *THX 1138* and the sci-fi hit *The Andromeda Strain*. But the Hugo trophy went to a Stanley Kubrick film, his eagerly anticipated follow-up to *2001*: an adaptation of Anthony Burgess's 1962 sci-fi novel *A Clockwork Orange*. The movie became a sensation, and for good reason. With the war in Vietnam still raging, protests erupting in the streets, and the social order perceived to be unraveling, Kubrick's vision of a dystopian future rife with incomprehensible slang, torturous behavioral conditioning, and gleefully sadistic "ultraviolence" struck a nerve.

But *A Clockwork Orange* sounded a deeper note through its use of music. Kubrick had already proven the power of music in *2001*, with Strauss's *Also sprach Zarathustra* becoming a vital part of the film's impact. Music played an even more integral role in *A Clockwork Orange*. More than a soundtrack, the selection of songs sprinkled throughout the film—haunting arrangements of classical strings and otherworldly electronics, played by synthesizer pioneer Wendy Carlos—are essential to the narrative, setting an alienating, ironic tension between tradition and futurism, grace and brutality. It wasn't pop music per se, but the sum total of *A Clockwork Orange* made a huge impression on certain popular musicians—especially those drawn toward science fiction. Bowie would soon adopt some of its imagery and slang for his next fictional incarnation. And in 1974, three years after *A Clockwork Orange*'s release, David Bowie and his friend Marc Bolan, leader of the glam band T. Rex, spent days in a hotel room binge-watching the film, which by that point had become one of the templates for the still embryonic aesthetic of punk.

Bolan's interest in science fiction, like Bowie's, was rooted in childhood. Born Mark Feld in 1947, the same year as Bowie, Bolan grew up devouring the literature of fantasy, from Tolkien to C. S. Lewis. But when he was eight years old, in 1955, in bed with the measles, he read Ray Bradbury's 1952 short story "A Sound of Thunder," one of sci-fi's most famous time-travel tales. In it, hunters from the future use a time machine to go to prehistoric eras and hunt dinosaurs—with the warning that any infinitesimal changes in the past can snowball into massive changes in the present.

In his fevered state, the young man who would become Marc Bolan absorbed these images of great lizards, which dovetailed with his obsessions with dragons. Years later, he launched a music career in the midst of London's late-'60s flowering of psychedelic creativity. The band in which he established himself was called Tyrannosaurus Rex, later shortened to T. Rex. At first the group was a folk-styled duo, but by 1971 they'd expanded to a full ensemble headed in a harder, more rock-inflected direction. He'd also befriended Bowie, a kindred spirit in many ways, and the two shared Tony Visconti as a producer as the '70s began; Bolan even played guitar on 1970's "The Prettiest Star" and "Memory of a Free Festival," Bowie's two singles immediately following "Space Oddity." Despite its title, "Prettiest Star" isn't sci-fi—but "Memory of a Free Festival" segues from hippie reverie into a more pointed exhibit of science fiction, with flying "machines of every shape and size" and "Venusians passing through." But Bolan's preoccupation with fantasy contrasted sharply with Bowie's love of science fiction. That said, a hint of sci-fi did creep into T. Rex's breakthrough album from 1971, *Electric Warrior*—specifically in the song "Planet Queen" and its refrain of "Flying saucer, take me away." Bolan had more to contribute to the decade's body of sci-fi music, but early on, he was still barely dipping his toes into deep space.

Bowie himself kept his science fiction subtle in 1971. He issued an album that year whose sci-fi content was coded and deceptively elusive. Arriving in December of that year, *Hunky Dory* drew immediate attention through a song titled "Life on Mars?", which gave the immediate impression that Bowie had returned to his "Space Oddity" themes of interplanetary speculation. In 1971, Mars was almost as much on people's minds as the Moon had been in 1969. In May, the United States' Mariner 9 probe entered into orbit around Mars, becoming the first spacecraft in history to orbit another planet; in December, the USSR's Mars 3 landed there, becoming the first spacecraft to make a soft landing on the surface of another planet. These developments sparked rampant discussion about the feasibility of human travel to Mars, which was the next obvious goal after the conquering of the Moon. Stoking this conversation was the long lineage of Mars exploration in science fiction. Since the late nineteenth century, the red planet, being Earth's closest neighbor, had been a steady subject of speculative fiction. H. G. Wells's *The War of the Worlds* in

1898, which depicted an alien invasion of Earth by Martians; Edgar Rice Burroughs's series of Mars novels, including the John Carter books so beloved by the Deviants' Mick Farren; Ray Bradbury's many Mars-based stories, starting with *The Martian Chronicles* in 1950: thanks to works like these and hundreds of others, Mars loomed large in the collective consciousness.

Being the consummate contrarian and trickster, Bowie didn't add a smidgen of sci-fi to "Life on Mars?" Rather, Bowie called the sweeping, epic song "a sensitive young girl's reaction to the media," a subject that couldn't have been further from Major Tom's ascent into cosmic purgatory. Now with a bit of fame under his belt, Bowie was learning to revel in the subversion of expectations—and also in deepening his use of metaphor in songwriting. Just as sci-fi novels are often allegorical and reflective of contemporary earthly concerns, "Life on Mars?" used a sci-fi hook to symbolize alienation of a more intimate and plausible sort.

Still, Bowie added a tinge of science fiction elsewhere on *Hunky Dory*. The song "The Bewlay Brothers" may not have an overtly sci-fi title, but its stream-of-consciousness account of its two mythic main characters refers to them at one point as "moon boys." It's a small detail, but one that crystallizes the rest of the song's surreal imagery of "wings that bark" and "the crust of the sun" into something strangely science fictional. And in 1971, when asked about the lyrics of "The Bewlay Brothers," Bowie described the song as *"Star Trek* in a leather jacket."

In the BBC documentary *Hawkwind: Do Not Panic*, Lemmy described Hawkwind as *"Star Trek* with long hair and drugs," as if modifying Bowie's self-assessment. The clash of sci-fi concepts and rock 'n' roll imagery was not only potent, it was seeping into the zeitgeist. As it turned out, *"Star Trek* in a leather jacket" was also a succinct premonition of Bowie's next album. In 1972, he would no longer simply dance with sci-fi. He was going to reincarnate himself as a living piece of science fiction itself.

I'M THE
SPACE INVADER:
1972

A SMALL CROWD OF SIXTY OR SO MUSIC FANS STOOD IN THE DANCE hall of the Toby Jug pub in Tolworth, a suburban neighborhood in southwest London, on the night of February 10, 1972. The backs of their hands had been freshly stamped by the doorman. A DJ played records to warm up the crowd for the main act. The hall was nothing fancy, little more than "an ordinary function room." The two-story brick building that housed it—"a gaunt fortress of a pub on the edge of an underpass"—had played host to numerous rock acts over the past few years, including Led Zeppelin, Jethro Tull, and Fleetwood Mac. Sci-fi music had even graced the otherwise earthy Toby Jug, thanks to recent headliners King Crimson and Hawkwind, and exactly one week earlier, on February 3, the band Stray performed, quite likely playing their sci-fi song "Time Machine." The concertgoers on the tenth, however, had no idea that they would soon witness the most crucial event in the history of sci-fi music.

Most of them already knew who David Bowie was—the singer who, three years earlier, had sung "Space Oddity," and who had appeared very seldom in public since, focusing instead on making records that barely dented the charts. His relatively low profile in recent years hadn't helped his latest single, "Changes," which had come out in January. Despite its soaring, anthemic sound, it failed to find immediate success in England. But the lyrics of the song seemed to signal an impending metamorphosis, hinted at again in late January when Bowie declared in a *Melody Maker* interview, "I'm gay and always have been" and unabashedly predicted, "I'm going to be huge, and it's quite frightening in a way." Bowie clearly had a big plan up his immaculately tailored sleeve. But what could it be?

Before Bowie took the stage of the Toby Jug, an orchestral crescendo announced him. It was a recording of Beethoven's Ninth Symphony, drawn from the soundtrack to *A Clockwork Orange*. To anyone who'd seen the film, the music carried a sinister feeling, superimposed as it was over Kubrick's visions of grim dystopia and ultraviolence. Grandiloquence mixed with foreboding, shot through with sci-fi: it couldn't have been a better backdrop for what the pint-clutching attendees of the Toby Jug were about to behold.

At around 9:00 p.m., the houselights were extinguished. A spotlight sliced the darkness. Bowie took the stage. But was it really him? In a strictly physical sense, it must have been. But this was Bowie as no one had seen him before. His hair—which appeared blond and flowing on the cover of *Hunky Dory*, released just three months earlier—was now chopped at severe angles and dyed bright orange, the color of a B-movie laser beam. His face was lavishly slathered with cosmetics. He wore a jumpsuit with a plunging neckline, revealing his delicate, bone-pale chest, and his knee-high wrestling boots were fire-engine red. Bowie had never been conservative in dress, but even for him, this was a quantum leap into the unknown.

Then he began to play. His band—dubbed the Spiders from Mars and comprising guitarist Mick Ronson, bassist Trevor Bolder, and drummer Woody Woodmansey—was lean, efficient, and powerful, clad in gleaming, metallic outfits that mimicked spacesuits, reminiscent of the costumes from the campy 1968 sci-fi romp *Barbarella*. The Jane Fonda vehicle had been a huge hit in England, and it became a cult film in the United States, thanks to its titillating portrayal of a future where sensuality is rediscovered after a lifetime of sterile, virtual sex.

In the same way, Bowie's new incarnation was shocking, lurid, and supercharged with sexual energy. Combined with his recent admission of either homosexuality or bisexuality, as he was then married to his first wife, Angela, Bowie's new persona oozed futuristic mystique, which Bowie biographer David Buckley described as "a blurring of 'found' symbols from science fiction—space-age high heels, glitter suits, and the like."

But what bewitched the audience most was the music. Amid a set of established songs such as "Andy Warhol," "Wild Eyed Boy from Freecloud," and, naturally, "Space Oddity," the Spiders from Mars injected a handful of new tunes, including "Hang On to Yourself" and "Suffragette City," that had yet to appear on record. Propulsive, infectious, and awash in dizzying imagery, this was a new Bowie—cut less from the thoughtful, singer-songwriter mold and more from some new hybrid of thespian rocker and sci-fi myth. These songs bounced off the walls of the Toby Jug's no-longer-ordinary function room. The audience, whistling and cheering, was entranced. A show eye-popping enough to dazzle an entire arena was being glimpsed in the most intimate of watering holes.

Although the crowd was sparse, people stood on tables and chairs to get the best possible view. The stage was only two feet high, but it may as well have been twenty, or two million—an elevator to outer space designed to launch Bowie into an orbit far more enduring than that of Major Tom in "Space Oddity."

At some point, amid the swirl and spectacle of the two-hour set, Bowie announced from the stage the name of his new identity: Ziggy Stardust.

LIKE AN ARTIFACT FROM SOME alien civilization, Bowie's fifth album, *The Rise and Fall of Ziggy Stardust and the Spiders from Mars*, was unveiled on June 16, 1972. By then, Ziggy had become a sensation. After the Toby Jug gig in February, concertgoers embraced Bowie's new persona in music venues around the UK. Attendance swelled each night, as did a growing legion of followers who dressed themselves in homemade approximations of Bowie's outlandish attire.

Just as the album was released, he and the Spiders appeared on the BBC's revered *Top of the Pops* program, performing the record's centerpiece: the song "Starman." For many of a certain age, watching Bowie on their family's television that evening was tantamount to the Beatles' legendary spot on *The Ed Sullivan Show* in the United States eight years earlier. "He was so vivid. So luminous. So fluorescent. We had one of the first color TVs on our street, and David Bowie was the reason to have a color TV," remembered Bono of U2, who was twelve at the time. "It was like a creature falling from the sky. Americans put a man on the moon. We had our own British guy from space."

Musically, "Starman" was an exquisite and striking slice of pop songcraft, exactly what Bowie needed at that point in his career. Lyrically, he smuggled in a sci-fi story that centers around Ziggy Stardust, who was both Bowie's alter ego and the fictional protagonist of the *Rise and Fall* concept album, as loose as it was in that regard—it is more a fugue of ideas that coalesce into a concept. Through the radio and TV, an alien announces his existence to Earth, which Bowie describes in lovingly rendered sci-fi verse: "A slow voice on a wave of phase." The young people of the world become enchanted and hope to lure the alien down: "Look out your window, you can see his light / If we can sparkle, he may land tonight." But that alien is reticent, and his shyness makes him all the more magnetic.

Bowie sang the song on *Top of the Pops* clad in a multicolored, reptilian-textured jumpsuit, which *Melody Maker* called, "*Vogue*'s idea of what the well-dressed astronaut should be wearing." In that sense, "Starman" is a self-fulfilling prophecy: before he could truly know the impact the song would have, he used it to describe its effect on Great Britain's young people in perfect detail. He was the starman waiting in the sky, and the kids who saw him on TV soon began to dress like him, hoping to sparkle so that he may land tonight.

If Bowie intended "Starman" to be an overt reference to Heinlein's *Starman Jones*, the book he loved as a kid, he never publicly confessed to it. But the admittedly sketchy story line of *Rise and Fall* parallels another Heinlein work: *Stranger in a Strange Land*, the novel that had influenced David Crosby in the '60s and, later, many other sci-fi musicians of the '70s. The book's hero, Valentine Michael Smith, comes to Earth from Mars; in *Rise and Fall*, Mars is built into the title. And both Valentine and Ziggy become messiahs of a kind—androgynous, libertine heralds of a new age of human awareness. Bowie claimed he'd turned down offers to star in a film production of *Stranger in a Strange Land* and had few positive words to say about the book, calling it "staggeringly, awesomely trite." Be that as it may, he clearly had read the book and developed a strong opinion of it—perhaps enough for some of its themes and iconography to seep into his own work.

The opening song of *Rise and Fall*, "Five Years," elegiacally delivers a dystopian forecast: the world will end in five years due to a lack of resources, and society is disintegrating into a slow-motion parade of perversity and moral paralysis. It's a countdown to doomsday, with the clock set at five years. The song's ominous refrain, "We've got five years," is sung by Bowie with increasing histrionics, his voice sounding more panicked and deranged as he repeats the phrase. "The whole thing was to try and get a mocking angle at the future," Bowie said in 1972. "If I can mock something and deride it, one isn't so scared of it"—with "it" being the apocalypse.

"Five Years" set a chilling tone, but *Rise and Fall* didn't entirely wallow in it. The coming of an alien rock star named Ziggy Stardust is relayed in a multi-song story that's equally melancholy and ecstatic, tragic and triumphant. On tracks such as "Moonage Daydream," "Star," and "Lady Stardust," Bowie wields terms such as "ray gun" and "wild mutation." He also claims, "I'm the space invader," as though he were channeling the ideas of his sci-fi heroes Stanley Kubrick or William S. Burroughs, particularly the latter's 1971 novel, *The Wild Boys*.

As Bowie explained, "It was a cross between [*The Wild Boys*] and *A Clockwork Orange* that really started to put together the shape and the look of what Ziggy and the Spiders were going to become. They were both powerful pieces of work, especially the marauding boy gangs of Burroughs's *Wild Boys* with their bowie knives. I got straight on to that. I read everything into everything. Everything had to be infinitely symbolic." The photos of the Spiders from Mars inside the album sleeve of *Rise and Fall* were even patterned after the gang of Droogs of *A Clockwork Orange*; Droogs are mentioned by name in the *Rise and Fall* song "Suffragette City." Furthermore, Bowie posed on the back cover of the album, peering out of a phone booth—just as though he were that other cryptic British alien who regularly regenerates himself and is often seen in a phone booth (specifically a police call box), the Doctor from *Doctor Who*.

Bowie also drew from work of the Legendary Stardust Cowboy. Born Norman Carl Odam, the Texan rockabilly artist released a twangy, oddball 1968 single titled "I Took a Trip (On a Gemini Spaceship)" that Bowie wound up covering in 2002; it was from Odam that Bowie borrowed Ziggy's surname. And after going on a record-buying spree while touring the United States in 1971, he bought *Fun House* by the Michigan proto-punk band the Stooges, whose outrageous lead singer was named Iggy Pop. He jotted down ideas on hotel stationary while traveling the States, resulting in a name that was a mash-up of Iggy Pop and the Legendary Stardust Cowboy. Ziggy Stardust was a fabricated rock star, one whose sleek facade flew in the face of the era's reigning rock aesthetic of laid-back, unpretentious authenticity. Instead, Bowie wanted to puncture that illusion by taking rock showmanship to a previously unseen, self-referential extreme.

When it came to Bowie's urge toward collage and deconstruction, Burroughs remained a prime inspiration. A pioneer of postmodern sci-fi pastiche as well as the literary cut-up technique, in which snippets of text were randomly rearranged to form a new syntax, Burroughs straddled both pulp sci-fi and the avant-garde, exactly the same liminal space Bowie now occupied. Rock critic Lester Bangs accused Bowie of "trying to be George Orwell and William Burroughs" while dismissing him as appearing to be "deposited onstage after seemingly being dipped in vats of green slime and pursued by Venusian crab boys"—a description that sounded like it could have been cribbed straight from a Burroughs book.

In 1973, Burroughs met Bowie in the latter's London home. The meeting was arranged by A. Craig Copetas from *Rolling Stone*, and the resulting exchange was published in the magazine a few months later. In the article, Copetas observed that Bowie's house was "decorated in a science-fiction mode," and that Bowie greeted them "wearing three-tone NASA jodhpurs." The ensuing conversation ranged across many topics, but it circled around science fiction—and in particular, the similarity Bowie saw between *Rise and Fall* and Burroughs's 1964 novel *Nova Express*, a surreal sci-fi parable about mind control and the tyranny of language.

In an effort to convince Burroughs of the similarity, Bowie offered one of the most revealing analyses of *Rise and Fall* as a work of science fiction:

> The time is five years to go before the end of the Earth. It has been
> announced that the world will end because of a lack of natural
> resources. Ziggy is in a position where all the kids have access to
> things that they thought they wanted. The older people have all

lost touch with reality, and the kids are left on their own to plunder anything. Ziggy was in a rock & roll band, and the kids no longer wanted to play rock & roll. There's no electricity to play it.

Bowie went on:

[The environmental apocalypse] does not cause the end of the world for Ziggy. The end comes when the infinites arrive. They really are a black hole, but I've made them people because it would be very hard to explain a black hole onstage.

Curiously, it took him another twenty-six years before casually revealing in an interview that a sci-fi song called "Black Hole Kids" was recorded as an outtake during the sessions for *Rise and Fall*. He called the song "fabulous," adding, "I have no idea why it wasn't on the original album. Maybe I forgot."

But Bowie dropped the biggest revelation about *Rise and Fall* in the 1973 conversation with Burroughs. Ziggy Stardust, according to his creator, is not an alien himself; instead, he's an earthling who makes contact with extra-dimensional beings, who then use him as a charismatic vessel for their own nefarious invasion plan. But like Frankenstein's monster being erroneously called "Frankenstein" to the point where it seems senseless to quibble with that usage, Ziggy Stardust continues to be widely considered the alien entity of *Rise and Fall*. Considering the shifting identity and gender of Bowie's most famous alter ego, that ambiguity may well have been his intention. Talking to Burroughs, he ultimately labels *Rise and Fall* "a science-fiction fantasy of today" before reiterating its similarity to *Nova Express*, to which Burroughs responds, "The parallels are definitely there."

Rise and Fall has always been as fluid as Bowie's facade itself. Michael Moorcock's Eternal Champion cast a shadow over Ziggy Stardust, especially the glammy incarnation of the many-faced character known as Jerry Cornelius—who was adapted to the big screen in 1973 for the feature film *The Final Programme*. It coincided with Ziggy's own ascendency, not to mention the New Wave of Science Fiction and its preference for fractured narratives and multiple interpretations over linear stories and pat endings.

During their mutual interview, Burroughs brought up the then-current rumor that Bowie might play Valentine Michael Smith in a film adaptation of

Heinlein's *Stranger in a Strange Land*. Bowie again dismissed it. "It seemed a bit too flower-powery, and that made me a bit wary." For his part, Bowie's fellow sci-fi musician Mick Farren of the Deviants later admitted he always thought Michael Valentine Smith was a major influence on Ziggy Stardust. "I was certain someone would call him out for plagiarism," Farren said. "Nobody did."

Bowie may have denied his affinity for *Stranger in a Strange Land* by his boyhood go-to author Heinlein, but he was not shy about professing his love for one of the authors Lester Bangs compared him to: George Orwell. Almost as a footnote, Bowie told Burroughs, "Now I'm doing Orwell's *Nineteen Eighty-Four* on television." That project would never come to pass, but it would lay the groundwork for his next, less famous sci-fi concept album—a jagged, atmospheric song cycle that plunged Bowie into the darkest extremes of dystopia.

IN JANUARY OF 1972, THE month before Bowie unveiled Ziggy Stardust at the Toby Jug, a fellow rising star in the glam movement took his own leap into outer space. Aided by producer Gus Dudgeon, who had helmed the sessions for "Space Oddity," the up-and-coming singer-songwriter Elton John recorded a song called "Rocket Man" for his next album, *Honky Château*. Released as a single in May of '72, "Rocket Man" bore some striking similarities to "Space Oddity": in a downbeat, first-person narrative from the point of view of a Mars-bound astronaut, the song cuts to the heart of space-age loneliness and isolation. "I miss the Earth so much, I miss my wife," John sang, echoing Bowie's "Tell my wife I love her very much" line from "Space Oddity." And like Major Tom, the unnamed narrator of "Rocket Man" seems more befuddled than heroic about being an astronaut, confessing, "All of this science I don't understand."

John's lyric writer, Bernie Taupin has acknowledged the influence of Pearls Before Swine's 1970 song "Rocket Man" on his own composition. Thanks to Taupin acting as the sci-fi middle man, Ray Bradbury's short story "The Rocket Man" filtered into John's song, then into the rock mainstream.

John's "Rocket Man" became a hit on both sides of the Atlantic that year. John's delivery is straightforward and accessible, and in many ways, it gave the space-fixated public a more palatable version of Bowie's musically and intellectually challenging work on *Rise and Fall*. The similarities weren't lost on Bowie. The month "Rocket Man" was released, he recorded "Space Oddity" in a radio session for the BBC—and in the middle of his new rendition, he injected the line, "I'm just a rocket man!"

Tom Rapp of Pearls Before Swine had more to contribute to sci-fi music in 1972 than indirectly influencing one of rock's biggest sci-fi songs. His solo album *Stardancer* came out that year, and while its title track didn't set any pop charts on fire, it's one of the most heart-stopping songs about the emotional cost of space exploration ever written. It sketches the same scenario of John's "Rocket Man," only from the perspective of the astronaut's family who has been left behind on Earth. As the song continues, it becomes clear that Rapp has drawn from another Bradbury story for his lyrics—this time "Kaleidoscope," the same tale of astronauts adrift in space that bore eerie parallels to "Space Oddity" three years earlier. And on "For the Dead in Space," another song from *Stardancer*, Rapp adopts the guise of a spaceman who pines poetically for the beauty of an extraterrestrial meadow: "The magic flowers of Mars / They are so far from me."

The red planet also shows up in T. Rex's 1972 "Ballroom of Mars," a typically surreal swirl of words and images from Marc Bolan imagining how "We'll dance our lives away / In the ballrooms of Mars." While not as committed to sci-fi as was Bowie, Bolan counterbalanced his friend's darker tendencies with a dreamier kind of star-love. As journalist Rob Young stated, the two were "Pied Pipers . . . transporting their young listeners from immersion in a speculative, mythological past and repositioning pop music in a future of plastic, glitter, and tin."

Another of Bowie's old friends in sci-fi fandom, Alex Harvey, surfaced with a sci-fi song in 1972 titled "Flying Saucer's Daughter." Recorded by the Sensational Alex Harvey Band, the song fell somewhere between Bowie's ethereality and Hawkwind's raw hypnotics; amid jarring sound manipulation and spikey riffs, Harvey sings of a woman who is a "space captain's daughter" and an "intergalactic celebrity."

Not every artist on the newly energized sci-fi bandwagon had ties to Bowie, though. A young prog group called Genesis released "Watcher of the Skies," the single off their 1972 album *Foxtrot*, and its sweeping yet ominous grandeur interpreted some of Arthur C. Clarke's ideas from *Childhood's End*—as did Pink Floyd's more blatantly named song "Childhood's End," also released that year.

The notion of aliens visiting Earth for reasons villainous, benevolent, or simply unknowable had taken hold in 1972, fueling a fresh wave of sci-fi songs. But the less philosophical sci-fi conceit—simply hopping in a spaceship and cruising the galaxy—wasn't going away. Ray Davies, who had shared Bowie's love of *2001: A Space Odyssey* back in 1968, released the single "Supersonic Rocket Ship" with his band the Kinks in 1972. Instead of trying to bring a sonic approximation of futurism to the song, however, the song was downright vaudevillian, concerned more with witty social satire than sci-fi itself. Not that Davies was averse to using sci-fi more earnestly; in the Kinks' 1970 song "This Time Tomorrow," he pensively asks, "This time tomorrow, where will we be? / On a spaceship somewhere, sailing across an empty sea?"

Heavy metal and hard rock—both genres still in their infancy in 1972—produced a sci-fi milestone that year in the form of "Space Truckin'" by Deep Purple. The long-running band had been drifting toward a harder, faster sound since its psychedelic days in the '60s, and "Space Truckin'" combined the best of the band's old and new approaches: raging riffs with spacey lyrics about how "We got music in our solar system / We're space truckin' 'round the stars." The song's unpretentious stomp—it was, in essence, Steppenwolf's "Born to Be Wild" recast for outer-space Hells Angels—helped cement the growing affinity between sci-fi and metal. So did the self-titled debut album by the group Captain Beyond. Led by former Deep Purple lead singer Rod Evans, the band fixated on astral mysticism and space travel as a means of exploring inner space. Its thematic ambition and progressive edge have been relegated to Deep Purple's shadow, despite being one of the most compelling sci-fi albums of 1972.

With the success of Bowie's Ziggy Stardust persona—and with sci-fi music becoming increasingly accepted thanks to 1972's explosion of space-related singles—it was inevitable that novelty would again creep in. Ricky Wilde, an eleven-year-old kid from England, scored a hit late in 1972 with "I Am an Astronaut." Charming yet atmospheric, it sounded like a kid's-eye-view of "Space Oddity," a kind of bubblegum Bowie. By year's end, even prepubescent children had their sci-fi music idol. Thanks to Ziggy Stardust's media saturation in 1972, parodies began to pop up. The British folk-rock band the Strawbs released a song titled "Backside" under the joking name "Ciggy Barlust and the Whales from Venus." They wouldn't be the last band to imitate the name Ziggy Stardust and the Spiders from Mars throughout the decade.

"Space Oddity" may have been Bowie's first major association with sci-fi, but *The Rise and Fall of Ziggy Stardust and the Spiders from Mars* made him the public face of it in the pop world. And this was a time when sci-fi across all media was looming larger than ever—and when visions of the future came with an anxious mix of both dread and hope.

✳ **THE GRAND BALLROOM OF THE** Statler Hilton Hotel—known originally and currently as the Hotel Pennsylvania—vibrated with excitement. Huge posters of William Shatner adorned the walls. Busts of Leonard Nimoy covered a table. Buttons reading I GROK MR. SPOCK and T-shirts with the slogan STAR TREK LIVES! were on conspicuous display. Publicity photos, prop replicas, and episode scripts were being traded and sold. Passersby gawked at moon rocks and an astronaut suit on loan from NASA. Isaac Asimov and Gene Roddenberry could be seen moving among the hundreds of fans gathered for an event that everyone in attendance recognized as historic.

What is generally considered to be the first true *Star Trek* convention took place on the weekend of January 21 through 23, 1972, at the Statler Hilton, located across the street from Madison Square Garden in Manhattan. Titled Star Trek Lives! by its organizers, the convention was a culmination of years of devoted fandom following the show's cancelation by NBC in 1969. *Star Trek* had been in syndication ever since, and its popularity had only grown. As NASA's space program expanded, so did the public's hunger for Roddenberry's vision of a bright, optimistic future where all the nations and ethnicities of Earth had managed to band together for the intrepid purpose of exploring the cosmos. *The Village Voice* called the convention's organizers "adult sci-fi freaks and show buffs," but no amount of condescension could curb this convocation of a new pop-culture tribe.

In addition to innovating the fandom convention, which influenced everything from the megalithic San Diego Comic-Con on down, Star Trek Lives! helped widely spread two enduring rituals of sci-fi fandom: fanfic and cosplay. These portmanteaux, standing for "fan fiction" and "costume play," demonstrated a new kind of engagement with popular culture. For the approximately three thousand *Trek* fans who showed up at the Statler Hilton, science fiction wasn't something to absorb passively, as was the expected mode of media consumption at the time. Writing one's own fiction using the characters and universe of a favorite sci-fi property—or publicly dressing up in costumes inspired by them—was a way of moving fandom beyond mere entertainment and into the realm of lifestyle, even of personal identity.

It's highly unlikely that any attendees of Star Trek Lives! also witnessed one of Bowie's Ziggy Stardust gigs across the Atlantic that spring. Yet the collective unconscious of sci-fi seemed to be in harmony. With Bowie fans starting to show up at his gigs clad in their handmade approximations of Ziggy's glittery spaceman garb, cosplay had also spontaneously appeared in the arena of sci-fi music.

Sci-fi fandom needed that agency. In 1972, themes of powerlessness, disenfranchisement, and oppression had settled into science fiction. Films and television programs that year such as *Silent Running*, *Solaris*, *Slaughterhouse-Five*, *Doomwatch*, and *The People*—the last being an ABC made-for-TV movie starring William Shatner—presented strange tomorrows full of societies and psychologies being taken over and confined. Folk singer Joan Baez's theme song for *Silent Running*, also titled "Silent Running," converted the movie's ecologically devastated postapocalypse into a haunting reminder of our severed connection to Mother Nature, leaving humanity increasingly estranged from its source of existence.

One of the year's biggest sci-fi novels, Asimov's Hugo Award-winning *The Gods Themselves*, was a cocktail of speculative nightmares, including alien depredation, human arrogance, societal collapse, and the imminent destruction of the Sun. Meanwhile, another book from 1972, Christopher Priest's *Fugue for a Darkening Island*, imagined a bleak near future where right-wing England has become flooded with African refugees and must face its xenophobia and insularity. And Barry N. Malzberg's 1972 novel, *Beyond Apollo*, called out NASA by name while depicting astronauts driven mad amid the corruption of government-funded space travel. The real-life Apollo program wound down in December of 1972. The completion of its final manned mission to the moon, Apollo 17, left the United States and the world wondering how, where, and when we would go next. That is, if we went farther at all.

In Martin Caidin's 1972 novel, *Cyborg*, the fictional astronaut Steve Austin is a crewmember of Apollo 17, who, after an accident, must be rebuilt back on Earth with robotic body parts. The next year, the TV movie *The Six Million Dollar Man* (and its subsequent weekly series) would be based on *Cyborg*, reinforcing the notion that science fiction might be more exciting here on Earth than out among the stars.

The most terrifying vision in 1972 of what might be in store for humanity came from another book adaptation. However, it wasn't a work of science fiction, but of science nonfiction. Orson Welles—the man whose authoritative voice caused a panic in 1938 when he performed a radio adaptation of H. G. Wells's classic alien-invasion story *The War of the Worlds*—narrated a documentary based on Alvin Toffler's phenomenally successful 1970 nonfiction book *Future Shock*. The bestseller contended that the twentieth century's exponential advances in technology had outpaced the human race's ability to process and cope with such massive upheavals. As Welles says in the film, "We live in an age of anxiety, a time of stress. With all our sophistication, we are in fact the victims of our own technological strength." Following Toffler's alarmist checklist, he goes on to consider everything from the hippie movement to X-rated cinema as possible symptoms of humanity's technological malaise.

The term "future shock" had firmly entered the popular lexicon by 1972; the following year, soul artist Curtis Mayfield released a single by the same name, a funky yet bloodcurdling account of the wrong direction in which society was heading, including Toffler's projections of ecological disasters and urban epidemics. "The future need not be blindly accepted. Author Alvin Toffler finds this conviction spreading among young people throughout the world," Welles intones in *Future Shock*. At film's end, Toffler himself addresses the viewer, adding, "We can no longer just allow technology to come roaring down at us." After decades of hopefully cautious and cautiously hopeful science and sci-fi, it was becoming the widespread belief by 1972 that someone ought to slam on the brakes.

"FUTURE SHOCK HAD ARRIVED." SO wrote Robert Hilburn in the *Los Angeles Times* on October 23, 1972. He was not, however, talking about Alvin Toffler. Nor was he commenting on pollution, overpopulation, or the imminent demise of the Apollo program. He was talking about David Bowie.

The Santa Monica Civic Auditorium played host to Bowie three days before the *Times'* review. The concert was later immortalized as the live album *Santa Monica '72*, one of the definitive live documents of Bowie's Ziggy Stardust era. As Hilburn observed, in detail that dripped science fiction, "The flashing strobe lights and strains of Beethoven's 'Ode to Joy' combined perfectly with the band's futuristic spacesuits and Bowie's own bisexual image to provide an aura of *A Clockwork Orange*, not so much in the sense of violence as in the incredible sense of 'nowness' and the wave of the future."

His fans were on the same wavelength. In the 1975 Bowie documentary

Cracked Actor, American fans are interviewed outside a Los Angeles concert. According to one woman, costumed dazzlingly in accordance with the Ziggy aesthetic as if she were a Trekker wearing Spock ears at a convention, "Bowie, he represents it all to me. Excitement. Space. See, I'm just a space cadet. He's the commander." Later a young blond man from Phoenix states, "He's from his own universe." When the interviewer asks, "What universe is that?" the kid replies, "The Bowie universe." Another fan at the time went on record saying that Bowie "was science fiction personified . . . I really believed he was an alien of some kind."

Bowie himself might have briefly harbored this belief. His wife, Angela, suggested that the obsession he'd held with science fiction and UFOs since childhood was more than just a hobby. The couple put forth the notion that Bowie was a member of a race called the Light People, advanced beings who came to Earth at various points throughout history to help enhance technology and culture. Other Light People included "Leonardo, Galileo, Newton, Gandhi, Churchill, and, closer to home, Dylan, Lennon, and Hendrix." Speaking to the *New Musical Express* (known mostly as *NME*) in 1972, Bowie's fellow sci-fi musician Robert Fripp of King Crimson said this: "You know, spirits from other places can take on physical bodies on this planet. Examples of people from other places? Jimi Hendrix, Marc Bolan, David Bowie." Regardless of whether Bowie believed he was a Light Person, or whether it was just another phase of his self-publicity, a new type of stardom coalesced around him: the image of the pop star as an otherworldly savior, a celebrity of superhuman dimensions with the power to transcend mundane reality and liberate the consciousness of the listener.

Just as the androgynous Bowie blurred the lines between genders, so did Ziggy Stardust blur the line between human and alien. Notes scholar Philip Auslander, "Bowie's alien persona was emblematic of his bisexual alienation from the heterosexual, male-dominated world of rock music.'" Whether he was actually an alien was not important. What mattered was his intrinsic ability to challenge one of the bedrock principles of rock music, that of authenticity. From its inception, rock had been all about realness, earthiness, grit, physicality. Through Ziggy, Bowie had disregarded this principle just as flagrantly as sci-fi authors had with their literature. Instead of trying to portray emotional and empirical reality as something objective, they relied on imagination, fabulism, and fluidity.

Still, Bowie existed in the real world, and not even Ziggy Stardust could transcend the pull of entropy. As hope for humanity's technological future fought to remain relevant amid the gloomy forecasts of the early '70s, Bowie told the NME in 1972 that he wanted to face "the inevitability of the apocalypse, in whatever forms it takes" while also "[promoting] some feeling of optimism in the future." Caught in this contradiction, the ongoing onstage saga of Ziggy Stardust—suffused with both wonder and horror—wore thin.

Ziggy Stardust made his final appearance on July 3, 1973. After a sold-out concert at London's Hammersmith Odeon Theatre, Bowie retired the character that had catapulted him to superstardom. A premonition of the artist's inner turmoil and disillusionment came four months prior, when he said, "Now here's the crunch. So an astronaut goes to the moon, takes a photograph of the Earth, comes back, and sets up an archetypal Earth which is no longer useful. It's not in the past. People are cleaning it up—ecology and so on. So where are we now? What's the next step after that one?"

He may as well have been talking about his own role as a sci-fi artist. First with "Space Oddity" and then more comprehensively with *The Rise and Fall of Ziggy Stardust and the Spiders from Mars,* he had gone into outer space, looked at rock music from a revolutionary new vantage, and returned only to find popular culture possibly worse than when he had left it. Rather than embracing his innovative use of sci-fi, speculative ambiguity, and futurist allegory, pop music accepted him only as an outlier. He had won converts, comrades, and imitators, but he was still seen as an anomaly. When he posed the question, "What's the next step after this one?" the future of his career and science fiction itself seemed to be caught up in it.

But Bowie wasn't done with the infinite possibility of sci-fi, the only canvas truly vast enough to host his creative ambition. Neither was a fresh contingent of musicians hailing from continental Europe who would profoundly change the way sci-fi and music could intermingle—musicians who would also wind up exerting a vital influence on Bowie and the entire sonic architecture of the future.

5

COMET MELODY:
1973

THEY CALLED IT "THE COMET OF THE CENTURY." MEDIA BUZZ SUR-
rounded the imminent arrival of the comet named Kohoutek throughout
1973. The solar-system-circling traveler had been discovered in March of that
year at the Hamburg Observatory in Germany. For that moment, Germany
was the center of the astronomical world. When, in December, the comet
reached perihelion—the closest point in its orbit to the Sun—humanity was
fortuitously prepared. Two space crews, the American Skylab 4 and the Soviet
Soyuz 13, were already scheduled to be in space that December. Those astronauts and cosmonauts became the first to observe a comet from space. The
Skylab crew photographed it in all its glory on Christmas Day, 1973, captur-

ing a sight that would not be seen again from Earth for another 75,000 years.

Only it wasn't as glorious as hoped. Overhyped for months on end, Kohoutek fell short of expectations, due in part to the comet's partial disintegration near the Sun just prior to its flyby of Earth. It wasn't long before "Kohoutek" became synonymous with "dud." As a curious postscript to the story, the three Skylab 4 astronauts—Gerald P. Carr, Edward G. Gibson, and William R. Pogue—suspended radio communications with NASA for the entire day of December 28, just as Kohoutek reached its historic nearest point to the Sun. The incident came to be known, a bit exaggeratedly, as the Skylab mutiny. Overworked and stressed after six weeks in space, the longest time any astronauts had spent away from Earth, the crew decided to go on strike for a day and do nothing but gaze out the windows of the space station, peering into the cosmos in contemplation.

If a single month illustrated the fatigue and disillusionment with space exploration that had set in by the early '70s, December of 1973 was it. For years, science fiction—including *Marooned*, written by Martin Caidin of *Cyborg/The Six Million Dollar Man* fame; Stanislaw Lem's philosophical interplanetary parable *Solaris*; and Barry N. Malzberg's novel *Beyond Apollo*—had been predicting that space travel might have its share of psychological as well as existential pitfalls. Technology had taken us so far, so fast. Miracles had become so commonplace that a once-in-a-thousand-lifetimes comet wound up being little more than a laughingstock.

In Germany, the cradle of Kohoutek's discovery, two men were not laughing. Ralf Hütter and Florian Schneider, residents of Düsseldorf, performed in a music group called Kraftwerk. It was not, to say the least, a conventional rock band. Formed in 1969 as an experimental group using mostly orthodox instruments, Kraftwerk—German for "power station"—had by 1973 morphed into something unrecognizable to contemporaneous audiences. The duo gradually replaced acoustic instruments, including drums, violin, and flute, with synthesizers, drum machines, and homemade electronics.

Thematically, their songs were innocuous; their 1973 album *Ralf und Florian* contained songs such as "Tanzmusik" ("Dance Music") and "Kristallo" ("Crystals"). But in December of 1973, they released a single—their first—that marked a profound shift in vision. Titled "Kohoutek-Kometenmelodie," or "Kohoutek Comet Melody," the single attempted to capitalize on the Kohoutek craze, much in the same way Bowie's "Space Oddity" had with the Apollo 11 mission four years earlier. Similarly, Sun Ra held a concert in tribute to Kohoutek in

December of 1973, and Hawkwind did the same a month earlier at a lecture about the comet sponsored by New York's famed Hayden Planetarium. Two years later, Journey—not yet a platinum-selling act—were late to the party with their instrumental "Kohoutek."

Kraftwerk's "Kohoutek-Kometenmelodie," like the comet itself, was somewhat of a flop. But its droning, pinging, synthesized outer-space daydream signaled a sea change. From there, the group clicked into a new identity. They recruited drummer Wolfgang Flür in 1973 to man the electronic drum pads that formed the stiff, brittle backbeat of their songs. They shed the last remaining vestiges of their hippie-era style and began dressing in crisp, severe outfits, like an apparition of what the 1930s might have imagined the twenty-third century to look like. Their music grew colder, starker, more robotic. They took to calling their recording studio "their laboratory." When asked by Lester Bangs in a 1975 interview for the *NME* how Kraftwerk felt about the idea of getting brain implants that would instantly translate their thoughts into music, Hütter replied, "Yes. This would be fantastic." A year later the *NME* also noted in a concert review, "If Hawkwind are the Michael Moorcock end of space rock, then Kraftwerk are closer to Asimov."

Kraftwerk's clinical, hardwired sound changed the way music, science, and humanity interfaced. "Kohoutek-Kometenmelodie" was just the beginning. A reworked version of the song appeared on their 1974 album *Autobahn*—a bracingly original record that bore no actual sci-fi lyrics but that dispassionately glorified the modern joys of industrialization, motorization, and technology. Many groups before them had sung about science fiction—but soon, Kraftwerk would embody science fiction.

KRAFTWERK WERE PART OF A loose conglomeration of German bands in the '70s that became lumped under a category called Krautrock. The bands involved hated the name, unflattering and reductive as it is, but it stuck; a lesser-used synonym for Krautrock, however, is "kosmische musik," or "cosmic music." An outgrowth of the German psychedelic rock scene of the '60s, Krautrock was only occasionally obsessed with outer space, and it rarely referenced works of sci-fi by name as did many American and British musicians of the era. Instead, as with Kraftwerk, a sense of technological restlessness and galactic resonance permeated a large portion of Krautrock.

One of the genre's originators, the group Amon Düül II, featured British bassist Dave Anderson before he left to join Hawkwind in time for the latter group's revolutionary early '70s releases. While with Amon Düül II, though, he helped conjure a constellation of Pink Floyd–influenced rhythm and texture intent on delivering the listener to other places and times. Lester Bangs compared them to the writing of William S. Burroughs, describing their 1971 song "Eye-Shaking King" as "overpowering the listener and turning his brain into the resinous extract of Burroughsian Mugwump spinal fluid." And on 1971's magnificent *Tanz der Lemminge*, there's a more targeted sci-fi inspiration to the incendiary track "H.G. Wells' Take-Off."

By 1973, Anderson had left for Hawkwind, carrying a marked Krautrock influence along with him—and Amon Düül II continued swimming in intergalactic waves. "Apocalyptic Bore" from that year's *Vive La Trance* album spoke in awestruck tones of a time when "We saw the UFOs fly by" and "Every now could explore the past / 'Cause the time-continuum robot was invented." Their 1974 album *Hijack* included the songs "Explode Like a Star" and "Archy the Robot"; in the latter, "Archy is my metal archaeopteryx," a heroic machine-man whose victory over evil is celebrated "in hi-fi, in sci-fi, marching bands belling." The cover of *Hijack* was an illustration of an alien taking a tethered spacewalk toward another craft with the words "Düül Amon" painted on its top. A letter written at the time by the band's management company explained that Amon Düül's "cosmic music liberates the listener in his own fantasia, and gives him the liberty of a voyager through time."

Another Krautrock pioneer, Can, alluded toward sci-fi vistas with their 1973 album *Future Days*; years before, they'd titled their first tape of psychedelic jams *Prehistoric Future*. The group Guru Guru paid homage to extraterrestrial life in 1970 and 1971 with their songs "UFO" and "Spaceship"—the latter containing what sounded like eerie, static-riddled radio broadcasts as well as ambient passages that might have been the voices of inquisitive quasars. Or, at the very least, B-movie sound effects gone prog. A 1973 album by Dzyan titled *Time Machine* was entirely instrumental, but its tricky, shifting tempos metaphorically depicted the dumbfounding confusion and revelation of time travel. Similarly, Cornucopia's "Humanoid Robot Show" from 1973 came on like a distorted nightmare of some android invasion.

The mesmerizing lull of ambient sound was just as paramount in Krautrock as was the abrasiveness of electronic noise. Ash Ra Tempel injected plenty of ambience into 1973's "Timeship," just one of many songs in which the band equated sonic weightlessness with psychedelic exploration. Time travel also played a central role in Achim Reichel's 1972 album *Echo*, released under the name A.R. & Machines, a jazzy, minimalist pulse of tribal futurism with song names like "The Echo of the Future." Echoes also featured heavily in *Alpha Centauri*, the 1971 album by Tangerine Dream. Led by the visionary guitarist and keyboardist Edgar Froese, the instrumental outfit turned Alpha Centauri—the closest star to our Sun, thus a favorite destination in science fiction from *The Twilight Zone* and *Star Trek* to Isaac Asimov's 1940 short story "Homo Sol" and Philip K. Dick's 1964 novel, *Clans of the Alphane Moon*—into an object of worship. With reverberating synths and oscillating drones, Froese and company produced the most compelling musical metaphor for outer space to date; he even gave the members of his band a score written on graph paper, lending it the air of an astronomical chart. He dedicated the album "to all people who feel obliged to space."

Klaus Schulze was a journeyman member of both Ash Ra Tempel and Tangerine Dream around this time, but his role in sci-fi music would ultimately be much more pronounced. His second solo album, *Cyborg*, was released in 1973—and while it bears no clear relation to the Caidin novel of the same name that inspired *The Six Million Dollar Man* television movies the same year, he has readily admitted that "I was a huge fan of science fiction stories." *Cyborg* does not dispute that claim. Drawing on classic sci-fi material about human-android hybrids, album tracks like "Chromengel" ("Chrome Angel") and "Neuronengesang" ("Neuro-Song") were written and recorded primarily on synthesizers, evoking a future-forward symbiosis between the instrument and its operator. As Schulze himself said, the synthesizer is "a dialogue partner for the musician," and when playing it, "you must be simultaneously rational and emotional."

Schulze's synthesized symphony fell somewhere between the astral, instrumental dreaminess of Tangerine Dream and the pulsing, beeping mechanization of Kraftwerk. Taken together, *Cyborg* and "Kohoutek-Kometenmelodie" helped turn 1973 into a banner year for the musical marriage of man and machine. Kraftwerk's own cyborg tendencies would become even more prominent as the '70s progressed, and Schulze would go on to compose music based on and titled after specific sci-fi novels, making his allegiance to the genre explicit rather than implied. While the majority of their Krautrock brethren would either disband or stray away from cosmic themes, Klaus Schulze and Kraftwerk eventually delved deeper into sci-fi by decade's end: Schulze by representing it, Kraftwerk by reflecting it.

KRAUTROCK IN MANY WAYS PARALLELED prog. Both favored long songs, synthesizers, and thematic ambition. But where prog was largely complicated, Krautrock was largely repetitive; Kraftwerk's industrial groove became known by the term "motorik." Still, a minority of German prog bands in the early '70s strayed into the cosmic territory dominated by their Krautrock neighbors. Lush and elaborate, the music of Hannover-based Eloy fell decisively on the side of prog. On their 1973 album *Inside*, the song "Land of Nobody" takes place during an interplanetary exodus: "We just leave the Earth's ground / On the way to see the new star." Like a less militant Paul Kantner's *Blows Against the Empire*, it's about fleeing our dying planet in the hope that a colony on a new world will prove more advanced and enlightened.

The flip side of this concept was found on another track from *Inside* titled "Future City," a warning about urban alienation and overcrowding in which frontman Frank Bornemann sings, "And you think about cities growing up / Until it's crushing you." From there, Eloy would go on to release numerous sci-fi concept albums, the first being 1975's sprawling *Power and the Passion*, a time-travel saga that takes place across centuries. Fittingly, Bornemann named the band after the Eloi—one of the two races of humanoids descended from Homo sapiens in the far future of H. G. Wells's 1895 novel *The Time Machine*. "This book grabbed me by the throat, and the story touched me deeply," Bornemann explained. "How these people, the Eloi, had to build everything up from scratch and created a new culture reminded me of what we were trying to do as a band." Eloy was, for him, "a start into an unknown future."

The members of Nektar may not have been German by birth, but the group of English expatriates came together in Hamburg in 1969. Along with Eloy, they became leading lights of the German prog scene—and they also became swept up in science fiction. Their 1971 debut album, *Journey to the Centre of the Eye*, was one of rock's first sci-fi concept albums, chronicling an astronaut's consciousness-altering trip to another galaxy after aliens abduct him on his way to Saturn. On their next sci-fi concept album, 1973's *Remember the Future*, the grand apparatus of spacetime itself became the engine, reflecting the kind of astrophysics-meets-metaphysics posited by the likes of Arthur C. Clarke and Roger Zelazny.

Germany's community of sci-fi musicians was a loose confederation at best, but in Southern England, there existed a more tightly knit cabal. Like a bucolic version of London's Ladbroke Grove, the music scene in Canterbury teemed with science fiction. Australian-born Daevid Allen cofounded the Soft Machine in 1966, naming the band after the William S. Burroughs novel; a massive fan of the author's surreal, taboo-shattering sci-fi, he'd actually met Burroughs in the '60s. Allen left the Soft Machine—which became a regular presence onstage at London's UFO Club—the following year. He settled in Paris and formed the band Gong.

From there he pushed his twisty, whimsical rock into the bizarre fringes of sci-fi. The group's Radio Gnome Invisible trilogy—which comprised the albums *Flying Teapot, Angel's Egg,* and *You,* released between 1972 and 1974—revolved around an outer-space protagonist named Zero the Hero who journeys to Planet Gong. There he accepts the noble mission to enlighten earthlings by playing them Planet Gong's indigenous music, which will unlock their nascent evolution. Allen quit Gong in 1975 after claiming that "an invisible forcefield" was keeping him from getting onstage with the rest of the group; before long he launched a series of new groups using variations on the Gong name (Planet Gong included) and claimed he was working on a Zero the Hero novel—which the *NME* referred to as "a Tolkien-scale history of the planet Gong." A song from *Flying Teapot,* "The Octave Doctors and the Crystal Machine," meshed with Allen's belief that he had been contacted by aliens he referred to as "the octave doctors."

Flying Teapot marked the first appearance of Gong's new guitarist, Steve Hillage. He was no stranger to space music. In 1969 he'd played in the psychedelic Canterbury band Arzachel, named after a crater on the Moon. Following that, he led the group Kahn. Borrowing their moniker from one of *Star Trek's* most beloved villains, the genetically engineered superhuman Khan Noonien Singh, the band also counted among its roster Nick Greenwood, who had already tasted sci-fi rock as a former bassist for Arthur Brown.

Khan's sole album, *Space Shanty,* from 1972, featured two songs in particular that stretched into the cosmos. The nine-minute epic "Space Shanty" and the slightly more modest "Stargazers" featured lyrics such as "Future comes, all you know is that you'll share / Suns and moons, many cycles, millions of days" and riffs that sounded like the band used astrophysics equations in place of sheet music. To top it all off, *Space Shanty's* cover boasted one of the most fully realized pieces of sci-fi album art up to that point: an ultra-detailed painting of a spaceship that wasn't slick or cartoonish, but eerily realistic, as if it were a mirage of a machine that might one day take humankind to the stars. In the interim, Khan was happy to supply the space-port music.

Elsewhere in England, prog continued to incorporate science fiction, although often superficially. Pink Floyd's *The Dark Side of the Moon* came out in 1973, becoming a benchmark for the band as well as a sales phenomenon. The group had finally succeeded in transitioning from a cult act to a stadium-filler, and they did so by returning—albeit mostly in name—to the Moon obsession first heard in 1969, when they jammed "Moonhead" as the Apollo 11 astronauts strode across the lunar surface. *The Dark Side of the Moon*, however, also marked a point where using astronomical terminology and imagery in prog started to become more of a stylistic strategy or vague metaphor, rather than the springboard for a substantive foray into sci-fi. Manfred Mann's Earth Band issued the album *Solar Fire* later in 1973. It seemed at first glance to be a concept album about the solar system—but that concept was fuzzy and lacking narrative cohesion, regardless of the majesty of the music. Yes's 1973 album *Tales from Topographic Oceans* also appeared to be a sci-fi opus thanks to its Roger Dean–designed cover depicting an ethereal alien panorama, not to mention song titles such as "The Revealing Science of God (Dance of the Dawn)." In actuality, the album was inspired by the writing of the Indian yogi Paramahansa Yogananda.

Plenty of bands were still using sci-fi as more than window dressing. In Electric Light Orchestra's gorgeous 1973 song "From the Sun to the World," mastermind Jeff Lynne sings cryptically of "People shouting from towers in the city / While their babies grow in test tubes overnight." In 1981, after using an increasing amount of spaceship imagery on his record covers and in his elaborate stage show, Lynne would write a sci-fi concept album, ELO's *Time*. A former ELO member, Roy Wood, released an even more impressive sci-fi song in 1973. "Miss Clarke and the Computer" is a tender folk-based pop number in which a robot, smitten with his owner, pleads not to be dismantled. At the end of the song, Wood's voice is electronically slowed down in pitch, as if the robot is gradually, tragically running out of power.

By the early '70s, King Crimson had moved away from the dystopian doom of 1969's "21st Century Schizoid Man." But in a 1973 profile on guitarist and leader Robert Fripp in *Melody Maker*, the interviewer observed that Fripp's home prominently displayed "shelves of sci-fi paperbacks." One of them might have been Philip K. Dick's *The Man in the High Castle*, the 1962 novel that imagined a world where the Nazis had won World War II. References to the book appear on *(No Pussyfooting)*, a groundbreaking 1973 album of ambient drones and loops that teamed Fripp with keyboardist Brian Eno.

Eno had just left Roxy Music, the Bryan Ferry–fronted glam band that luxuriated in a retro-futuristic image. Crisp and sterile, Ferry exuded anachronistic dazzle, as if he had traveled both forward and backward in time—like the Doctor of *Doctor Who*—and accumulated a synthesis of sartorial tips along the way. He once confessed that he was a fan of sci-fi films during his younger days, and that as a teenager he would take his dates to see them. That said, he didn't fully dive into sci-fi in his lyrics. Even the song "Ladytron," from the group's self-titled 1972 debut album, bore no trace of android lovers, despite its evocative title—although his 1978 solo song "This Island Earth" clearly called back to the 1955 sci-fi movie of the same name, a classic he likely saw in the cinemas of his youth. Roxy Music's guitarist Phil Manzanera, however, had previously played in Quiet Sun, a group from the Canterbury scene who had a song titled "Mummy Was an Asteroid, Daddy Was a Small Non-Stick Kitchen Utensil." The band's name also bore a distinct resemblance to *The Year of the Quiet Sun*, a Hugo-nominated sci-fi novel by Wilson Tucker published in 1970.

While Roxy Music didn't sing explicitly about sci-fi, Eno had an affinity for the work of Philip K. Dick that resonated with Fripp. The keyboardist suggested that one of the two lengthy instrumental tracks on *(No Pussyfooting)* be titled "The Heavenly Music Corporation," after a brand of marijuana cigarettes mentioned in *The Man in the High Castle*. The album's second track was called "Swastika Girls," which, keeping in mind the Nazi concept of Dick's novel, is either another *High Castle* reference or a remarkable coincidence. Eno's 1975 solo song "St. Elmo's Fire," from the album *Another Green World*, has the sci-fi-friendly line "Splitting ions in the ether," which his biographer David Sheppard described as "Samuel Taylor Coleridge by way of Philip K. Dick." Dick eventually returned the favor; the fictional electronic-music composer Brent Mini, a character in his 1981 novel *VALIS*, was based on Eno.

Another Green World doesn't come across as a sci-fi concept album, but sci-fi informed the record's entire contemplative tone. Said Eno,

> The album had a mood established before I started. I was thinking about escaping. I read a science fiction story a long time ago where these people are exploring space and they finally find this habitable planet—and it turns out to be identical to Earth in every detail. And

I thought that was the supreme irony: that they'd originally left to find something better and arrived in the end—which was actually the same place. Which is how I feel about myself. I'm always trying to project myself at a tangent and always seem eventually to arrive back at the same place. It's a loop. You actually can't escape.

Early in his career, Eno asserted that he'd traveled to Earth from his true home, a planet called Xenon, much in the same way Bowie had dubbed himself a Light Person. The same fictional planet of Xenon is cited in the tour program of Hawkwind's 1972 Space Ritual Tour—something Eno could have very well been in possession of. Such outlandish claims became routine in the glam scene of the early '70s. Bowie may have retreated from science fiction in 1973—retiring Ziggy Stardust and sprinkling just a handful of sci-fi images into that year's *Aladdin Sane* album, such as the "strung out on lasers" line from "The Jean Genie"—but the impact of "Space Oddity" as a harbinger of so much subsequent sci-fi music only reaffirmed his association with outer space in the mind of the public.

The United States unleashed its own answer to Bowie that year. The self-titled debut album by Jobriath, a Texas-raised singer-songwriter, came out in 1973, and his over-the-top, glam-alien appearance signaled an obvious attempt to catch Bowie's rising star, as did the album's blend of elegant piano, strutting rhythms, raygun sound effects, unearthly snarl, and gay sexuality. Tracks like "Space Clown," "Earthling," and "Morning Starship" drove the point home; superficial and extravagant yet wholly catchy and fun, *Jobriath* had all the makings of a hit. But it failed to find purchase, proving that Bowie's sui generis strangeness was not something that could be effectively mass-produced. Jobriath faded from the music industry, tragically dying of AIDS in 1983 before gaining posthumous recognition as a trailblazer of sci-fi rock.

Jobriath's failure underscored a fundamental difference in audiences on either side of the Atlantic, particularly between American and British ones. Sporadic works of sci-fi rock did manage to pop up in North America in 1973: "I'm a Stranger Here," a song about alien visitation by Canada's the Five Man Electrical Band; *Cosmic Furnace*, an album of spacey, synth-driven prog by Roger Powell, the keyboardist of Todd Rundgren's Utopia; and "Space Station #5" by the hard-rock band Montrose, featuring future Van Halen frontman Sammy Hagar, who would later revisit sci-fi in his 1976 solo song "Silver Lights," an account of an apocalypse triggered by mass alien abduction.

Overall, though, sci-fi music in the United States simply had not caught on—or even coalesced into a recognizable entity—the way it had in Germany and England. Tuneful sci-fi songs like "On Our Way to Hana" by the folk-pop group Mu failed to find a foothold; melodic and well produced, the 1973 single mentioned the appearance of "silver saucers" in the opening verse, which was enough to keep most radio programmers away.

While shows like *Doctor Who* were a staple of mainstream culture in the UK, sci-fi in the United States remained mostly a cult preoccupation. British programs aimed specifically at younger viewers, such as *The Tomorrow People*—which ran from 1973 to 1979—helped cement sci-fi in the minds of a generation raised on TV. *The Tomorrow People* posited an emerging population of adolescent superhumans, known alternately as Homo novis and Homo superior, not dissimilar from Marvel Comics' X-Men. The term "Homo superior" had been coined by sci-fi author Olaf Stapledon in his 1953 novel *Odd John*, and it surfaced in Bowie's 1971 song "Oh! You Pretty Things," where he sings that we mere Homo sapiens "Gotta make way for the Homo superior," meaning the next stage of our own evolution. It's entirely possible Bowie picked it up from *Odd John*, but Roger Price, the creator of *The Tomorrow People*, remembered a conversation he had with Bowie where he told the singer about his series-in-progress. The term "Homo superior" came up, and Price believed it influenced Bowie to write "Oh! You Pretty Things."

American sci-fi television did experience an uptick in 1973. *The Six Million Dollar Man*'s three pilot episodes launched that franchise. And Gene Roddenberry experienced a small post–*Star Trek* victory in the form of a feature-length pilot for CBS titled *Genesis II*, the postapocalyptic story of a man who wakes up to a chaotic future after being placed in chemical hibernation for centuries. *Genesis II* was not picked up as a series, but Roddenberry wasn't hurting for work that year. After years of fan outcry and increasing demand due to reruns and conventions like Star Trek Lives! in New York in 1972, *Star Trek* returned to the airwaves. And although the original cast had been rehired, they wouldn't be appearing onscreen: The new *Star Trek* series was a cartoon. *Star Trek: The Animated Series* ran from 1973 to 1975, not touching the original series in quality, but galvanizing fans and bringing many more into the fold. It was also the first major step toward reigniting the *Star Trek* live-action franchise on the silver screen, which would in turn help revive science fiction as a pervasive force by decade's end.

Star Trek: The Motion Picture was still six years away. In 1973, very few sci-fi moviemakers had their cameras trained on outer space. The fifth and final of the original *Planet of the Apes* movies, *Battle for the Planet of the Apes*, came out that summer, and like all the installments of the series, it was set on Earth. So were the 1973 sci-fi films *Westworld*, an adaptation of Michael Crichton's paranoid-about-androids novel; *Soylent Green*, based on Harry Harrison's novel *Make Room! Make Room!*, to which Bowie's 1967 song "The Hungry Men" bore such a strong resemblance; and *Sleeper*, Woody Allen's spoof of the Rip-Van-Winkle-goes-sci-fi concept that Roddenberry had used the same year in *Genesis II*. These three movies were markedly different—although all of them were nominated for Hugo Awards for Best Dramatic Presentation the following year, with *Sleeper* being the dark-horse winner—but they all focused squarely on our own planet. In the aftermath of *Future Shock*, sci-fi cinema centered on earthly characters and concerns, including ecological, political, and societal fears. No one was making breathtaking, eye-popping, space-opera spectacles, which in the early '70s were considered passé, if not downright kitsch.

One young auteur, however, saw things differently. George Lucas, two years after making his sci-fi debut with *THX 1138*, celebrated the release of *American Graffiti*, his coming-of-age story about a California teen in the early '60s. There was nothing remotely sci-fi about it. But it was nominated for an Academy Award for Best Picture, and that earned Lucas the clout to start working in earnest on the script he'd begun in January of 1973. Spurred by his recent, failed attempt to reboot the *Flash Gordon* franchise, as well as his admiration for the scope and romance of Akira Kurosawa's samurai master-piece *The Hidden Fortress*, Lucas began sketching out names of exotic-sounding characters and places. He gathered these notes into a synopsis he called *Journal of the Whills*; in it, a young man named CJ Thorpe becomes apprenticed to a master named Mace Windy, hoping to learn the esoteric ways of a corps of space-commandos known as the Jedi-Bendu. Three months later, the synopsis had grown into a thirteen-page treatment. Lucas changed its working title to *The Star Wars*.

JAMES EARL JONES PRESUMABLY HAD no idea what Lucas was up to in 1973. He was busy trying to wrap his head around an entirely different kind of science fiction. A musical kind. Four years before loaning his stentorian voice to the greatest sci-fi villain in history, Jones stood on the set of his variety show, *Black Omnibus*, and watched a grown man dance like a robot.

Black Omnibus lasted twelve episodes and came after Jones's breakout Hollywood role in 1970's *The Great White Hope*, which netted him an Academy Award nomination for Best Actor. The short-lived but barrier-breaking show featured African American authors and entertainers, from comedian Richard Pryor to author Alex Haley to the soul group the Spinners, who were interviewed by Jones before giving a performance. His guest on this episode was Rufus Thomas, the former Memphis radio DJ who had spun his showmanship and gift for gab into a recording career. One of the mainstays of Stax Records, second only to Motown in the R & B industry, Thomas specialized in songs that either capitalized on or sought to create dance crazes. "Walking the Dog," "Do the Funky Chicken," "Do the Funky Penguin"—his discography of singles read like a shopping list of outrageous dances.

Thomas was on *Black Omnibus* to promote his most outrageous dance single to date: "Funky Robot." Released in 1973, the song didn't feel futuristic in any way; like most of Thomas's singles, it was a gritty, straightforward tune drawn directly from the Stax template. The closest it came to approximating the sound of a robot was a distorted guitar line in the intro that seemed to simulate the mechanized buzz, or perhaps even the voice, of a robot from a sci-fi film. During his performance of the song, Thomas doesn't do the Funky Robot himself. Instead he invites a young woman in a T-shirt and immaculate Afro to the stage, where she demonstrates the dance by locking her limbs and torso into a series of stiff, angular poses that somehow flow together into something deceptively graceful—even while illustrating the eeriness of the human body simulating a machine that simulates the human body.

"I don't really know how these youngsters are these days," Thomas candidly confessed to Jones during the interview segment of the program. Thomas was fifty-six, and his lurid, voluminous, hot-pink cape and silver boots were dramatically offset by his bald pate and salt-and-pepper sideburns. He then added, speaking about the origins of dance crazes in general: "You don't really know where they start or how." All the clarity he could provide was, "The kids came up with another one called the Funky Robot."

If there's one true origin of the Funky Robot dance (alternately shortened to "the Robot"), it's not generally known. By the late '60s, however, the dancer Charles "Robot" Washington—inspired partly by the iconic Robby the Robot from the influential 1956 sci-fi film *Forbidden Planet* and the popular '60s show *Lost in Space*—was among those who had begun to popularize the dance under the leadership of the inventive choreographer Don Campbell. Washington began appearing on a relatively new, nationally syndicated television show called *Soul Train*, which showcased African American music and dancers. From there the Robot spread. By 1973, it had trickled all the way up to the king of funky dance crazes, Rufus Thomas.

Bespectacled and dressed conservatively, Jones chuckled as he introduced Thomas and his dance: "Okay, let's have a look at the . . . Funky Robot." He didn't bother to hide a hint of condescending amusement while reacting to Thomas's outlandish dress and robotic nonsense—oblivious to the fact that, in four short years, Jones himself would become inextricably associated not only with robots and voluminous capes, but with cyborgs, spaceships, and the whole of science fiction.

THOMAS'S "FUNKY ROBOT" WASN'T THE first song to harness the robot dance craze of the late '60s and early '70s. Nor was it the first to have that name. In 1972, organist Dave "Baby" Cortez issued his own, totally different song called "Funky Robot." Like Thomas's song, it bore little sonic resemblance to science fiction, although the chant of "Robot! Robot! Do the Funky Robot!" at the start of the track had a vaguely mechanical intonation. The Solicitors' "Robot Strut," also from 1972, might have been attempting to mimic the sharp, jerky articulation of a robot—but what's more clearly science fictional is the spasm of harsh, jagged static that serves as a solo in the middle of the song.

"Electric Robot" by Harvey Scales was released in 1974, one of the final singles of the original Funky Robot wave. His lyrics perfectly summed up the aesthetic of the dance while offering a succinct tutorial: "I got a dance I want to show to you, yeah, yeah / It's like something from the future, yeah, yeah" he scats over a funky vamp, then adds, "Walk around like a mechanical man!"

One of the most exciting Funky Robot songs was 1972's "Do the Robot" by the Family. The group was a side project of MSFB, the Philadelphia-based collective of musicians that provided much of the backing for the city's booming soul and funk scene, including acts such as the Spinners and the O'Jays—not to mention providing the theme song for *Soul Train*. "Do the Robot" stood out not only for its inspired, driving arrangement, but for a break in which a vocalist intones in a deep bass voice, "Robot! / Do it to it! / Robot!" Bathed in reverb and machinelike in its low register, it wasn't dissimilar from how Jones would later sound as Darth Vader. It also prefigured the imminent use of two devices, the talk box and the vocoder, that would be commonly employed in music by the end of the decade to convert the human voice into something shockingly robotic. It was as though the Family already had the inhuman tone of the talk box and the vocoder in their heads, but they had yet to become aware of the emerging technology that could bring it convincingly to life.

"Do the Robot," like most Funky Robot songs, made little impact on the charts. But in October of 1973, a fifteen-year-old singer appeared on *Soul Train*. Not only did this young man perfect the Funky Robot, turning it into a thing of pop performance art in the eyes of Americans, he cemented his burgeoning image as an entertainer just as virtuosic at dancing as he was at singing. His name was Michael Jackson.

He and the Jackson 5 were booked onto *Soul Train* to promote their latest single, "Dancing Machine." It was a major shift away from the candy-coated soul of "ABC" and toward a more mature, polished, danceable sound, one that would become more recognizable as disco by the end of the '70s. The lyrics alluded to an android-like woman, an "automatic, systematic" dance partner "filled with space-age design." When the group took the stage of *Soul Train* to the beat of their own recording, something magical happened. After being introduced by *Soul Train*'s dignified creator and host, Don Cornelius, Michael commanded the performance. As his brothers shuffled humbly along at his side, he broke out into a breathtaking exhibition of the Funky Robot, complete with a coldly metallic facial expression and moves that looked more robotic than an actual robot might have mustered.

The Funky Robot, having run the course of all trends, fell out of vogue soon after, before being resuscitated in the '80s. But Jackson's 1973 demonstration of the dance made an indelible impression on hundreds of thousands of viewers: funk music and science fiction not only made sense together, they could exist in symbiotic harmony. Funk was already one of the most innovative forms of music of the time, but here, on the national platform of *Soul Train*, it was finally being paired with imagery and movement that suited funk's latent futurism.

As for Jackson, another decade would pass before he debuted a new dance on television—one that he didn't invent but indisputably perfected, one that would grow far larger than the Funky Robot, one that carried similar sci-fi overtones. It was called the Moonwalk.

✦ **ROBOTICS WASN'T THE ONLY KIND** of science fiction manifesting in funk and soul music in 1973. The Newcomers—a group on Stax, the same label as Rufus Thomas, and who quite openly sounded like the Jackson 5—released a catchy cover version that year of "The Martian Hop," a 1963 novelty song by the Ran-Dells about an entirely imaginary dance craze taking place on Mars. It wasn't funk by any stretch, and that fact itself made the Newcomers' single ever more of a novelty. While funk's rhythmic and instrumental mutation of R & B was beginning to click in sympathy with the forward-looking vision of science fiction, soul music—which was more rooted in earnest, conventional pop songcraft—never took to sci-fi in any significant way. Another exception is Jay & the Techniques' 1972 Motown single "Robot Man," a song that had nothing to do with the Funky Robot but instead used robots as a metaphor for a man who obeys his unfaithful lover without question.

In the early '70s, a smattering of instrumental songs married sci-fi titles to funk jams. The most famous is 1971's "Outa-Space" by keyboardist Billy Preston, who was just coming off a profile-raising stint as a session musician for the Beatles. Apart from a slightly trippy organ break, nothing about the song, apart from its name, feels particularly sci-fi—and the same can be said for 1972's "Space Monster" by the band Lunar Funk, a track that reaffirms funk's affinity with sci-fi without actually contributing anything to the dialogue between the two. Recorded around the same time, the far more obscure single "U.F.O." by the Texas outfit Mickey & Them delivered a bit more on the premise of its title. The layered organs and synthesizers, played by organist and bandleader Mickey Foster, melt into an atmospheric wash of cosmic hum and flying-saucer blips—supported by the funkiest of backbeats.

Mugo ventured beyond instrumental funk. The young eight-piece band—formed by students at McKinley Technical High School in Washington, D.C.—released the single "Space Travel" at the same time Ziggy Stardust was beaming through the cosmos to infinitely greater attention across the Atlantic. The lyrics tentatively touched on sci-fi, as heard in lines like "I'm reaching through space and time," plus a spirited refrain of "I like space travel!" But the song also contained a bubbly, straight-out-of-*Star-Trek* synth solo on par with Foster's, reinforcing the link between funk, synthesizers, and science fiction.

The first fully formed sci-fi funk song was "Escape from Planet Earth" by a vocal quartet from Camden, New Jersey, called the Continental Four. Not only did their 1972 single have an unmistakably sci-fi title, it came with a complete sci-fi narrative. The intro alone is a thing of wonder: Over swooshing rocket effects and radar-like beeps, a voice that identifies itself as being from Mission Control hails one of its spaceships. A reverse countdown ensues, after which the craft lands on alien planet. The astronaut in charge of the mission then turns to his companion, presumably a woman, and says, "Well, here we are, darling, millions and millions of miles from planet Earth." Then a slinky, midtempo funk track kicks in, and the entire story is told: The ship's occupants have traveled across the galaxy to flee Earth's social disintegration and start a new civilization. They're bound to become an extraterrestrial Adam and Eve who "start a new generation in this distant land." Naturally, a spacey synthesizer appears in the song, but it manages to transcend any trace of novelty. The Garden-of-Eden-in-space theme had a canonical sci-fi precedent: it's the premise of a 1963 episode of *The Twilight Zone* titled "Probe 7, Over and Out."

A current of sci-fi utopianism runs subtly through "Escape from Planet Earth." The lyrics don't focus on the problems of African Americans at home, as so much socially conscious funk of the time did (most notably Curtis Mayfield's Alvin Toffler-inspired "Future Shock"). Rather, they look forward to overcoming the inertia of oppression on Earth and venturing intrepidly into outer space, with a strain of religious awe worked into the concept. As little known and largely forgotten as the song is, it was one of the first pieces of popular music—if not *the* first—to positively depict African Americans among the stars.

In this way, "Escape from Planet Earth" is a textbook example of Afrofuturism. Sun Ra had been embodying Afrofuturism for decades, and his 1971 university lectures in Berkeley helped introduce a new generation of the counterculture to his cosmic ideas. Others were picking up on it, including jazz keyboardist Lonnie Liston Smith, whose 1974 song "Cosmic Funk" codified the nascent sound.

Sci-fi funk had been set in motion. Before the '70s finished, it would surpass sci-fi rock as the most profound vessel for science fiction in popular music. Yet in 1973, the man who would become the foremost figure in sci-fi funk hadn't taken up his mantle. *Cosmic Slop,* by the band Funkadelic, came out that year, a record whose architect was the Detroit composer and multi-instrumentalist George Clinton. He also led the group Parliament; the overlapping outfits became known collectively as P-Funk.

Despite song titles such as "Cosmic Slop" and "No Compute," the album didn't have much to do with science fiction, dwelling instead on more terrestrial topics like ghetto life and raunchy sex. A bigger premonition came on the track "Mommy, What's a Funkadelic?," the opening song of Funkadelic's self-titled 1970 debut album, which featured the line, "By the way, my name is Funk / I am not of your world." Reinforcing that point, the album's closing song, "What Is Soul," also slyly nods toward one of Clinton's largest influences, Jimi Hendrix's trailblazing sci-fi-inspired song "Purple Haze"— the lyrics go "Orange haze, orange haze, it ain't purple no more." Clinton's lifelong interest in sci-fi was starting to seep into his increasingly advanced theories about funk, recording techniques, and Afrofuturism. Music would never be the same.

6

SECRETS OF THE CIRCUITRY MIND: *1974*

AMID A CASCADE OF UNEARTHLY ELECTRIC PIANO COMING FROM stage right, the singer leaned toward his microphone. His face was obscured by a thick beard, bushy hair, dark glasses, and long shadows. His outfit was a tight leather jumpsuit unzipped from chest to navel, and strange symbols adorned it, delineated in rhinestones. He raised his hand, crooked his fingers, and gestured at the audience like a mad scientist explaining his nefarious plan. Then he sang, in a voice dripping ancient mystery: "Clock strikes twelve, and moon-drops burst / Out at you from their hiding place."

The song, called "Astronomy," was a high point of Blue Öyster Cult's concert sets in 1974. It closed the New York group's third and most recent album,

Secret Treaties, released in April of that year. Singer-guitarist Eric Bloom delivers the song's foreboding lines with delicious drama, but he didn't write them. They were drawn from pages of verse written by BÖC's manager and lyrical collaborator, Sandy Pearlman—the aspiring songwriter who had praised the sci-fi elements of the Byrds' *Younger Than Yesterday* in 1967. Comprising an epic work of unpublished poetry titled *The Soft Doctrines of Imaginos*, Pearlman's story involves a cabal of aliens known as Les Invisibles who grant a superhuman named Imaginos the ability to jump through time, influencing history according to their hidden and sinister agenda.

"Astronomy" is one of many BÖC songs written throughout the band's existence that drew from Pearlman's Imaginos writings. He'd been with the band, in effect an unofficial extra member, since the Long Island–spawned rock outfit had gestated under different incarnations in the late '60s. He'd been a music journalist for *Crawdaddy* then, the zine that sci-fi authors such as Samuel R. Delaney had written for, and whose publisher, Paul Williams, was one of Philip K. Dick's most passionate champions. Much like Les Invisibles pulling the strings of Imaginos for their own purposes, Pearlman utilized the very willing members of BÖC as his ministers of disruption. Hard-edged and cloaked in a supernatural aura, the group benefited immensely from the guidance and input of Pearlman, who sought to mix alchemy and the occult with science fiction. According to friend Bolle Gregmar, Pearlman was "very fascinated by the old druids and all that stuff. But he wanted to put it in context with the future rather than going backwards."

In addition to Sandy Pearlman, two other writers who weren't actual members of Blue Öyster Cult contributed to the lyrics of *Secret Treaties*. One was rock critic Richard Meltzer, who had also cut his teeth in the pages of *Crawdaddy* in the '60s. The other was Patti Smith.

In 1974, the future icon, punk poet laureate, and Rock and Roll Hall of Fame inductee was living with her boyfriend, BÖC keyboardist Allen Lanier. A rising star in the New York literary scene, she made her debut as a lyricist on record as the coauthor of "Baby Ice Dog" on BÖC's 1973 album *Tyranny and Mutation*. Her collaboration with the band allowed their sci-fi obsessions to bleed into her own, but she was no stranger to science fiction. While living at the fabled Chelsea Hotel in the early '70s, she would wander the halls hoping to run into Arthur C. Clarke, who was also a resident at the time; following his death in 2008, she staged a series of events in his memory, during which she read her prose poem "Arthur and Patti." And while she never devoted herself to sci-fi music as such, a handful of her songs with the Patti Smith Group in the '70s—"Birdland," "Distance Fingers," "Space Monkey"—show a preoccupation with UFOs. "Birdland" in particular is one of the most arresting and hallucinatory accounts of alien abduction ever set to music: "Take me up quick, take me up, up to the belly of a ship," Smith sang. "And the ship slides open, and I go inside of it, where I am not human."

Smith formed the Patti Smith Group in 1974 with guitarist Lenny Kaye, who had his own affinity for science fiction. Prior to picking up a guitar professionally, he was an avid participant in sci-fi zine culture. He published his first zine about science fiction at the age of fifteen; titled *Obelisk*, it was followed by others such as *Sadistic Sphinx* and *Hieroglyph*. Kaye was also close with the members of BÖC, although it's probably only synchronicity that *Sadistic Sphinx* and *Hieroglyph* could easily have been names of BÖC songs.

BÖC's first blush of science fiction had come on their self-titled 1972 debut album. It contained "Workshop of the Telescopes," a track rife with alchemical imagery and a ritualistic exhortation to "Rise to claim Saturn, ring and sky." Pearlman said, "It's really what I call a gothic technology song . . . It has kind of a Frankenstein's laboratory, techno-gothic take on how things would be transformed, and what the transformative mechanism would be." That theme of metamorphosis carried over to the title of their next album, *Tyranny and Mutation*, whose striking black-and-white cover featured an illustration of a cryptic, futuristic ziggurat—the kind that might have been built by ancient alien visitors. BÖC's bassist Joe Bouchard considered it "very futuristic, definitely otherworldly. I think it fit the kind of music we were doing, our futuristic, science-fiction-leaning thing."

Secret Treaties, though, was the band's most upfront sci-fi statement to date. The track "Subhuman" takes place amid "warm weather and a holocaust," and along with "Astronomy," it's a pivotal song in the Imaginos cycle, establishing the concept that would eventually culminate in the 1988 album *Imaginos*. The liner notes of *Secret Treaties* spoke enigmatically of a covert agreement between the aliens and Earth, concluding with a dire assessment: "These treaties founded a secret science from the stars. Astronomy. The career of evil."

There's no small amount of camp and melodrama to BÖC's sci-fi mythologizing, but it's superbly balanced by Pearlman's earnest love of speculative fiction in all its forms: horror, fantasy, and science fiction. On "Flaming Telepaths," one of the most vivid tracks from *Secret Treaties*, the narrator cuts loose in a cry of hubris: "Yes, I know the secrets of the circuitry mind / It's a flaming wonder telepath." Pearlman said he meant to deal with supernatural themes "in a scientific way . . . It's about this scientist who attempts to mutate consciousness, and he just can't do it; he's failed too many times. But the scientist has this poisonous pride, and he's got to keep on trying, beating his head against this barrier."

In much the same way, BÖC beat their heads against a barrier—the one that prevented most sci-fi bands from reaching the upper tier of stardom. As if by self-fulfilling prophecy, Blue Öyster Cult became a cult band. They would enjoy the occasional hit single, including 1976's "(Don't Fear) The Reaper" and 1981's "Burnin' for You," but neither were sci-fi songs. It was as though two parallel-universe versions of BÖC existed alongside each other: one was an underground cabal communicating in coded, sci-fi narratives, and the other was a band for chugging beer to.

As with science fiction across all media in the mid-'70s, creators and fans seemed resigned to the fact that stories and songs about "rising to claim Saturn" and "the circuitry mind" were going to remain—with a few fluke exceptions, like the work of David Bowie—niche obsessions. This would be proven hugely wrong just three years after the release of *Secret Treaties*. But for the time being, the forces of sci-fi continued to dwell mostly in the shadows, where BÖC thrived, only occasionally bursting from their hiding place.

DAVID BOWIE DARTED AROUND HIS conjoined hotel suites at the venerable Pierre in Manhattan's Upper East Side. Instead of a guitar, he wielded scissors and glue. Movie cameras and video editing equipment were strewn throughout his rooms. He'd been in New York just a few days; he'd trekked up from Philadelphia, where he'd been recording his upcoming album *Young Americans*. The plan was to finish working on *Young Americans* at the famed Record Plant studio in New York. On this night, however, Bowie wasn't obsessing over his current album-in-progress or even entertaining his habitual retinue of groupies. With images from his most recent record, *Diamond Dogs*, dancing through his mind, he was building a model.

Diamond Dogs came out in May of 1974, and its vision of a postapocalyptic urban hellscape had come to consume him. In New York, he was surrounded by skyrocketing crime and urban decay. A nationwide recession deepened in the wake of 1973's stock market crash. The oil crisis was fueling global unrest and fears of long-term energy scarcity. Richard Nixon's resignation in August laid bare the fragility of democracy. *Diamond Dogs* resonated.

Bowie wanted to turn the album into a movie. In an interview years later, he recalled that he wanted it set in a world ravaged by fuel shortages and populated by cyborgs. He knew he needed a treatment of some kind to show Hollywood producers, but rather than typing up a simple synopsis, he rented camera equipment and hired a film crew to come to his suites at the Pierre. There they would capture on celluloid a half-hour teaser for the big-screen adaptation of *Diamond Dogs*, as Bowie envisioned it.

The model he was building for the teaser was of a city. It was called "Hunger City," a crumbling metropolis rife with social and economic collapse where—according to "Future Legend," the album's ominous opening track—"corpses lay rotting on the slimy thoroughfare." From the tops of skyscrapers, "red mutant eyes gaze down" on the city's scavenging tribes of barely human survivors. *Melody Maker* called the song "doom through science fiction."

In his hotel room, Bowie hung a piece of black fabric. When his model of Hunger City was finished, he installed it in front of that canvas, evoking an aura of eternal night. Then, as his producer Tony Visconti remembered, "He videoed his set for thirty minutes against a black cloth backdrop. Afterwards he played back the tape and he walked against the black cloth background and narrated his story treatment. We combined the prerecorded tape and live David, many times reduced, onto a second machine via the console, and it appeared as if he was actually in the city . . . The Lilliputian-sized David was at the right scale for the set, and it all looked very convincing."

Visconti never saw the film again, and it's never surfaced since. One can only imagine the stupefying strangeness of a low-budget short starring a miniaturized David Bowie strolling through his own handmade model of the dystopian Hunger City, sterile skyscrapers looming and red mutant eyes gazing down.

Then again, the *Diamond Dogs* album itself is all that's needed. Grim and oppressive, it was Bowie's return to science fiction after the success of *The Rise and Fall of Ziggy Stardust and the Spiders from Mars*. With his Ziggy persona retired, he found himself drawn to a different strain of sci-fi. Visconti, who contributed to the production of *Diamond Dogs*, called it a work of "future shock," using the Alvin Toffler titular term that the *Los Angeles Times* had also deployed while reviewing Bowie's historic Santa Monica concert in 1972. Indeed, the album brought the cosmic speculation of "Space Oddity" and *Rise and Fall* plummeting horrifically back down to Earth's own tomorrow. Bowie had explored terrestrial sci-fi before, most notably in 1967's "We Are Hungry Men," whose spoken-word intro presaged Bowie's eerie opening monologue in *Diamond Dogs'* "Future Legend."

Bowie was reaching beyond his own penchant for future shock. More blatantly than he ever had or ever would again, he cited specific works of science fiction in his music—especially one of his favorite books, George Orwell's *Nineteen Eighty-Four*, just as he'd promised William S. Burroughs, in a way, when he'd boasted during their conversation for *Rolling Stone* in 1973, "Now I'm doing Orwell's *Nineteen Eighty-Four* on television." Where Bowie's 1970 dystopian song "Saviour Machine" featured the Big Brother–like President Joe, *Diamond Dogs* contained numerous direct references to literature's most enduring work of dystopian fiction. The song "We Are the Dead" is a line from the novel, something the book's protagonist Winston says to his lover, Julia, as the Thought Police come to arrest Winston for his crimes against the state. Bowie sang, "I hear them on the stairs"; Orwell wrote, "There was a stampede of boots up the stairs." Even more explicit are the songs that immediately follow, "1984" and "Big Brother." In the latter song, Bowie appears to call back to "Saviour Machine" with the lines "Please, savior, savior, show us." He also squeezes in a little lingering Ziggy-esque space imagery, as if to purge it from his system: "Give me pulsars unreal." It was a line that could have served as the title of a sci-fi manifesto.

Diamond Dogs' debt to *Nineteen Eighty-Four* makes perfect sense. The album began as an adaptation of the book. Bowie first pictured it as a combination stage production, feature film, and concept album that retold Orwell's cautionary tale about tyranny and conformity. He dove into the ambitious multimedia project, but he soon ran into a unbeatable opponent: Sonia Orwell, the author's widow and executor of his literary estate. Unhappy with prior adaptations of her late husband's work, she refused to grant Bowie permission to adapt his book. As Bowie remarked, "I found out that if I dared touch [*Nineteen Eighty-Four*], Mrs. George Orwell would sue or something. So I suddenly had to change about in midstream, in the middle of recording."

That change encompassed a complete overhaul of the story line, including grafting remnants of his Orwell adaptation to an entirely original setting: his mutant-infested Hunger City tableau. It made for a patchy, uneven narrative—

there's even less of a coherent tale to *Diamond Dogs* as there is to *Rise and Fall*—but it also gave Bowie poetic license to completely reframe the aftermath of the apocalyptic. The triptych of "We Are the Dead," "1984," and "Big Brother" was grandfathered in from the original adaptation plan; it's entirely possible that part of Bowie's reason for including these openly Orwell-quoting songs was simply out of spite.

As he explained years later, still fuming, "At the end of 1973 George Orwell's widow, Sonia, withheld permission for the *Nineteen Eighty-Four* project. Mrs. Orwell refused to let us have the rights, point blank. For a person who married a socialist with communist leanings, she was the biggest upper-class snob I've ever met in my life. 'Good heavens, put it to *music?*' It really was like that." In some quarters, the prejudice against pop music being a valid vehicle for serious science fiction held.

Nineteen Eighty-Four wasn't the only work of sci-fi that went into the seething, murky stew of *Diamond Dogs*. Bowie seemed happy to point them out; they were, after all, works he'd been championing for years just combined in a different way. "I had in my mind this kind of half [Burroughs's] *Wild Boys* and *Nineteen Eighty-Four* world," he said. "There were these ragamuffins, but they were a bit more violent than ragamuffins. I guess they staggered through from *A Clockwork Orange* too." He went so far as to cast himself as one of those ragamuffins, "a real cool cat who lives on top of Manhattan Chase" named Halloween Jack who is mentioned in *Diamond Dogs*' title track and whose decadent, shock-haired, eye-patched visage could have belonged to an alternate-reality version of Ziggy Stardust. For that matter, both of them could just as easily have been hitherto unknown incarnations of Michael Moorcock's Eternal Champion, alongside Elric of Melniboné and Jerry Cornelius.

Metropolis, Fritz Lang's 1927 sci-fi classic, loomed large over the project as well. The pioneering silent film takes place in a futuristic city where severe class divisions give rise to revolution and one of cinema's first and most compelling robots indelibly brands the screen. Bowie claimed it was just as important as Orwell's work in his conception of the album, stating, "I know the impetus for *Diamond Dogs* was both *Metropolis* and *Nineteen Eighty-Four*—those were the two things that went into it." On the resulting tour to support *Diamond Dogs*, he indicated that *Metropolis*'s stark illusion of tomorrow should be an element of the set. The set also contained a hydraulic arm that hoisted Bowie seventy feet above the stage for his nightly rendition of "Space Oddity." The man who created the astronaut Major Tom, however, was afraid of heights and had to conquer his phobia in order to perform. During one show, the hydraulic arm malfunctioned, leaving Bowie hovering perilously over the audience for six songs—much the same way Major Tom had become stranded in space.

Since the days of "Space Oddity," Bowie had been as interested in sonically representing science fiction as he was in lyrically representing it. He took that a step further on *Diamond Dogs*. Visconti used an array of new digital effects technology on the recording, including the space-age sounds of noise gates, flangers, and phasers—equipment that would later become commonplace but still seemed startlingly futuristic in 1974. Most strikingly, the album ends with "Chant of the Ever Circling Skeletal Family," a song whose coda is a sampled loop of the single syllable "bro" from the word "brother." Recalled Visconti, "David asked if I could capture the word 'brother' at the end of the last track, 'Chant of the Ever Circling Skeletal Family,' and repeat it ad infinitum. Of course I could, but lo and behold, that short word was too long for the puny memory banks in the machine. Storage was very limited in those days. So I managed to capture just 'bro' with a snare drum hit, and that actually sounded amazing, like a robot with AI that was not working very well singing it."

It all added up to an alarming, end-times soundtrack that Bowie himself regarded as "desperate, almost panicked." Looking back, he called *Diamond Dogs* a "very English, apocalyptic kind of view of our city life" with "obvious inspirations from the Orwellian holocaust trip. It was pretty despondent." In 2016, bestselling speculative author Neil Gaiman was asked to pick a favorite Bowie album. He chose *Diamond Dogs*

> . . . because it was kind of *mine*. It was science fiction, it came out when I was thirteen-and-a-half, and it was a weird mash-up of this strange, dystopian, mutant-y *Nineteen Eighty-Four*. It filled my head. I loved the imagery. I loved trying to work out what it was about . . . Talking to [fellow author] Alan Moore, who's a little bit older than I am, we both fed on Bowie imagery and absorbed it, and it went into that early melting pot where you believe it, you take it in, and you let it grow.

If Bowie had known how much his sci-fi music—which was directly inspired by his favorite authors—would go on to inspire future sci-fi authors, he might have thought differently about his next stop. *Young Americans*, the album he was working on while building his Hunger City model in the Pierre in December of 1974, had nothing to do with science fiction. Newly immersed in contemporaneous R & B, it's the point at which Bowie resurrected himself as a soul singer—and in 1974, nothing screamed sci-fi less than soul music, at least compared to the likes of glam. Yet on *Diamond Dogs*, Bowie forged an intriguing fusion of funk and sci-fi; the song "1984" mixes Orwell's nightmare with music clearly influenced by Isaac Hayes's 1971 blaxploitation anthem "Theme from Shaft." But he abandoned this fleeting experiment in sci-fi funk just as others were about to pick up that idea and run with it—and in the process rival Bowie as the decade's preeminent practitioners of science fiction in popular music.

Bowie wasn't done with sci-fi, though, and definitely not permanently. He may have abandoned his plans to turn *Diamond Dogs* into a movie—despite his elaborate efforts in filming a treatment for it—but he was prescient about one thing: his next big sci-fi project was going to be cinematic.

ZIGGY STARDUST HAD DEPARTED THE planet by 1974, replaced by Halloween Jack and other guises Bowie had in the works. But in the collective consciousness, Ziggy's renown only grew. Imitation, as always, was the sincerest form of flattery. Following the Strawbs' parody of Ziggy Stardust and the Spiders from Mars—namely, their 1972 alter ego Ciggy Barlust and the Whales from Venus—two bands in the glam pantheon similarly riffed on the indelible name of Ziggy and his band. Bowie's old friend Marc Bolan released an album by his band T. Rex called *Zinc Alloy and the Hidden Riders of Tomorrow*, and a group called Be-Bop Deluxe followed suit with the song "Jet Silver and the Dolls of Venus."

By 1974, Bowie had eclipsed T. Rex as an international phenomenon, and Bolan—already a fading teen pinup in England—was playing second fiddle. Not only was *Zinc Alloy* an obvious nod to *Ziggy Stardust*, the album contained some of Bolan's most outright sci-fi song titles: "Venus Loon," "Galaxy," and "Interstellar Soul." As with earlier T. Rex tracks like "Ballrooms of Mars," these song titles did not signal a true slide into sci-fi. Bolan was always much more of a fantasist—and a great one, at that—than a sci-fi artist, crafting surreal, nursery-rhyme lyrics that alluded to mythical creatures and magical worlds. His childhood love of sci-fi stories like Ray Bradbury's time-travel classic "A Sound of Thunder" never translated into a complete embrace of sci-fi music. Yet in 1971, Bolan referred to himself as "a science fiction writer who sings," although he may have been using the common shorthand of lumping both fantasy and sci-fi together under the term "science fiction."

At the same time, speculative fiction was enjoying a renaissance of science fantasy: a combination of science fiction and fantasy. Novels of the late '60s and early '70s such as Roger Zelazny's *Lord of Light* and Anne McCaffrey's Dragonriders of Pern series allowed elements of myth and magic to mingle with advanced technology and futuristic settings. For example, the Pern books took place on a planet colonized by humans but whose inhabitants had genetically engineered the small, winged lizard they found on the planet so that they resembled dragons from legend.

Interestingly, T. Rex released an album in 1976 titled *Futuristic Dragon*. If Bolan read McCaffrey, he never mentioned it in interviews. But the album's cover art would not have been out of place on the cover of a Pern novel; it depicted an armored warrior riding the back of a great winged lizard. It was painted by George Underwood, an acclaimed illustrator whose work graced many sci-fi novels of the decade—who also happened to be a boyhood friend of David Bowie. Like Bowie's "Future Legend" from *Diamond Dogs*, the eponymous opening track of *Futuristic Dragon* is a spooky, spoken-word introduction. It's also Bolan's most exquisitely executed piece of science fantasy, one that heralds the terrible arrival of "A thunderbolt master, a 'lectronic savior / A cold galactic raver, the Futuristic Dragon."

Bill Nelson, leader of the British band Be-Bop Deluxe, also winked at Ziggy Stardust and the Spiders from Mars in 1974. The group released "Jet Silver and the Dolls of Venus" on their debut album *Axe Victim*. The lyrics even went so far as to mimic Bowie's basic premise: a fictional, planet-hopping troupe of musicians "span the space between us with a tune." It wasn't mere mimicry, though; Nelson was a devoted sci-fi fan. In the early '70s he was in a psychedelic band called Lightyears Away who had a song called "Astral Navigator," and sci-fi would show itself persistently throughout his career in the '70s.

"I'd long had an interest in sci-fi and projections of the future," Nelson said. At a young age, he shared Syd Barrett's love of the comic-book space hero Dan Dare, created by Frank Hampton: "His images of the future, particularly of future cities, had an inventiveness and elegance that was very seductive." Nelson, like Bowie, was also captivated by *Metropolis*: "I remember seeing stills from *Metropolis* when I was a young boy and being fascinated by the architecture of Lang's imagined future city." Be-Bop Deluxe would sometimes perform with scenes from *Metropolis* synchronized to their music, and a still from the film—depicting its iconic robot—adorns the cover of their 1977 live album *Live! In the Air Age*.

An inventive guitarist, Nelson didn't play straightforward glam rock. He was just as adept at the twists and turns of progressive rock, and he packed the virtuosity and ambition of prog into concise chunks of catchy songwriting. By blending the two dominant forms of sci-fi rock at the time, he created the ideal foundation for singing about robots, astronauts, and technological wonder. Unlike Bowie's fearful assessment of the future on *Diamond Dogs*, Nelson's shimmering mirages of tomorrow were largely upbeat, even when dwelling on isolation, alienation, and destruction. His 1976 song "Life in the Air Age" detailed how "All the oceans have run dry / It's grim enough to make a robot cry," but it did so against bright, infectious music.

Nelson considered himself equally influenced by the science fiction of Bradbury and Kurt Vonnegut as he was by that pioneer of sci-fi rock, Jimi Hendrix. Accordingly, the Be-Bop Deluxe song "Honeymoon on Mars" scans like vintage Bradbury circa *The Martian Chronicles*, while the satirical title of "Dance of the Uncle Sam Humanoids" could have been swiped from an unpublished Vonnegut novel. Both songs appear on the 1976 album *Modern Music*. On the cover, Nelson—dressed in a suit and tie, his hair cut neatly short—shows off a TV wristwatch, like a scientist out of a '50s sci-fi film. In a few years, the explosion of new wave music would popularize that shiny, retro-futuristic aesthetic. But in the mid-'70s, Nelson already personified it.

Glam was still popular, but its link to sci-fi was weakening as it went more mainstream. Acts like Gary Glitter and the Sweet brought glam mainstream acceptance while using sci-fi as a superficial stylistic reference only. However, an American expatriate in London released one of the year's most compelling sci-fi-glam singles. Brett Smiley was only eighteen when "Space Ace" came out in 1974. The New Yorker had hooked up with Andrew Loog Oldham, former manager and producer of the Rolling Stones, to record the song, a gloriously dreamlike paean to extraterrestrial loneliness in which Smiley croons, "I'm on the wrong planet, so out of place / I'm gonna go back and be a space ace." Despite its gorgeousness, the single tanked, and Smiley wound up written off as another would-be Bowie like Jobriath, trying to emulate Ziggy Stardust after Bowie himself had already given up on that persona. And like Jobriath, Smiley eventually died of AIDS—but in a cosmic twist of coincidence, he passed away on January 8, 2016, just two days before Bowie.

Some of the veterans of prog reawakened their interest in sci-fi in 1974. Rick Wakeman, keyboardist of Yes—whose appearance on Bowie's "Space Oddity" had set him on the sci-fi path five years prior—released the solo album *Journey to the Centre of the Earth*. Both a sci-fi concept album and an adaptation of Jules Verne's 1864 novel about adventurers who descend into a strange, subterranean world, it instantly hit the top of the British album charts. In this regard, Wakeman succeeded where Bowie failed—he managed to not only successfully adapt one of his favorite sci-fi books, he did so to enormous commercial acclaim. Granted, Wakeman was aided immeasurably by the fact that his source material had passed into the public domain, so no one could deny him the rights to use it. Lavish, overripe with orchestral pomp, and undeniably fun, *Journey to the Centre of the Earth* remains one of the best-known and most loved sci-fi albums of the '70s—while being an unwittingly misleading representation of the breadth and depth of the decade's sci-fi music.

Peter Hammill of Van Der Graaf Generator also touched base with his sci-fi roots with the song "Red Shift," off his 1974 solo album *The Silent Corner and the Empty Stage*. Over eight minutes in length, it's practically a mini-album in and of itself, brimming with echoes, cosmic sound effects, and lyrics about "being displaced now in time and relativity" and "in the depths of the galaxies." Guesting on guitar was Randy California of the group Spirit, whose early sci-fi rock anthems include "1984"—no relation to Bowie's "1984" from *Diamond Dogs*, apart from the Orwell influence. Hammill had just come off a sci-fi project that was not his own: in 1974, the English-language version of *Felona e Sorona*—an album by the Italian prog group Le Orme—was released, and Hammill had translated the lyrics. The album concerned twin planets named Felona and Sorona who orbit each other, one utopian, the other dystopian.

In Germany, sci-fi music was continuing to spread—although in one case, the musicians themselves weren't aware it was happening. Between 1974 and 1976, four records by the Krautrock band the Cosmic Jokers were released by Ohr Records on their Kosmische imprint, bearing titles such as "Intergalactic Nightclub" and "Cosmic Joke." The joke, purportedly, was on the people who played on the album. The tracks were culled from jam sessions by various Krautrock luminaries, including Manuel Göttsching of Ash Ra Tempel and Klaus Schulze, then released without their knowledge or consent. Whether or not that's entirely true, the Cosmic Jokers were a winning self-caricature of sci-fi Krautrock, right down to the press release sent out by Ohr's founder,

Rolf-Ulrich Kaiser: "The time ship floats through the galaxy of joy. In the sounds of electronics. In the flashes of light. Here you will discover Science Fiction, the planet of COSMIC JOKERS, the GALACTIC SUPERMARKET, and the SCI-FI PARTY. That is the new sound. Space. Telepathy. Melodies. Joy." Meanwhile, Kaiser continued to release more sober sci-fi music like "Your Lunar Friends," the eleven-and-a-half-minute alien-themed symphony by the band Wallenstein.

In North America, a scattering of bands were making sci-fi music, often more with an experimental intent than with any hope of reaching popular audiences. Simply Saucer hailed from Hamilton, Ontario, and their raw, harshly hypnotic drone gave sci-fi music a new context—somewhere between the MC5's proto-punk and Hawkwind's cosmic throb. Although Simply Saucer never released an album during the '70s, they recorded one in 1974 that later saw the light of day under the name *Cyborgs Revisited*. It's a fitting title. Songs such as "Here Come the Cyborgs" and "Dance the Mutation" were built of mechanical riffs and burbling synthesizers. The album was produced by Daniel Lanois, who later rose to fame as a producer for U2 and a collaborator with one of the most eminent sci-fi musicians, Brian Eno, with whom he created the theme song to David Lynch's 1982 adaptation of Frank Herbert's *Dune*.

Polished and progressive, the American outfit Stardrive had little in common with Simply Saucer. Yet their two albums, *Intergalactic Trot* from 1973 and *Stardrive* from 1974, went equally unrecognized. With titles like "Pulsar" and "Jupiterjump," the funky electronic band used synth-driven instrumentals to elicit the icy, technological precision of the future; they also foreshadowed the imminent digital revolution with keyboard lines that sound downright glitchy.

Kraftwerk were the vanguard of electronic music in 1974 with *Autobahn*, but others were plugging into the same circuits. A budding young guitar-and-synthesizer wizard from France named Richard Pinhas unveiled the debut album by his band, Heldon. Dubbed *Electronique Guerilla*, it loaded abrasive layers of synth into angular prog not far from King Crimson. It sounded nothing like Kraftwerk or even Krautrock, but it used similar technology to create a wholly unique reaction to industrialized society—one that turned its own automated rhythms against it. That year he was finishing his PhD in philosophy, studying at the Sorbonne under French philosopher Gilles Deleuze; his dissertation was titled "Science Fiction, the Unconscious, and Other Things," and it cited, among his many sacred sci-fi tomes, Frank Herbert's *Dune*.

Pinhas dedicated *Electronique Guerilla* to two of his favorite authors, William S. Burroughs and the anarchist sci-fi writer Norman Spinrad. Pinhas even named Heldon after a genocidal nation in Spinrad's 1972 book *The Iron Dream*. Spinrad's premise is dismaying: a portion of it is a novel within a novel written by Adolf Hitler, who in an alternate timeline becomes the author of a sci-fi book called *Lord of the Swastika*. *Electronique Guerilla* would begin a musical association with sci-fi in general—and Spinrad and Herbert in particular—that Pinhas would cultivate even more deeply throughout the decade and beyond.

KEN ELLIOTT WAS YET ONE more musician in awe of the way synthesizers could be made to channel science fiction. With fellow keyboardist Kieran O'Connor, he formed the prog synth duo Seventh Wave and released two albums in 1974 and 1975, *Things to Come* and *Psi-Fi*. The titles alone were big tip-offs; the songs overflowed with science fiction, from the H. G. Wells–referencing "Dance of the Eloi" to the breathtaking, science-fantasy epic "Star Palace of the Sombre Warrior." Unknowingly, Seventh Wave build a bridge between progressive rock and the coming synth-pop revolution. Elliott also contributed to another genre-spanning sci-fi album: *Interstellar Reggae Drive*, a one-off project named Colonel Elliott & the Lunatics.

A reggae album made by a prog keyboardist with a serious sci-fi bent might seem like the recipe for a novelty record of the worst kind. Instead, *Interstellar Reggae Drive* is fascinating. Instrumental and atmospheric, tracks like "Jumping Jupiter" and "Guns of the Martian Giants"—the latter an interplanetary reworking of the Skatalites' ska classic "Guns of Navarone"—allowed Elliott to show off his talents on his synthesizer of choice, the Moog ARP 2600, while proving that the deep syncopation of reggae was just as viable a blank slate for sci-fi as any other form of music. Elliott traveled to Jamaica to record the album at King Tubby's studio in Kingston. Born Osbourne Ruddock, King Tubby was one of the most sought-after producers in Jamaica at the time, thanks to his innovative use of sound manipulation and the mixing board as an instrument—a technique that birthed the cavernous, otherworldly thrum of dub. "King Tubby truly understood sound in a scientific sense," said one of his compatriots, the reggae singer and producer Mikey Dread. "He knew how the circuits worked and what the electrons did."

Other reggae songs dabbled in space themes in the early '70s, including "U.F.O." by Harry J. Allstars, "Outta Space" by the Upsetters, "Your Ace from Space" by U-Roy, and "Space Flight" by I-Roy. The last, released in 1973, was produced by one of King Tubby's associates, Lee "Scratch" Perry. Pierced by laser-like synths and deep rumbles of cosmic bass, Perry's ethereal music ventured even further into the galaxy than Elliott and Tubby's *Interstellar Reggae Drive*. "We're going on a space flight to Venus and Mars!" yelps I-Roy, your enthusiastic tour guide into the unknown.

Born in 1936 in Jamaica, Perry was a well-established reggae artist in 1973, when he built his Black Ark studio in Kingston. It quickly became legendary. Like King Tubby and other innovators at the time, Perry invented new ways to sculpt raw sound using technology. Later in his career he would embrace science fiction more openly, but I-Roy's "Space Flight"—written and produced by Perry—was the first indication of Perry's belief that he was "an alien from the other world, from outta space . . . I live in space. I'm only a visitor here." After establishing his mastery of sci-fi reggae, he furthermore admitted, "I love science fiction. It is about bringing the impossible to life and making it look real." While Tony Visconti was concocting new ways to use the recording studio as a launchpad for sci-fi music with Bowie's *Diamond Dogs*, Perry paralleled him in Kingston. "Lee Perry's productions and theory fictions open up an entirely new field: the MythScience of the mixing desk," wrote music journalist Kodwo Eshun. He "taps into the secret life of sound machines, opens the cybernetics of the studio."

Meanwhile, Perry's fellow space traveler, Sun Ra, was readying his sci-fi opus—a cinematic one. Released in 1974, his film was *Space Is the Place*. Filmed in 1972, the movie spun off from Sun Ra's 1971 lectures at UC Berkeley. In it, Sun Ra—playing himself—struggles for the liberation of the black race through technology and the colonization of the stars. The plot involves scheming NASA scientists, an "outer space employment agency," and, of course, the expansive free jazz of Sun Ra's Arkestra, the means by which he can teleport himself and others to planets beyond this one.

Space Is the Place is a keystone of Afrofuturism, and while it wasn't widely distributed at the time, it epitomized a current that had been running through jazz in the first half of the '70s. Albums such as Ornette Coleman's *Science Fiction* from 1971, Return to Forever's *Hymn of the Seventh Galaxy* from 1973, and Charles Earland's *Leaving This Planet* from 1974 strengthened the bond between jazz and sci-fi, one John Coltrane had solidified in the late '60s. One of Coltrane's albums, *Interstellar Space*, was released posthumously in 1974; despite the fact that it had been recorded seven years prior, it resonated profoundly in the Afrofuturist climate epitomized by *Space Is the Place*.

As the '70s progressed, black music began filling the vacuum left by the retreat of glam and prog from sci-fi themes. On *Hymns to the Seventh Galaxy*, a masterpiece of celestial, futuristic jazz fusion, the multiracial Return to Forever included a song called "Theme to the Mothership." Nine minutes in length, it's an alternately frenetic and spacious odyssey propelled by guitar and keyboard. The term "mothership" aligned perfectly with the premise of *Space Is the Place*: that some sort of vessel, like Sun Ra's teleportational concert stage or even Lee "Scratch" Perry's sound-warping Black Ark, might deliver black people to a promised land among the stars. The biggest, brightest, and most righteous mothership of them all, however, had yet to land.

YOUR MEMORY BANKS HAVE FORGOTTEN THIS FUNK: *1975*

GEORGE CLINTON LOVED TO FISH. EVER SINCE HE WAS A BOY, HE would count the minutes until he could carry his fishing rod and tackle box to the nearest lake or creek and sink a line, hoping to score a prize catch. It mellowed him out, and for someone whose brain incessantly buzzed with as much music and creativity as his, the tranquility of fishing was a welcome relief.

One trip out on the water, however, was anything but tranquil. Clinton, now an adult and the leader of the overlapping funk groups Parliament and Funkadelic, had chartered a Haitian skipper in Miami to take him and his bandmate, bassist Bootsy Collins, into the Atlantic for a fishing expedition.

A couple days into the voyage, the boat found itself deep in the Bermuda Triangle. He and Collins had just taken some tabs of LSD, their fishing drug of choice, when a storm rolled in. It wasn't a typical storm: thick, metallic-gray clouds washed over the boat, obscuring all vision. And instead of rain, drops of what appeared to be mercury began pelting them, spattering into silvery liquid droplets across the deck.

Gripped by a mix of dread and psychedelic elation, Clinton suddenly realized what was happening. This wasn't a storm. It was a visitation. A UFO. It became clear to him that aliens were attempting to abduct them. Collins, who had arrived at the same conclusion, started screaming about "the Space Limousine" that had come to take them to "the Mothership." While the skipper cowered in the cabin with a bottle of booze, Clinton and Collins ripped off their shirts and bared their chests to the violent sky, letting the deluge of mercury envelope them as they danced and laughed.

Gradually the storm subsided. With the skipper now drunk, the awestruck Clinton and Collins steered the boat back to harbor. Apparently, the alien pilots of the UFO, after snagging their catch so firmly on the hook, had decided to let them go.

Clinton has many variations of this tale. In one account, he and Bootsy were in a car, not a boat. It was eleven in the morning, near their adopted home of Detroit and during broad daylight, when "suddenly a beam of light from a UFO hit us, and we couldn't see a thing." When he arrived home, he discovered that almost half a day had magically passed. "I'm telling you, time disappeared on that journey. We were taken to a weird place!" Clinton later said. According to another version, he and Collins weren't in the United States—or even on LSD. "Bootsy and I both, as high as we stayed, we weren't high that particular time!" he recounted. "We had just went into the border into Canada. And [we saw] a light, straight out of the clouds, straight to the ground. In daylight! Three or four minutes later, again right through the trees. [The light] hit one side of the street, the other side of the street, and the third one, it hit the car we were in! [Afterward] I called Bootsy up and made him repeat everything that happened. It spooked both of us."

It's not unusual for those who have encountered UFOs to remember their experiences inconsistently. In his bestselling 1972 book *The UFO Experience*, astronomer J. Allen Hynek classified possible alien visitations by a First, Second, and Third Encounter system—clearly Steven Spielberg was taking notes, as his *Close Encounters of the Third Kind* would appear five years later—

and set off a fresh wave of speculation about extraterrestrial takeovers. In a Close Encounter of the Second Kind, one potential symptom is what Hynek dubbed "lost time"—gaps and distortions in one's memory due to a brush with alien technology.

Of course, the LSD might have had something to do with Clinton's fuzzy recollection. Not to mention his penchant for dazzlingly complex self-mythology. Parliament had formed as a New Jersey doo-wop group called the Parliaments in 1955, when Clinton was only fourteen; throughout the '60s, he was a songwriter for the famed Brill Building as well as for Motown, and he moved the Parliaments to Detroit in 1967 in an unsuccessful attempt to get his own band signed to Berry Gordy's legendary label. But since the early '70s, both Parliament and Funkadelic had been evolving into something far more advanced than the average funk band. They conjured hallucinatory images of outer space and other worlds in their songs. But in 1975—just as Hynek's second popular book about UFOs, *The Edge of Reality*, flew off the shelves—Parliament flew deeper into the unknown with a spearheading album of unidentified sci-fi funk called *Mothership Connection*.

"Face it, even your memory banks have forgotten this funk," sings Clinton, gently yet firmly chiding the human race, on "Mothership Connection (Star Child)." The signature track on *Mothership Connection*, it's delivered from the perspective of Star Child—Clinton's newly established alter ego, a "Citizen of the Universe" who's come to liberate the human race from a chronic state of funklessness. Naturally, the Star Child references the Bermuda Triangle, the alleged site—or at least one of them—of Clinton's real-life UFO encounter.

It all marked the genesis of a sprawling new cosmology invented by Clinton and company, one that took Sun Ra's esoteric strain of Afrofuturism and reverse-engineered it for the dance floor. On "Unfunky UFO," aliens "here from the sun" come to Earth to steal "the funk," and they don't just mean the music. In Clinton's view of reality, wrote Kodwo Eshun, "funk—like ovaries, sperm, or the sandworm spice in *Dune*—is the vital force, the *élan vital* that visiting aliens want to extract and extort." Or, for that matter, like another powerful, arcane form of energy that would soon appear in sci-fi: the Force.

Just as David Bowie was temporarily relinquishing his leadership of sci-fi music—ironically enough, in order to explore funk on *Young Americans*—Clinton picked up the baton and fused funk and sci-fi on a scale that had never been attempted before. On *Mothership Connection*'s opening track,

"P. Funk (Wants to Get Funked Up)," a voice from "the Chocolate Milky Way" takes over Earth's airwaves to herald the arrival of the Mothership, "home of the extraterrestrial brothers, dealers of funky music." At the time, blaxploitation cinema was positioning African American actors, for the first time, as leading men and women in action films; Parliament was doing the same thing, only musically, and with science fiction. On *Chocolate City*, Parliament's album right before *Mothership Connection*, "we had imagined a black man in the White House," Clinton said. "For *Mothership Connection* we went even further afield and imagined a black man in space . . . In my mind, the concept of *Mothership Connection* wasn't just *Star Trek* in the ghetto, but pirate radio coming in from outer space."

Conceptually, *Mothership Connection* recalled the "slow voice on a wave of phase" that took over the radio on Bowie's "Starman" from three years prior. As if to call out Bowie for his abandonment of space music in favor of plain old earthbound funk, Clinton mentioned him by name on "P. Funk (Wants to Get Funked Up)," singing, "Then I was down south and I heard some funk with some main ingredients / Like Doobie Brothers, Blue Magic, David Bowie."

Parliament did more than simply inject funk with sci-fi themes, as a handful of artists had done before. They were reprogramming funk in order to launch it into tomorrow. Parliament and Funkadelic—now known collectively by the portmanteau P-Funk—converted the psychedelic thrum of their formative work into rocket fuel, utilizing synthesizers, jazzy intricacy, and studio technology to mutate funk's DNA. In the same way pioneering sci-fi novels of the '60s like Anne McCaffrey's *The Ship Who Sang* and Frank Herbert's *Dune* had imagined how humans could scientifically enhance themselves in an interplanetary culture, so did *Mothership Connection* scientifically enhance funk so that it might cope with the rigors of an increasingly grim future—or, as "Unfunky UFO" claims with no shortage of pulp heroics, "to save a dying world."

Playfulness became a weapon of progress. Composer Shawn Wallace said one of P-Funk's strengths was their virtuosity at repurposing and layering language in their lyrics, to the point where "they were almost speaking in code. Almost like the old Negro spirituals, we're going to talk about three things in this one line, and you almost have to be in the club to understand." That density became part of the appeal—similar to how the complicated worldbuilding and technobabble of sci-fi novels and films drew in those who relished the effort of decrypting it. Afrofuturists such as Clinton "enjoy challenging their listeners on their path to enlightenment," said author Ytasha L. Womack. "They enjoy pulling the rug out from under the smugness of reality. Whether it's through chord changes, oddity, or sheer boldness, they get a kick out of tossing their listeners into the far reaches of outer space."

The same year *Mothership Connection* materialized, Samuel R. Delany's opus, *Dhalgren*, was published. The Afrofuturist author used narrative circularity and self-referential text to render his parable of American dystopia a work of profound disorientation; meanwhile, a rising African American sci-fi writer named Octavia E. Butler, who had already drawn acclaim for her short stories, was readying her debut novel. Titled *Patternmaster* and published in 1976, it pictured a future of genetically engineered humans locked in a strict caste system. The remaining books in the series would reveal a hidden history of human development that stretched back to Ancient Egypt. Clinton, like Sun Ra before him, held similar theories. "The descendants of the Thumpasorus Peoples knew Funk was its own reward," state the liner notes of the P-Funk collection *Tear the Roof Off: 1974–1980*, referring to "Night of the Thumpasorus Peoples," the last song on *Mothership Connection*. "They tried to remain true to the pure, uncut Funk. But it became impossible in a world wooed by power and greed. So they locked away the secret of Clone Funk with kings and pharaohs deep in the Egyptian pyramids and fled to outer space to party on the Mothership and await the time they could safely return to refunkatize the planet."

Clinton's affinity for sci-fi stretched back to his boyhood in Plainfield, New Jersey. A child of the TV age, he grew up with alien beings and otherworldly realms beamed nightly into his living room. "*Buck Rogers* was the beginning of television," he said, speaking of the iconic early '50s space adventure series; little did he know in 1975 that it would be rebooted by NBC at the end of the '70s. As he grew older, more sophisticated shows like *The Outer Limits* and *Star Trek* sustained his fascination with sci-fi. "I did love science fiction, of course, especially *Star Trek*, because it moved along on its ideas," he said. "They came up with some brilliant concepts and developed amazing realities." Bootsy Collins was likewise immersed in the "amazing realities" of sci-fi as a kid: "I kind of grew up with it on TV, watching *Star Trek*, *Lost in Space*, *Flash Gordon*, I mean all of this stuff." Clinton also gave Collins a crash course in some of the popular pseudo-science books of the day, most notably *Chariots of the Gods?* by Erich von Däniken. Published in 1968, it became a bestseller on par with

Toffler's *Future Shock* and Hynek's *The UFO Experience*, thanks to von Däniken's claim that aliens visited Earth in the distant past—inspiring many of the world's religions as well as granting advanced technology to ancient peoples. That theory became central to P-Funk's gleefully anachronistic narrative.

As they had with Bowie, Stanley Kubrick's instant sci-fi classics exerted a strong pull on P-Funk. Parliament's stage shows involved a replica of the Mothership, as it appeared on the cover of *Mothership Connection* in all its UFO-tastic glory, from which Clinton would pop out, dressed like the rest of the group in elaborate, glittery, futuristic costumes—ones that might have been made out of mercury. "When *A Clockwork Orange* brought the codpiece to our attention, Clinton had to wear one the size of a loaf of Wonder Bread, covered in rabbit fur," said author Pagan Kennedy. And Clinton's adopted guise of Star Child carried traces of *2001: A Space Odyssey*, in which the astronaut Dave Bowman is reborn as the celestially evolved Star Child.

Coincidentally or not, another band in 1975—who happened to be Parliament's labelmates on Casablanca Records—was using the Star Child name for one of their members. Paul Stanley of Kiss, the makeup-masked, hard-rock group who had their big breakthrough in 1975 with the live album *Alive!*, had taken to calling himself the Starchild. Along with his cosmic-themed comrade Ace "Space Ace" Frehley, Stanley brought a trace of sci-fi to Kiss's outrageous aesthetic—an otherwise latent love that would fully (and bizarrely) blossom on the small screen before the decade was over.

Like a sci-fi movie franchise or series of novels, the saga that Clinton launched with *Mothership Connection* continued. Until the start of the '80s, Parliament released an album each year—*The Clones of Dr. Funkenstein* in 1976, *Funkentelechy Vs. the Placebo Syndrome* in 1977, *Motor Booty Affair* in 1978, *Gloryhallastoopid* in 1979, and *Trombipulation* in 1980—that expanded, to some degree, the cosmic mythology of the P-Funk universe, including new characters like the villainous space trickster Sir Nose D'Voidoffunk. It was a place populated, in Clinton's words, by "Afronauts capable of funkitizing galaxies." Like Sun Ra, Clinton moved forward and backward in time, from the starships of the future to the pyramids of Ancient Egypt. Cloning, genetic engineering, prehistoric technology: Parliament swirled it all into a pulsing mass of sci-fi spectacle. It all revolved around the Mothership. A symbol of liberation on par with Noah's Ark—or Sun Ra's Arkestra—the Mothership "took funkateers out of the disco-dominated dance scene, which smelled clean and felt rigid, and returned them to the belly of the cosmos, where it smells skanky and feels rubbery," emblemizing "the possibility of a spiritual, not a physical, return to blood and to roots, to the swirling gasses and dust of cosmic conception."

Disco was indeed dominating the dance scene in 1975, although it had yet to make its biggest mainstream breakthrough. Parliament was already offering itself as an alternative to what it viewed as a slick, simplified, ultimately soulless substitute for funk; in two years, Clinton would begin referring to disco as "the Placebo Syndrome." As alternative as it was, *Mothership Connection* went mainstream too, going gold and eventually platinum. Meanwhile, disco, P-Funk's avowed enemy, was preparing to become an enormous vessel for science fiction as well, thanks in part to the unwitting influence of P-Funk themselves. The trigger, however, was not an album, but a film. And in two short years, that trigger would be pulled.

JOE HARRIS DID NOT KNOW about George Clinton or his encounter with aliens in the Bermuda Triangle, but he might as well have been there. "Every day people report strange flying objects with bright shiny lights / They ain't done a thing to us, so why are we getting uptight?" went the lyrics of "UFO's," a 1975 single by Harris's funk group, the Undisputed Truth.

Overshadowed by the upheaval that was Parliament's *Mothership Connection*, the Undisputed Truth's "UFO's" nonetheless epitomized '70s sci-fi funk. It boasted synthesized flying-saucer noises and robotic chanting. It took psychedelic funk and made it futuristic. And it offered a profound meditation on the possibility of UFO sightings and our connection to an alien race that transcended the superficiality of the sci-fi novelty song.

The Undisputed Truth was brought together by Norman Whitfield, the Motown producer whose cavernous, atmospheric sound revolutionized soul music in the late '60s. By the early '70s, his success with artists such as the Temptations—whose dark, apocalyptic "Ball of Confusion" set the tone for songs like Curtis Mayfield's "Future Shock"—earned him the leeway to assemble his own group from scratch. Initially comprising the Motown session singers Harris, Brenda Evans, and Billie Calvin, the Undisputed Truth enjoyed modest popularity until the mid-'70s, when the group reinvented itself. As seen on the cover of *Cosmic Truth*, the 1975 album that contained "UFO's," Harris and crew had adopted a sci-fi image, with illustrations of their faces floating within a surreal firmament of stars, gaseous shapes, and geometric forms.

"UFO's" was no fluke. *Cosmic Truth* also sported "Spaced Out," in which the intensity of a sexual tryst is wrapped up in an outer-space motif. More to the sci-fi point, the song "1990"—more or less "Ball of Confusion" set in the future—predicts the proliferation of dystopian, *Future Shock* social ills: joblessness, corruption, pollution. Rather than promoting space travel with wide-eyed wonder, "1990"—like Gil Scott-Heron's "Whitey on the Moon" before it— summed up the sour mood that had settled in regarding its cost: "How in the world can you spend another dollar on the space race / When families at home are starving right in front of your face?" The song ends in a flurry of chaotic malfunctioning-computer beeps.

Whitfield called the Undisputed Truth's sci-fi look and sound "the cosmic thing." But Harris, the group's leader and only consistent member through-out its many lineup changes, said that he wasn't just following Whitfield's lead, and that he had more influence over the band's direction than most people thought: "We've been into the cosmic thing for a long time, and our albums have always had cosmic sleeves to them. We have always designed our own sleeves—in fact, as leader of the group, that has always been one of the jobs that's left to me. I have always worked closely with Norman in terms of general direction for the group."

The Undisputed Truth released a second album in 1975, *Higher Than High*. Although light on actual sci-fi content—mostly on the title track, which fea-tured plenty of B-movie raygun effects—the record doubled down on visuals. The front cover depicts the band's members drifting through space in glit-tering jumpsuits, silver makeup, and frosted Afros—almost a cross between the costumes of Parliament and Kiss. When the gatefold cover was opened, a striking photo of the band in similar garb seals the deal. This was not just album art, but reality: the Undisputed Truth began appearing onstage in their space-age getups at the same time Parliament was ramping up their intergalactic theatrics in anticipation of *Mothership Connection*, which came out in December of 1975.

On the Undisputed Truth's next album, 1976's *Method to the Madness*, a roster shakeup led to the addition of singer Taka Boom. The younger sister of funk star Chaka Khan, Boom had appeared on various P-Funk records, including singing backup on *Mothership Connection*, on which she was credited as Taka Khan. *Method to the Madness* begins with a four-minute, clearly Clinton-inspired monologue by a squeaky-voiced alien who beams the Undisputed Truth aboard his spaceship in order to satisfy his curiosity about humankind. "We're the Undisputed Truth, and we've been waiting," a member of the band tells the alien. "Waiting to become a part of a new world. Perhaps you have room for us in your world?"

The Undisputed Truth's sci-fi funk never took root the way P-Funk's did. At no point did their music sound as innovative or uniquely futuristic as Clinton's, and they never attempted a multi-album narrative completely with an underlying mythology. Clinton was obviously aware of the Undisputed Truth; beyond the Boom connection, both groups were based out of Detroit at the time, and a decade later Harris even supplied guest vocals to Clinton's 1986 solo album, *R&B Skeletons in the Closet*.

By then, the Undisputed Truth had broken up. Their swan song was 1979's *Smokin'*, an album that contained a pair of winning sci-fi funk songs: "Atomic Funk," which offered dancing as the antidote to paranoia about nuclear warfare, and "Space Machine," a song swimming in scintillating space effects. "The space machine is not a dream," went the lyrics. "There's life on other planets for sure." The space journey that had begun with "UFO's" four years earlier came to a close. The Undisputed Truth may not have had the reality-rattling impact of P-Funk, but they stuck to their passions long enough to leave behind a respectable contribution to the canon of sci-fi funk.

Labelle didn't add as much to sci-fi-funk as the Undisputed Truth, but they did so with dazzle and depth. The group—Patti LaBelle, Sarah Dash, and Nona Hendryx—began in the '60s as the Philadelphia outfit Patti LaBelle and the Bluebelles, but like Clinton and his Parliaments, they decided to reinvent themselves in the early '70s. Emboldened by glam and the increasing sophistication of funk, they had an early disco hit with 1974's "Lady Marmalade." The B side of that single, however, headed in a different direction entirely. Musically, "Space Children" wasn't far from "Lady Marmalade," but lyrically it dealt with "space children, universal lovers" who are urged to find enlightenment in "greater stars in galaxies."

"Space Children" predated Clinton's "Mothership Connection (Space Child)," but together they harmonized. Labelle offered a smooth, refined, but no less adventurous take on sci-fi funk, thanks largely to the writing input of Hendryx. Their stage costumes resembled chrome-plated space-suits sculpted into formfitting elegance; during performances, they would sometimes glide down from the rafters using harnesses as if they were space visitors descending upon the audience. The overall impact combined both feminism and Afrofuturism. According to an interview with *The New York Times* in 1974,

> Nona's working clothes are futuristic. She represents the energy usually associated with space-age independence, the rage to live and discover what is new. Boots, pants, silver ensembles helped define a personality that sees tomorrow and its possibilities belonging—at least in part—to her.

Labelle shared a costume designer with both P-Funk and Kiss. Larry LeGaspi operated out of a studio in New York called Moonstone, and he specialized in futuristic fashion for the burgeoning rock-star market. "My design ideas come from my childhood fantasies. I dream of other planets," LeGaspi explained. "I'm always finding myself in very strange places in my imagination! The other night I had this dream of climbing up a cliff behind some sort of insect people. They had these incredible legs, or boots, and I woke up to sketch out the image of an idea. Space seemed the only direction for me to go, because the '70s just seem to be a repeat of the '30s through the '60s. I see my work as a kind of 'Space Deco.'"

In 1975, Labelle released the album *Phoenix*. It featured the track "Cosmic Dancer"—no relation to the T. Rex song of the same name—a sumptuous romantic fantasia with a celestial sweep. More solidly in a sci-fi vein was "Black Holes in the Sky." Harrowingly beautiful, the song prompted the listener to "Behold black holes in the sky," then got downright astrophysical with the line, "A shining star turned itself inside out." The rock magazine *Creem* called the song "a kind of feminist 'Rocket Man,'" referencing Elton John's astronaut anthem. The reviewer might not have been aware that John, before he found massive fame as a songsmith with sci-fi flair, was a pianist in Patti LaBelle and the Bluebelles' touring band in the late '60s.

"I was very into science fiction and futuristic ways of thinking," said Nona Hendryx, referring to her input into Labelle's music and image. She avidly read "books about dreams and human consciousness; cybernetics is also a subject that fascinates me." After embarking on a solo career in the late '70s, she became even better known for her sci-fi sympathies and eventually worked with Brian Eno. But it wasn't until the twenty-first century and the spread of online genealogy searches that she discovered she was a distant cousin—despite a slight difference in surnames—to one of the godfathers of sci-fi music: Jimi Hendrix.

✳ **WHILE FUNK, GLAM, AND PROG** bands were the main sources of sci-fi music, a handful of soft-rock artists adapted to the sci-fi climate in 1975. By mid-decade, the trend of singer-songwriters led by Carole King and James Taylor had boomed, and it was inevitable that a few of them would gaze into outer space for inspiration. A year earlier, Clifford T. Ward's "Jayne (From Andromeda Spiral)" had set the tone for a new kind of space rock: one that was tuneful, lushly arranged, and projected heartbreak into the cosmos. Released at the end of 1975, Gary Wright's hit single "Dream Weaver" seemed like a wispy ballad of spiritual romanticism, but it also mused about traveling to the stars—and it was played entirely on synthesizers, with the exception of acoustic drums, further popularizing the association between synths and space. A similarly religious tone suffused Chris de Burgh's song from the same year, "A Spaceman Came Travelling," which unsubtly smuggled a Christian message into a tale of alien visitation.

Al Stewart's "Sirens of Titan" was the most forthright sci-fi soft-rock song—an unabashed adaptation of Kurt Vonnegut's 1959 novel *The Sirens of Titan*, complete with explicit mentions of the book's main character, Malachi Constant, and details taken straight from the story such as "I wander the endless Mercurian caves" and "So I came in the end under the shadow of Saturn." It was far more upbeat than Stewarts's usual, pillowy folk rock, but it still flew in the face of the challenging sounds that had come to typify sci-fi music by 1975. Along the same lines, Elton John's 1975 song "Dan Dare (Pilot of the Future)" was lyricist Bernie Taupin's bouncy tribute to the comic-book space colonel who had also enthralled the young Syd Barrett of Pink Floyd and Bill Nelson of Be-Bop Deluxe, along with an entire generation of British sci-fi musicians. Where "Rocket Man" brooded and yearned, "Dan Dare (Pilot of the Future)" wrapped up John's fleeting flirtation with sci-fi by celebrating the bright-eyed optimism of '50s pulp. Cheekily, though, the song ends with the confession, "Dan Dare doesn't know it / But I liked the Mekon"—referring to the green-skinned, egg-headed Venusian archenemy of Dan Dare.

Nostalgia and sentimentality had begun to creep into the alarmist, experimental sci-fi music of the '70s. "You were as futuristic as Colonel Dare,"

Robert Calvert sang from a stage on which Hawkwind was playing in the summer of 1975, adding with a twinge of loss, "There were voices among the stars." The group had just fired their bassist, Lemmy, after he was arrested for drug possession at the border between the United States and Canada while on tour that spring. Calvert, who had exited Hawkwind a year earlier amid his accelerating bipolar disorder, was rejoining them to perform and read his new poem, "Ode to Crystal Set." In it, he waxed maudlin about Dan Dare and the bright sci-fi of his youth. *Melody Maker* said he "looked like an alien being's idea of a Parisian Left Bank beat with his blue beret and manic staring eyes," while *Sounds* compared Hawkwind's new lineup to "the well-oiled Starship *Enterprise*." Even the "barbarians with machines" of Hawkwind had become professionals.

Michael Moorcock also continued to appear onstage with Hawkwind. Their 1975 album, the last with Lemmy on bass, was titled *Warrior on the Edge of Time*, and it would prove to be the most involved collaboration between the author and the band. Following their landmark sci-fi album, 1971's *In Search of Space*, they'd release three additional full-lengths—*Doremi Fasol Latido* in 1972; *The Space Ritual Alive in Liverpool and London*, known more commonly as *Space Ritual*, in 1973; and *Hall of the Mountain Grill* in 1974—that expanded their majestic, propulsive, cosmic drone and consolidated their cult of future-primitive, post-hippie explorers of the universe. *Warrior on the Edge of Time* felt different. Murkier and less focused, it wandered from Moorcock's spoken-word interludes like "The Wizard Blew His Horn" and "Warriors." The latter used the same sinister, cybernetic-sounding voice modulation that had been heard on "Sonic Attack" during his earliest performances with the group.

As before, this new Hawkwind material siphoned images and themes from Moorcock's Eternal Champion cycle. It breached the membrane between sci-fi and fantasy, allowing them to mingle and synergize. *Sounds* observed that Hawkwind "seem to be moving away from the science fiction thing and into the realms of science fantasy." The *Warrior* track "Standing at the Edge," cowritten by Moorcock, contained the evocative phrase "veteran of a thousand psychic wars"—one that would resurface later, after the author had begun collaborating with Hawkwind's conceptual cousins from New York, Blue Öyster Cult.

Moorcock and Calvert were doing more than appearing here and there with Hawkwind. Moorcock's own band, the Deep Fix, released their debut album *The New Worlds Fair* in 1975. Along with numerous links to the author's science fiction and fantasy, it included some Hawkwind personnel—most notably multi-instrumentalist Simon House. The album's title alluded to *New Worlds*, the magazine Moorcock had edited and published in the late '60s and early '70s, engendering the revolutionary New Wave of Science Fiction. The band faded away soon after; as Moorcock, who was much more accomplished as a writer than a musician, explained, "We grew tired of the record industry's increasing orthodoxy." Still, madly inspired songs from *The New Worlds Fair* such as "Starcruiser" remain worthy footnotes to Hawkwind's sci-fi legacy.

Never one to sit still, Moorcock also appeared—as a banjoist—on Calvert's 1975 solo album *Lucky Leif and the Longships*. It wasn't sci-fi, but Calvert's previous solo outing, *Captain Lockheed and the Starfighters* from 1974, decidedly was. The shambolic satire wove futuristic elements into a World War II story, incorporating interstitial skits and Calvert's energizing blend of the cosmic and the comic. Along with Moorcock, Brian Eno and Arthur Brown made appearances, making *Captain Lockheed* an all-star album of sorts—akin to a musical sci-fi convention caught on record.

While sci-fi funk, led by Parliament, boomed in 1975, sci-fi rock could not keep up. For every rock song about technology run amok, like "The Tale of the Giant Stone Eater" by the Sensational Alex Harvey Band, led by Bowie's old mentor in UFO-watching, or Alice Cooper's zany "Space Pirates," there was a far more vital jam coming from the funk realm. In "Space Age" by the Jimmy Castor Bunch, a P-Funk–level frenzy of asteroid-zapping synths and nebula-sized rhythms, Castor delivers the cautionary enjoinder, "Don't be a robot / You'll lose your soul."

Some sci-fi rock releases in 1977 rose above. Magma—the French prog band whose 1970 self-titled album had been one of the decade's first major works of sci-fi music—delivered *Live/Hhaï*, an in-concert recording building out the rich alien mythology that mastermind Christian Vander had earlier established. The artistic triumph of *Live/Hhaï* was a consolation prize for Vander. A passionate fan of *Dune*, he'd been contacted that year by the hallucinatory filmmaker Alejandro Jodorowsky, who was directing an ultimately failed adaption of the novel. Jodorowsky proposed that Magma should provide half the soundtrack for the film, with Pink Floyd supplying the rest. "We met Jodo several times in 1975. He had an office in Paris. You could see the first drawings prepared for the film on the walls," Vander remembered. "We exchanged ideas about how the music should sound. Then unfortunately the production stopped"—a victim of its own ambition and budget overruns. One can only imagine the soundtrack, let alone the film, that might have resulted.

Krautrock continued to thrive. But outside Kraftwerk's *Radio-Activity*, an album that upgraded their "Kohoutek-Kometenmelodie" breakthrough with shockingly futuristic electronic songs like "The Voice of Energy" and "Radio Stars," even that scene began to experience sci-fi fatigue. Some of the most compelling works of sci-fi music to emerge from Germany in 1975 weren't Krautrock at all. Nektar continued the speculative methodology of 1971's *Journey to the Centre of the Eye* and 1973's *Remember the Future* with a new concept album, *Recycled*. Prophesizing a dystopian era where energy scarcity rules all aspects of life, the tracks "Cybernetic Consumption" and "Automaton Horoscope" showed that prog still had plenty to say through sci-fi.

Hailing from Hanover, Germany, the Scorpions had a huge connection to Krautrock. Their new producer, Dieter Dierks, was one of the genre's architects, having worked with Amon Düül II, Ash Ra Tempel, and Tangerine Dream, among others. The Scorpions, on the other hand, existed in the liminal zone where hard rock was metamorphosing into heavy metal. Their 1975 song "Robot Man," with its staccato riffage and dark aggression, heralded metal's swiftly approaching future. At the same time, it reached back to Black Sabbath's "Iron Man," speeding it up for the accelerating mid-'70s. "Robot Man" featured a lyric that seemed to describe the song itself: "Do you feel him, the cold vibration? / Comes from everywhere, produce a crazy science-fiction creation." By coincidence, ace guitarist Michael Schenker had left the Scorpions two years earlier to join UFO, the British outfit behind the influential 1970 space-rock instrumental "Unidentified Flying Object." The Scorpions' "Robot Man" felt like just another outrageous song by an outrageous band, but it presaged a wave of sci-fi metal that was just beginning to awaken.

One of the new guard's most promising torchbearers was a curly-haired PhD student at Imperial College London named Brian May. He was nearing the completion of his doctorate in astrophysics, but his attention was torn. While studying diligently from 1970 to 1974, which included treks to Spain to spend time at the Teide Observatory in Tenerife, he lived a double life: he was also a rock guitarist. Following the dissolution of his group Smile—which had released the "Space Oddity"–like single "Earth" in 1969—the sci-fi fan had formed a new band in 1970. They called themselves Queen. And by 1974, they'd become popular enough that it was no longer feasible for May to divide his time. Weighing his options, he quit school and threw himself full-time into music.

You could take the guitarist out of science, but you couldn't take the science out of the guitarist. Queen's fourth album, *A Night at the Opera*, would forever change May's life—it contained "Bohemian Rhapsody," a song set to become one of the most beloved of all time—but it also looked back longingly at his past. Tucked near the middle of the record is a sci-fi folk song titled "'39." Written entirely by the guitarist, it sketched a melancholy, time-dilation scenario where Einstein's theory of special relativity comes to bear on an explorer who travels into space and returns over a lifetime later, only to find that he's barely aged.

Besides being one of the most scientifically rigorous sci-fi songs of the '70s, "'39" resembles one of Robert A. Heinlein's juveniles, the 1956 novel *Time for the Stars*, in which teen twin brothers—one space-bound, one earth-bound—experience a similar rift in time. May's story, however, is far more grim than Heinlein's, as befits the war-weary tenor of 1975. One of the hottest sci-fi novels was Joe Haldeman's *The Forever War*, published the year before and eventually winning the Hugo Award for Best Novel. Set in a space-opera future, it's a morally complex examination of warfare based in part on Haldeman's tour of duty in Vietnam.

Saigon fell in April of 1975, but the wounds the Vietnam War inflicted would be felt for decades to come—and sci-fi captured that. Films released that year included the politically charged *Death Race 2000*, where a race across the North American continent has become a dystopian nightmare. Taking place in a vaguely similar setting, *Rollerball* dealt with deadly roller-skating gladiators in the savage world of 2018. *The Ultimate Warrior*, which imagined New York in 2012, depicted street gangs in a pandemic-stricken urban wasteland. David Cronenberg's debut feature, *Shivers*, posited a horrific engineered parasite that's transmitted through sex, while *The Stepford Wives* pictured a modern-day suburban limbo where housewives have been replaced by androids. And a strange musical called *The Rocky Horror Picture Show*—which became a cult classic after hitting the midnight-movie circuit—combined glammed-up sleaze with vintage sci-fi, horror, and rock 'n' roll, delivering songs such as "Science Fiction/Double Feature." The track reveled in the glorious camp of yesteryear's sci-fi cinema, peppered with references to Buck Rogers and *The Day the Earth Stood Still*; that surely helped the film become a staple of sci-fi conventions after a triumphant screening at 1976's Worldcon in Kansas City, Missouri. It marked a new approach to sci-fi music—one that scavenged the genre's past with a gleeful disregard for self-seriousness or so-called good taste. By the end of the '70s, this kind of celebration of sci-fi as pop-art camp, rather than earnest subject matter, would take a tighter hold on the music world.

While uniform in neither topic nor tone, the major sci-fi films of 1975 had one thing in common: they could not have cared less about space. "The moon had been visited, and was found wanting, as interesting as anyone's holiday snaps," wrote media critic Andrew M. Butler of the mid-'70s space-exploration doldrums. From there, "much sci-fi shifted to more earthly concerns."

Parliament's *Mothership Connection*, on the other hand, projected its concerns onto the cosmos. By combining elements of funk, glam, and prog into a space-fixated hybrid, the album redefined the bond between sci-fi and popular music. Few of Parliament's rock 'n' roll peers could keep up. One rock band, though, was about to renew and expand what it meant to make sci-fi music. They weren't from the predictable hot spots of England, Germany, or the United States. They hailed from Canada.

8

WHAT CAN THIS STRANGE DEVICE BE?: *1976*

NEIL PEART, FAR FROM HIS TORONTO HOME, AMBLED OUT OF A PAWN-shop in Arkansas with a bulky machine tucked under his arm. Climbing aboard the chartered bus that was parked outside the shop, he found his designated area among the seats and tables and made a space for his new acquisition.

The year was 1976, and the band Peart belonged to, Rush, was touring the United States. After eight years of unimpressive sales, they'd finally started to gain momentum with their latest album, *2112*. Units were moving, and attendance at their shows was swelling. It was entirely possible, Peart surmised, that they were becoming rock stars. Introverted by nature, he preferred to keep to himself before and after their concerts, more likely to have his nose buried in a book than to be partying in a crowd. The debauchery that took place on tour buses in the '70s is legendary—but on that day in Arkansas, Peart had something else in mind. He opened up the device he'd just purchased, placed it on a table, and caressed its keys. Then, as his bandmates Geddy Lee and Alex Lifeson piled onto the bus and settled in for the long drive to the next stop on the tour, Peart inserted a piece of paper into the apparatus and began typing.

"I carried [the typewriter] with me on tour and made an attempt at the inevitable first novel," Peart remembered. The book was going to be "a science fiction story built around the songs from *2112*." Peart drummed for Rush, but he also wrote their lyrics—and his premise behind *2112* seemed to have tapped into something. Fans connected to the album in droves. At the start of 1976, their label, Mercury Records, was on the verge of dropping the Canadian hard-rock band. They warned the group that their upcoming fourth album needed to have hits; their immediately previous album, 1975's *Caress of Steel*, saw progressive elements start to dominate over more radio-friendly material. Two tracks, "The Necromancer" and "The Fountain of Lamneth," were lengthy songs dripping with fantasy. The former was heavily indebted to Tolkien, one of Peart's favorite fantasy authors.

Mercury urged Rush to pump out shorter, more digestible chunks of Led Zeppelin–like rock, as they'd done when they started out as a party band in the suburbs of Toronto. Peart did indeed take the band in a new direction in 1976—but not the one Mercury wanted. For their next album, *2112*, he shed the elves and wizards of the fantasy genre. Instead, he struck out into science fiction. The first side of the album comprises a story line set, unsurprisingly, in the year 2112—in the same way Orwell's *Nineteen Eighty-Four* is set in that year. And, like Orwell's novel, Peart's twenty-minute seven-part masterpiece concerns a totalitarian regime that controls all aspects of life and suppresses the freedom and individuality of its citizens. Rather than taking place on a mostly recognizable version of Earth, though, *2112* takes place in a postwar union of planets—one might even call it an empire—ruled by the Red Star of the Solar Federation. A cabal called the Priests of the Temple Syrinx controls the content and dissemination of all media, and by extension, all creativity.

That changes with the emergence of a hero. The character is established not in the album's music, but in the text of the Peart's liner notes, where the hero lives on a planet with twin moons, and he passes his days plugged into an entertainment machine that pumps Syrinx-sanctioned "Templevision" directly into his consciousness. One day, while visiting a cave, he stumbles across a different kind of entertainment machine: an electric guitar. "What can this strange device be?" he wonders, holding the instrument and strumming its strings. "It's got wires that vibrate and give music." But when he plays the guitar for the Priests, he's condemned for sedition and blasphemy. Ultimately, he meets a tragic end; the Priests crack down, and control over the Solar Federation is expanded and strengthened.

The music that accompanies Peart's sweeping cosmic chronicle is just as grandiose. The synthesizer, played by Lee, that opens the song-cycle could serve as the space-warping soundtrack to any number of sci-fi films, and the dynamic compositions by the group showcase Lifeson's supple precision on guitar, Peart's mathematical intricacy on the drums, and Lee's wailing, high-pitched expressiveness as a singer. Unlike much of the progressive rock emanating from England at the time, there was nothing reserved or abstract about 2112; it felt intimate and emotive, even at the peak of its conceptual bombast.

The second side of the album consisted of assorted unrelated songs, although one of them, "The Twilight Zone," paid homage to Rod Serling's influential sci-fi show. Peart's lyrics make a direct reference, spoilers and all, to the twist ending of "Will the Real Martian Please Stand Up?"—a 1961 episode of The Twilight Zone. It wasn't the end of Rush's sci-fi proclivities. They would go on to write numerous songs involving space travel, computers, and the pitfalls of advanced technology. Before the '70s were out, Peart would write another ambitious piece, "Cygnus X-1," about a space mission into a black hole; it was split into two parts and placed on two separate albums, 1977's A Farewell to Kings and 1978's Hemispheres, parallel to the way sci-fi cinema would start shifting toward a sequel-based model in the late '70s. Those who bought Farewell and got caught up in the story of "Cygnus X-1" needed to line up a year later to buy Hemispheres in order to find out how the story ended.

The album 2112 became Rush's breakthrough, cementing their identity forever with the genre of science fiction. Peart appreciated that. In 1969 and 1970, before joining Rush, the eighteen-year-old aspiring drummer lived in London, taking whatever gig he could in the hopes of finding success as a musician. He crashed in the flat of a friend, who happened to be a big sci-fi fan. Book by book, his friend's library made it into Peart's hands:

. . . especially one of them: a science-fiction epic called *Fall of the Towers* by Samuel R. Delany, which would have a profound effect on my life, in so many ways, both in my future reading and early lyric-writing, such as *2112* and 'Cygnus X-1.' In retrospect, how amazing I should come across that particular book, so poetic, richly imagined, and original, by that particular writer, who still ranks among the best in the genre, I think.

He also devoured the works of John Wyndham—the author that Paul Kantner admired and appropriated in Jefferson Airplane in the '60s—including the novels *The Day of the Triffids* and *The Midwich Cuckoos*.

Another author greatly inspired *2112*, although she's not usually considered a sci-fi writer—one whose reputation brought controversy to the album and Peart himself. Ayn Rand, whose novels *The Fountainhead* and *Atlas Shrugged* have become primers for libertarianism and the bizarre notion of altruism as a moral failing, had a sci-fi novella published in 1938 titled *Anthem*. In it, a dystopian society brings civilization to the brink of ruin after technological development is strictly overseen by the government and individual liberty is suppressed. It's an argument for unregulated capitalism. Peart based a Rush song, 1975's "Anthem," on Rand's book, and he included such anti-welfare lines like "Begging hands and bleeding hearts will only cry out for more."

When it came to injecting Rand's beliefs into sci-fi, Peart wasn't alone. The '70s saw an explosion in libertarian science fiction, catalyzed by Robert A. Heinlein's *The Moon Is a Harsh Mistress*, which imagines a revolution among the colonies of the Moon—and whose character of Mike, a sentient supercomputer, is compared to John Galt, the central figure of Rand's *Atlas Shrugged*. Peart later distanced himself from Rand's form of pro-selfishness science fiction:

> To a struggling, twenty-year-old musician, *The Fountainhead* was
> a revelation, an affirmation, an inspiration. Although I would
> eventually grow into and, largely, out of Ayn Rand's orbit, her
> writing was still a significant stepping stone or way station for me, a
> black-and-white starting point along the journey to a more nuanced
> philosophy and politics. Most of all, it was the notion of *individualism*
> that I needed—the idea that what I felt, believed, liked, and wanted
> was important and valid.

Peart has remained a sci-fi reader, and since *2112*, Rush has never strayed far from the genre. Few bands in history have synthesized sci-fi and music as seamlessly and passionately—and few lyricists have approached songwriting with such a novelist's eye, even though Peart never did finish pecking out that novelization of *2112* on his pawnshop typewriter. "In one of Wyndham's books, I read his definition of what [science fiction] should be: 'Extraordinary things happening to ordinary people,'" Peart said, "which I still think is pretty good, and transcends the genre to cover *all* storytelling, as the best science fiction can do."

WHILE RUSH BROKE THROUGH THE stratosphere in 1976, another band from Toronto began its own journey into sci-fi music. Klaatu borrowed their name from a sci-fi classic—*The Day the Earth Stood Still*, the 1951 film in which an alien named Klaatu and his ominous robot sentinel, Gort, land their flying saucer in Washington, D.C., with a mysterious message for humanity. The nod to the movie didn't stop there. The group's debut album, *3:47 EST*, came out in 1976, and it's a reference to the exact time Klaatu's ship lands on Earth. Aptly, the album's opening song—and a hit single the following year—was "Calling Occupants of Interplanetary Craft," a seven-minute daydream of soft, melodic prog and lyrics that urge the listener to send a telepathic invitation into the cosmos, one that might entice aliens to come to Earth.

The title of the song was also drawn from an intriguing source. As Klaatu cofounder John Woloschuk explained, "The idea for this track was suggested by an actual event that is described in *The Flying Saucer Reader*, a book by Jay David published in 1967. In March 1953, an organization known as the International Flying Saucer Bureau sent a bulletin to all its members, urging them to participate in an experiment termed World Contact Day whereby, at a predetermined date and time, they would attempt to collectively send out a telepathic message to visitors from outer space. The message began with the words . . . 'Calling occupants of interplanetary craft!'"

There was no fear of aliens in "Calling Occupants," only a wistful desire to make contact. That can't be said for another track on the album, "Anus of Uranus," a comedic song about an asshole of an alien who visits Earth and makes a nuisance of himself. The album ends with "Little Neutrino," a gorgeous piece of baroque, psychedelic pop featuring electronically altered vocals sung from the unique point of view of a neutrino emitted by the Sun.

Klaatu released an entire sci-fi concept album in 1977 called *Hope*. Recorded with the London Symphony Orchestra, it's a meditation on intergalactic loneliness concerning a powerful alien who's the last of his race and spends his days trying to help others—essentially the same premise as *Doctor Who*, although rendered with a rich, lush pathos. "Come aboard my ship / I've something to show you," the alien sings with benevolent mischief on "Around the Universe in Eighty Days," the title being a reference to Jules Verne's adventure novel *Around the World in Eighty Days*, one of the Father of Science Fiction's non-sci-fi books.

The group received a huge boost in 1977 when one of the biggest pop acts in the world, the Carpenters, recorded a cover of "Calling Occupants" that became a hit on its own. But Klaatu also drew attention for a less desirable reason: soon after the release of *3:47 EST*, a rumor began to circulate that the members of Klaatu were actually the Beatles—who had disbanded six years prior. As easy as it was to dispel, this conspiracy theory persisted for years, adding one more layer of mystique to the group's otherworldly symphonies.

A lesser-known band than the Carpenters also recorded a version of "Calling Occupants" in 1977. At the Langley School District of British Columbia, a music teacher named Hans Fenger had begun assembling elementary students in a school gym in suburban Vancouver. There he recorded them singing popular songs of the day. The kids' version of "Calling Occupants"— released on a small run of records in the '70s before being rediscovered and becoming cult hits in the twenty-first century—was haunting. Innocent yet oddly melancholy, their choral delivery of the song's plea for interplanetary connection takes on a forlorn dimension. The Langley Schools Music Project, as it became known, also recorded "Space Oddity" in 1976. It remains one of the song's most arresting cover versions. Bowie's lyrics about cosmic isolation and existential doubt sound even more chilling coming out of the mouths of babes—children of the Space Age, some of whom were born the year Neil Armstrong left his bootprint on the Moon.

Bowie himself could not escape "Space Oddity." Reissued in 1975, it far outsold its original release in 1969 and became his first chart-topping single in the UK. With *Diamond Dogs* in 1974, though, he seemed to have purged sci-fi from his blood in one last dystopian spasm. The soulful *Young Americans* from 1975 was free of sci-fi, unless you count its cover of the Beatles' "Across the Universe," and his 1976 album *Station to Station*—although a daring leap into futuristic sounds that would become more pronounced the following year—contained just one track that could be called sci-fi, and just barely. "TVC15" is about a woman who jumps into her television screen and is trapped there: "So hologramic, my TVC15," Bowie sang, coquettishly flirting with science fiction after having all but broken up with it.

WHEN ASKED ABOUT HIS POSSIBLE lead role in a big-screen adaptation of Heinlein's *Stranger in a Strange Land* earlier in the decade, Bowie said, "I didn't want to be involved with it because I thought it would be a bit typecast . . . I'd be alien for life. I'd just be stuck out there. All I'd be offered would be people with green skins and varying color hair." But if Bowie was trying to distance himself from being stereotyped as an artist immersed in outer space and aliens, he was doing a poor job. In 1976 he starred as an alien from outer space in Nicolas Roeg's *The Man Who Fell to Earth*.

Based on the 1963 novel by Walter Tevis, the film revolves around an alien who comes to Earth and takes the name Thomas Jerome Newton—the same first name, it turns out, as Major Tom. Newton's mission is to use his superior technological knowledge to amass wealth, enough to fund a private space mission that can save the few survivors of his race, the Antheans, who are dying of drought. Before he can fulfill his plan, he's arrested and tortured by the government. Finally, broken and alcoholic, he records an album of music with a message for his wife, with the futile hope that it will become popular enough to be broadcast on the radio, in which case the Antheans will be able to pick up the signal and relay it to her.

It was the same sci-fi trope Bowie had used on *The Rise and Fall of Ziggy Stardust and the Spiders from Mars* and George Clinton has used on *Mothership Connection*, in which the radio becomes the medium of extraterrestrial communication. As far back as the '50s, sci-fi writers such as Fredric Brown had employed this trope, often using it to explain how aliens have learned English and details of Earthling culture: they've picked it up from radio waves full of popular songs and advertisements. It had become such a cliché in sci-fi literature by the '70s that it was parodied in *Star Smashers of the Galaxy Rangers*, a 1973 novel by Harry Harrison—the author of *Make Room! Make Room!*, the novel that became the basis for the movie *Soylent Green*, and that also predated Bowie's similar theme in his 1967 sci-fi song "We Are Hungry Men."

Filmed in New Mexico, *The Man Who Fell to Earth* is visually stunning, pitting the elemental desert against the elemental Bowie, a creature seemingly carved out of quartz. When Roeg—the same director that Pete Townshend wanted to helm his *Lifehouse* sci-fi project—cast Bowie, he did so because the singer was "a strange and very different kind of human being," ideally suited to portraying an alien. Of course, Bowie had already made a career of doing so. As he recalled, "My snapshot memory of that film is not having to act. Just being me as I was was perfectly adequate for the role. I wasn't of this earth at that particular time." In fact, Bowie was battling substance abuse and depression at the time, and his gaunt, withdrawn appearance only added to his masterful performance and visual mythology. Bowie must have agreed; stills from the film were used in the cover art of both *Station to Station* and the album's follow-up, 1977's *Low*. Furthermore, his striking appearance in *The Man Who Fell to Earth* helped serve as the basis for his next fictional stage persona, the Thin White Duke—a character that also bore some resemblance to Moorcock's elegant, mercurial Jerry Cornelius.

Bowie was going to compose the soundtrack to the film as part of his contract, but he was overtaxed. The job went to the folk-pop songwriter John Phillips of the Mamas & the Papas, leaving the viewer to imagine what kind of chilling, out-of-this-world score Bowie might have produced.

While working with Paul Buckmaster—the composer who had done the orchestral arrangement on "Space Oddity"—on the ultimately abandoned soundtrack to *The Man Who Fell to Earth*, Bowie absorbed a major new inspiration. "We listened a lot to the Kraftwerk albums, *Autobahn* and *Radio-Activity*," Buckmaster said. "I was fascinated and tickled and amused by them. We both enjoyed their records very much indeed. We kind of took them seriously, but we kind of laughed as well. Not at it, but because the music had a kind of innocent quality which was very fetching, and a deadpan humor as well."

The admiration went both ways, especially after Bowie began trumpeting the genius of Kraftwerk in interviews. "That was very important for us, because it linked what we were doing with the rock mainstream," said Ralf Florian. "Bowie used to tell everyone that we were his favorite group, and in the mid-'70s the rock press used to hang on every word from his mouth like tablets of stone." When Bowie was on tour in Europe in 1976, accompanied by his friend and sometimes collaborator Iggy Pop, he met with Kraftwerk in Düsseldorf to exchange pleasantries and admiration. Kraftwerk recounted this summit of sci-fi-music giants in their 1977 song "Trans-Europe Express," going so far as to drop a sly mention of Bowie's most recent album: "From station to station / Back to Düsseldorf City / Meet Iggy Pop and David Bowie."

Kraftwerk being Kraftwerk, they didn't sound excited—they just coldly, robotically relayed the facts, like a camera eye clicking.

Later Bowie would say, "Much has been made of Kraftwerk's influence on our Berlin albums. Most of it lazy analysis, I believe." However, there's no denying that some amount of Kraftwerk's clinical, abstracted approach to pop music, not to mention their use of emerging electronics, made an impression on Bowie's next two albums, both released in 1977. Produced in conjunction with Brian Eno in Berlin, they weren't sci-fi in terms of lyric content—but they did adopt, perhaps unconsciously, Kraftwerk's aesthetic of embodying science fiction more thoroughly than singing about it.

Bowie and Marc Bolan, friendly rivals for years, had started out on a level field in the late '60s, when the two aspiring superstars launched their own musical space race. But by 1976, Bolan lagged far behind. He'd failed to sustain the success of T. Rex's string of hit singles in the early '70s, including his fluke U.S. smash, "Bang a Gong (Get It On)." Like Bowie, T. Rex struggled to strike a balance between singing about science fiction—and fantasy, much more prominent in Bolan's cosmology—and more down-to-earth concerns like sex, drugs, and rock 'n' roll itself.

Bolan, though, refused to give up. T. Rex's 1976 album *Futuristic Dragon* was his latest attempt at science-fantasy grandeur, and he released a non-album single that year titled "Laser Love." But his use of such imagery was beginning to feel shallow and scattered; he seemed to be recycling rather than innovating in the way Bowie was. Still, the sheer joy of dragons, planets, lasers, and all the trappings of pulp sci-fi sparkled through Bolan's glam-pop lens. In that sense, his love of sci-fi remained innocent and uncluttered compared to Bowie's fraught love affair with the genre.

"I DON'T HAVE A GREAT fascination for Bowie," Paul Kantner said in 1976 when asked if he'd seen *The Man Who Fell to Earth*. By that point, he might have been tired of hearing about Bowie. Kantner had been merging sci-fi with rock music for just as long, and Jefferson Airplane had released sci-fi songs that were heard by millions in the late '60s while Bowie's "Space Oddity" had still been on the launchpad. And while Bowie personified science fiction, Kantner was clearly more widely read in the genre—and he had a Hugo nomination under his belt by way of bona fides. *Blows Against the Empire*, however, hadn't garnered anywhere near the level of attention and sales as *The Rise and Fall of Ziggy Stardust and the Spiders from Mars* or *Diamond*

Dogs, so it was Bowie who had become the de facto figurehead of sci-fi rock. If Kantner didn't feel outright resentment, a slight twinge of jealousy was at least in order.

Since *Blows Against the Empire*'s unprecedented Hugo nod in 1971, Kantner had persisted with science fiction. Jefferson Airplane's 1971 album *Bark* contained a triptych of songs—"Rock and Roll Island," "When the Earth Moves Again," and "War Movie"—which interlock to form a story about human beings achieving enlightenment and liberation through technology and space travel. "Rock and Roll Island" features the line "Can you feel us singing electric in your body"—which may have been a reference to Walt Whitman's poem "I Sing the Body Electric," but more likely came from the robot-themed Ray Bradbury short story of the same name. Later in 1971, Kantner and Grace Slick released an album under their own names, titled *Sunfighter*. On it was the track "Holding Together," which detailed a trip to Andromeda while picking up where *Blows Against the Empire* left off: "I see the Empire is breaking down from the inside."

The album *Dragon Fly*, released in 1974, marked Kantner's final shift into the future. Jefferson Airplane and its allusion to contemporary technology was dead; the future-exploring Jefferson Starship had taken its place. Accordingly, the album featured a song called "Hyperdrive"; the lyrics were written by Slick and involved time travel through psychic, faster-than-light transportation: "I can think light years ahead / Or I could put myself back a thousand years ago." *Dragon Fly* may not have been nominated for a Hugo Award, but it was played during the opening ceremonies of the World Science Fiction Convention, the home of the Hugos, in Kansas City, Missouri, that summer.

Dragon Fly boasted another sci-fi song, but it was written by neither Kantner nor Slick. "All Fly Away" was penned by a Californian folk singer named Tom Pacheco who had befriended the couple. "Space city like a jewel on wings / Rocket ships like bees they sting" Kantner sings in a psychedelic reverie. Pacheco also loved sci-fi; his 1976 solo song "Judge Proctor's Windmill" was a twangy country song that chronicled, in great detail, the legendary UFO crash and alien burial in Aurora, Texas, that allegedly happened in 1879 and was even reported in an area newspaper at the time. Sci-fi country music was a rare species, but there had been a precedent: in 1974, the early John Carpenter sci-fi film *Dark Star*—which shared a name with the Grateful Dead's sci-fi opus—featured a country song called "Benson, Arizona." Written by Carpenter and sung by John Yager, the tune sounded like it could have been about driving trucks or roping cattle. Instead, it was about an astronaut who hurtles across the galaxy while pining for his girlfriend on Earth.

Jefferson Starship's next album, *Red Octopus*, appeared in 1975, and Kantner continued his tradition of placing at least one sci-fi song on each of his albums—in this case, the fairly self-explanatory "I Want to See Another World." *Spitfire* followed in 1976, and its track "Song to the Sun" was inspired by Arthur C. Clarke's *Childhood's End*: "In fact, the very words 'Childhood's End' are on [the song]," Kantner was proud to explain. He also spoke at the time about how Heinlein, his foremost muse on *Blows Against the Empire*— and the man who had personally given his blessing for Kantner to base songs on his work—had continued to influence Jefferson Airplane's music.

Additionally, Kantner had been captivated by another vintage sci-fi novel: 1957's *Wasp* by Eric Frank Russell. As Kantner enthused, "It was about dropping an earthman onto another planet to become a terrorist—to upset the government there—and they made his skin purple to match. He acts like a one man army to make the planet think there's a whole nest of invaders— wasps—all around by doing the stings here and there. The book was later taken out of print and turned up on the CIA reading list for terrorists, counterspies." It's no wonder that Kantner, who had long connected science fiction and revolutionary politics in his mind, would have been a fan.

Across the Atlantic, Peter Hammill had likewise been revisiting his well-thumbed copy of *Childhood's End*. The Van Der Graaf Generator leader also released a song in 1976 inspired by the book: "Childlike Faith in Childhood's End." But it took another British prog frontman to craft a gloriously original work of sci-fi music in 1976. Jon Anderson, the lead singer of Yes, unveiled his debut solo album *Olias of Sunhillow* in July. Its concept wasn't drawn from any particular book or author, nor did it hew strictly to sci-fi. Like T. Rex's *Futuristic Dragon*, it dealt in science fantasy—only in a far more developed way. It told the tale of Olias, an alien tasked with evacuating his race from their doomed planet to a new home. Although clearly a work of sci-fi, its pseudo-magical themes and imagery owed as much to fantasy; it also gave Anderson the opportunity to probe sci-fi to a degree that Yes never fully did.

A year earlier, Anderson had teamed up with a Greek keyboardist with the imposing name Evángelos Odysséas Papathanassiou. Wisely he went by the more manageable stage name Vangelis. After failing an audition as the new keyboardist for Yes—following Rick Wakeman's departure for a solo career, resulting in his hit sci-fi album *Journey to the Centre of the Earth*—Vangelis established a rapport with Anderson. The singer contributed vocals to "So Long Ago, So Clear," a song from Vangelis's 1975 solo album, *Heaven and Hell*. Although Anderson's lyrics mentioned "How we chased a million stars / And touched as only one can," it wasn't a sci-fi song. But in 1976, Vangelis released his next solo album, *Albedo 0.39*. Instrumental in nature, it was more of a science album than a sci-fi album; without lyrics to delineate any specific premise or narrative, it allowed the synergy between song titles and music to imply a kind of euphonic astrophysics. The term "albedo" comes from the language of physics, which Vangelis was happy to define on the notes of the album itself as "The reflecting power of a planet or other non-luminous body. A perfect reflector would have an Albedo of 100%. The Earth's Albedo is 39%, or 0.39." Dominated by synthesizer and sound samples such as the recordings of the Apollo 11 moon landing, *Albedo 0.39* contemplated the mechanism of the universe through cutting-edge technology—a musician using the methodology of the astronomer.

Increasingly, the synthesizer was being employed as a musical spaceship. In Australia, the group Cybotron—the first but not the last outfit of that name to use synths in the service of sci-fi music—issued a song called "Arrakis," a pulsating barrage of electronic sounds beholden to Krautrock and taking its title from the desert planet in *Dune*. Meanwhile, one of Krautrock's leaders, Klaus Schulze, also named works after some of his favorite books, staging live synthesizer performances of album-length pieces titled *The Andromeda Strain* and *Make Room! Make Room!*—aural interpretations of the novels by Michael Crichton and Harry Harrison. He also collaborated with Steve Winwood and Japanese musician Stomu Yamashta in the jazzy yet ambient group Go, whose self-titled album from 1976 featured "Space Theme," "Space Requiem," and "Space Song," haunting tributes to the future. The following year, Schulze began setting up concerts in venues that he felt were far more conducive to his music than concert halls: planetariums.

Even as Parliament unleashed their second salvo of hard-edged sci-fi funk, *The Clones of Dr. Funkenstein*, in 1976, the subgenre couldn't have gotten any softer than Stevie Wonder's "Saturn." On waves of sunny synthesizers, Wonder sailed away to a veritable Eden in space, leaving the turmoil of Earth far behind: "On Saturn, people live to be two hundred and five / Going back to Saturn where the people smile."

Equally smooth was Norman Connors's "You Are My Starship." Sung by former Miles Davis bassist Michael Henderson, the song swirled wispy jazz and sweet funk into a romantic cosmic confection. Charles Earland chased his 1974 album, *Leaving This Planet*, with another album that combined science fiction with jazz fusion: *Odyssey*, the phonographic vessel for tracks like "Intergalactic Love Song" and "Cosmic Fever." And Asha Puthli—an Indian singer who had contributed ethereal vocals to Ornette Coleman's *Science Fiction* album in 1972—released a silky, funky song called "Space Talk" that pleaded for romantic release among the stars, equating the zero-gravity yearning for sexual connection with an astronaut floating in space—the erotic inverse of Major Tom. "Taking a space walk / Still looking for love," she croons.

The most potent showing of jazzy sci-fi funk in 1976, though, emanated from Philadelphia. Dexter Wansel had been a respected but entirely behind-the-scenes session keyboardist before deciding to launch a solo career that year on Philadelphia International Records (PIR). It was his first unilateral musical statement to the world, but rather than playing it safe by sticking to the mainstream sound of PIR, the twenty-six-year-old dug down and aimed high, tapping into his lifelong passion for space exploration and science fiction.

The result was *Life on Mars*. It bore no relation to the Bowie song of the same name from 1971; instead, it left its own unique imprint in the annals of sci-fi music. Playfully funky, cleanly precise, and above all, deeply reverent toward the mysteries of outer space, songs such as "Stargazer," "One Million Miles from the Ground," "Themes from the Planets," "Rings of Saturn," and the album's synth-soaked title track propelled the humble Wansel into the upper echelon of '70s sci-fi musicians. "The one thing I realized at PIR was that I was different," he said. "I had to create something different for myself." He would go on to publish his sci-fi novel *Shortwave*, in 2011, joining the ranks of Julian Jay Savarin, Mick Farren, and the handful of other sci-fi musicians who have funneled their obsession with technology, futurism, and outer space into prose.

The flow of rock songs infused with sci-fi continued. Steely Dan released "Sign in Stranger" in 1976, a darkly humorous song that takes place on a planet of criminals named Mizar Five. The group's coleader Donald Fagen has spoken openly and often of his longtime attraction to sci-fi. "I sort of grew up with that," Fagen said.

> I was a member of the Science Fiction Book Club, and they used to send me these novels and stories . . . There were also some very

funny science fiction writers who knew how to use science fiction
to comment on the present. Frederik Pohl and C. M. Kornbluth,
for example. *Space Merchants* and novels like that were very good
social satire. Philip K. Dick could also be very funny, and Henry
Kuttner as well.

The same year, the group Automatic Man—who combined prog, funk,
hard rock, and just about every other genre it could get its hands on—injected
some extraterrestrial paranoia into their song "I.T.D. Interstellar Tracking
Devices." It appeared on their self-titled debut album as well as its follow-up,
1977's *Visitors*; not only did they both sport sci-fi songs, they both used the
same image of a chrome-skinned, large-headed alien for their covers. Heavy
metal continued to take shape, and with it, so did its sci-fi influence. Rainbow—a band made up of former members of Deep Purple as well as a previously little-known singer named Ronnie James Dio, later of Black Sabbath
and Dio fame—roared into science-fantasy legend with a song titled "Stargazer." It seemed at first to be strictly a fantasy song, until Dio asks the wizard
of the tale, where his home star is and, "When do we leave?"
An album appeared in the summer of 1976 that consolidated the iconography of rock and sci-fi. Ironically, the album had nothing whatsoever to do with
aliens, robots, or dystopias. The infectious hard-rock band Boston celebrated
their self-titled debut album in August, which was poised to become one of
the most popular records of the decade. Their songs were about loving hard,
working hard, and playing in a rock 'n' roll band—nothing remotely celestial.
But the album, soon to land in millions of homes, came with the most sci-fi
of covers. The artwork was a painting of a fleet of spaceships shaped like guitars. The mothership of the flotilla hovers over a planet, presumably Earth,
obliterating it with some superweapon.
The image became one of the most recognizable confluences of popular
music and sci-fi in history. It also marked the threshold where sci-fi became
a selling point rather than a commercial risk in the music industry. Just half
a decade earlier, trafficking in sci-fi music came with the potential of being
dismissed as a cult band—the musical equivalent of those who attended *Star
Trek* conventions, which were still decades away from becoming commonly
accepted mass-media gatherings. Slapping a spaceship on the cover of an
album was now an enticement. It also routinely became an act of false adver-

tising. Sci-fi music had begun to be reduced to its lowest graphic denominator, signifying little to nothing.

That said, Boston's leader Tom Scholz did indeed feel that his album's cover art—which he initially envisioned—symbolized something. As he succinctly put it, "The idea was escape; I thought of a spaceship guitar." On Rush's *2112*, a sci-fi guitar became an implement of defiance in the far-flung future. Four months later, the sci-fi guitar on *Boston* signified a different kind of liberation—from the everyday doldrums of post-Watergate, post-Vietnam, energy-crisis life circa the mid-'70s. "Come on, let us give your mind a ride," went the lyrics to "Feelin' Satisfied," a hit from Boston's second album, *Don't Look Back*, released in 1978 with the same guitar spaceship on the cover. If that wasn't the purpose of science fiction, what was?

PAUL McCARTNEY WAS HAVING A hectic summer. Aside from dodging questions about whether he was secretly a member of Klaatu, he and his current band Wings were spending 1976 on a global tour called Wings Over the World. He hadn't played a concert in the United States since the Beatles' final tour in 1966. The North American leg of the Wings Over the World tour concluded in June with a triumphant three-night engagement at the Forum in Inglewood, California, just outside Los Angeles.

During those three shows, Wings played both sides of one of their 1975 singles: "Venus and Mars/Rock Show" and "Magneto and Titanium Man." Despite its astronomical title, "Venus and Mars" had nothing to do with science fiction; that said, it was one of the songs the Langley Schools Music Project recorded in 1976 and 1977, alongside "Calling Occupants of Interplanetary Craft" and "Space Oddity." On the other hand, Wings' "Magneto and Titanium Man" was based on the Marvel Comics supervillains of the same name, with another Marvel character, the Crimson Dynamo, added in. While playing the song live, the band projected images from the comics onto a giant screen behind them. McCartney was such a fan of Marvel's mix of sci-fi and superheroics that he invited Jack Kirby—the cocreator of Magneto, as well as numerous other beloved characters such as Captain America, the X-Men, the Fantastic Four, and the Hulk—to be his guest at the concert, an invitation Kirby gladly accepted.

Kirby, however, wasn't the only famous creator of sci-fi that McCartney invited to the Forum. After one show ended and the audience of thousands began to file out of the stadium, McCartney went backstage to meet a writer and producer whose work he'd adored for a decade, ever since he was a twenty-three-year-old kid in the Beatles. Being Paul McCartney, he was used to people acting starstruck around him. But when he met this particular hero of his backstage—a middle-aged gray-haired man with twinkling eyes and a generous smile—McCartney was the one in awe. His guest was Gene Roddenberry. And McCartney wanted to do more than simply meet him, shake his hand, and thank him for *Star Trek*. He wanted to collaborate with him.

"Paul contacted him and was a *Star Trek* fan," said Susan Sackett, Roddenberry's longtime assistant. "He invited us to a concert, which was great, and we met him backstage, which was fun. Paul hired Gene to write a story about the band, which was Wings at the time, and it was a crazy story. Paul gave him an outline, and Gene was supposed to do something with it. It was bands from outer space, and they were having a competition. Gene was open to things at this point; *Star Trek* wasn't happening at that point, and he wasn't getting his scripts produced, and he had a family to feed. It's kind of fun when Paul McCartney contacts you."

Following pilots like 1973's *Genesis II* that didn't get picked up as series, plus the cancellation of *Star Trek: The Animated Series* in 1975, Roddenberry was scrambling for work. His efforts to capitalize on the cult sensation of *Star Trek* was a double-edged sword: his diehard fans wouldn't settle for anything less than the live-action return of Kirk and Spock, and Hollywood now viewed him as a one-trick sci-fi pony, regardless of his pre–*Star Trek* résumé, which included everything from Westerns to police procedurals. He'd been reduced to accepting speaking appearances at colleges for as low as six hundred dollars, supplementing that with guest-of-honor slots at sci-fi conventions, which had grown exponentially since Star Trek Lives! in 1972.

The offer from McCartney, one of the world's top rock stars, was a godsend. But the offer to collaborate on a sci-fi battle of the bands starring Wings was doomed. Roddenberry wrote some treatments of the idea for McCartney, but the project quickly fizzled out. Said Sackett, "I have no idea what happened to that. It's probably stuck in a file, like the end of *Raiders of the Lost Ark*."

As fortune would have it, Roddenberry had a good reason for letting the Wings collaboration lapse. Paramount, the studio behind *Star Trek*, had made a breakthrough. After years of cautious talk, aborted scripts, and dropped balls, they had a solid green light on the project Roddenberry wanted to do more than anything. He was going to direct a big-budget *Star Trek* feature film for the silver screen.

It's not hard to see why Paramount finally came to its senses regarding what would become *Star Trek: The Motion Picture*. Although public interest in space exploration had dipped to a low in 1975, it showed robust signs of revival in 1976. In September, NASA rolled out its newest spacecraft, one that was designed to revolutionize mankind's forays beyond Earth. It was called the Space Shuttle, and it was meant to be reused from mission to mission, an innovation that would save taxpayers billions while vastly expanding astronauts' capabilities. The first Shuttle was originally called the *Constitution*, but a massive letter-writing campaign to President Gerald R. Ford spurred him to change its name to the *Enterprise*. An exultant Roddenberry was there, along with most of the original cast of *Star Trek*, for the grand unveiling and rechristening of the Space Shuttle *Enterprise* on September 17, 1976, in Palmdale, California.

Space became exciting again. Two months before the *Enterprise*'s debut, NASA's Viking 1 became the first spacecraft to land successfully on the surface of Mars. A test performed on Martian soil by the subsequent Viking 2 lander in September set off a fresh debate about the possibility of microbial life on the planet—and about the ramifications of alien life in general. And in July, the IMAX documentary *To Fly!*—a rapturous history of manned flight from balloons to the moon landing and beyond—raked in millions, helping to rekindle the magic of space exploration in the public imagination.

A fictional movie, however, was about to alter the way people viewed spaceships, aliens, robots, and pop culture itself—with music very much included. At the end of 1976, that movie was still five months away. But one thing was already clear: people were hungering to return to the stars.

A DISTANT PLANET FROM WHERE I COME: 1977

"A LONG TIME AGO IN A GALAXY FAR, FAR, AWAY." DOMENICO MONARDO read those lines as they crawled up the movie screen, a shiver of anticipation shooting down his spine. The feeling seemed to crackle like electricity through the audience of the theater that day. Monardo, thirty-seven years old, sat next to kids and adults alike, all equally entranced as a series of incredible sounds and images exploded from the screen: spaceships, robots, aliens, laser swords, strange worlds, a galactic rebellion.

He'd seen sci-fi films before, many of them, but none like this. It wasn't campy, yet there was humor. It wasn't clichéd, yet it was familiar. There was a moral to the story, but it didn't have any of the heavy-handed sermonizing of so many of the new sci-fi movies he'd seen so far that decade. And while much of the swashbuckling tone reminded him of the pulp serials of his youth, like *Buck Rogers* and *Flash Gordon*, the special effects were cutting-edge, so vivid and believable. The film took everything about sci-fi that had captured his imagination as a boy, reduced it to its essence, and hurled it into the future—even though it took place "a long time ago."

The film's climax drew near. The brave pilots of the Rebellion, including the farmboy-turned-warrior Luke Skywalker, launched their assault on Darth Vader's planet-destroying Death Star. Monardo braced himself, although he already knew the ending. The date was Thursday, May 26, 1977, and the film had opened just the day before, but he was seeing it for the fourth time. And like David Bowie—who nine years earlier had viewed *2001: A Space Odyssey* over and over again in the theater, ultimately resulting in "Space Oddity"—Monardo was about to take inspiration from a groundbreaking piece of sci-fi cinema and with it make music history.

Star Wars revitalized science fiction. Bucking every setback and naysayer he had encountered in Hollywood over the past four years, George Lucas held true to the vision that had consumed him since 1973, when his treatment for a script titled *The Star Wars* had begun to make its rounds among producers. Studios wanted him to make something more like *American Graffiti*, his Oscar-nominated nostalgia piece about adolescent misadventures in the early '60s. But *Star Wars*, as Lucas came to shorten the title, was a nostalgia piece in a different way. It harnessed the wonder and fun of the admittedly corny sci-fi films of yore—including *Flash Gordon*, which Lucas had failed to reboot—then it added pioneering visual effects and hints of a deeper, mystic mythology. It was expected to bomb. Instead, by the summer of 1977, it became a phenomenon. Lines of repeat viewers like Monardo stretched from movie theaters across the world. Some fans would dress up as their heroes, in the same way *Star Trek* fans and Bowie fans had started doing earlier in the decade. Overnight, sci-fi had grown from a niche to the hottest ticket on the planet.

Monardo grew up on the same space-opera staples as Lucas, four years his junior. Born in the small town of Johnsonburg, Pennsylvania, halfway between Pittsburgh and Buffalo, he'd spent his childhood immersed in sci-fi. In addition to being a film buff, "I read every science fiction book there was," he said. He was also a jazz trombonist, and by the mid-'70s he'd become a producer in the burgeoning disco scene, which enabled him to pair his love of pop with his acumen for sweeping arrangements. Seeing *Star Wars* brought his hunger for sci-fi roaring back. "After I saw the film the first day, and fell in love with it, I went back and sat through four showings in a row. I had to confirm that what I had seen and heard was in fact what I had seen and heard," he said. "I recognized the genius of it. I recognized that it was going to be the biggest film of all time. And so it was easy for me after that to just fall in place."

What fell into place was *Star Wars and Other Galactic Funk*. Released under Monardo's mononymic nickname, Meco, in 1977, the album took John Williams's majestic, orchestral score for the film and transposed it into disco. Like Lucas's battle to get *Star Wars* made, Monardo's struggle to get *Galactic Funk* approved was hard fought. "I had to convince the record company people that it was going to be [successful] too, and that was difficult," he said. Eventually he won out and was vindicated: the lead single from the album, "Star Wars Theme/Cantina Band," hit the number-one spot on the *Billboard* charts in October, and the album went platinum.

Like disco as a whole—which by 1977 was already being unjustly dismissed as nothing but fluff for the dance floor—*Galactic Funk* was much more accomplished and substantive than it was given credit for. Monardo painstakingly reimagined Williams's original music, crafting a thrilling and thematically complex interpolation. There's no denying that Monardo saw the commercial potential of pairing one of the trendiest genres of music with the most buzzed-about film of the year. But disco and sci-fi weren't fads to him. They were forms of expression he deeply loved. Rather than being a cheap cash-in, as it was generally considered at the time, *Galactic Funk* was an extravagant tribute.

The album went on to be nominated for a Grammy Award for Best Instrumental Pop Performance in 1978. It lost, fairly enough, to John Williams's *Star Wars* score. Meco chased the success of *Galactic Funk* with another adaptation of a hit 1977 sci-fi film. *Encounters of Every Kind* capitalized on Steven Spielberg's alien-visitation blockbuster *Close Encounters of the Third Kind*. By 1979, he was emboldened to try his hand at a work of original sci-fi disco: *Moondancer*. As he described the album's premise on the back of its cover, "One night I dreamt that I was at a disco. What was so unusual about the dream was that the disco was on the Moon, and among the regular clientele were many Creatures of the Night. I asked the Intergalactic Council to teleport me there to see if such a place existed. Sure enough, there it was; just as I had imagined it to be!"

Monardo continued making sci-fi disco, along with other kind of music, but *Star Wars and Other Galactic Funk* remained the apex of his career. His lifetime of sci-fi output has been overlooked, and he's been lumped in with his many imitators. But *Galactic Funk* turned the tide of sci-fi music, popularizing it in a way that no one—not Bowie, not Parliament, not Rush—had been able to do before. It would prove to be for the better, and it would prove to be for the worse.

✦ **STAR WARS AND OTHER GALACTIC FUNK** blasted open the floodgates. Up to and including Monardo, musicians making sci-fi music risked ridicule, rejection, and, with a few exceptions, little more than cult status. Now, dabbling in sci-fi music—especially sci-fi disco—was a surefire way to get a record deal. With *Star Wars* being the most obvious touchstone—subtly reinforced by the fact that the Brooklyn discotheque prominently featured in that year's box-office triumph, *Saturday Night Fever*, was called 2001 Odyssey—1977 witnessed a profusion of funk and disco songs that were released in the wake of Meco's breakthrough. Even in their undisguised opportunism, though, many were intriguing. The group Cook County put a jazz-funk spin on cosmic music with "Star Wars," while the French group Droids took their name from the robots in Lucas's universe while delivering a sparse, synth-centered, Kraftwerkian homage titled "(Do You Have) the Force"—one of the best and most inspired of the '70s *Star Wars* songs. And in Jamaica, reggae legend Rico weighed in with the dub-inflected "Ska Wars."

Keyboardist David Matthews mashed up his various sci-fi passions with his 1977 album *Dune*, which included a dazzling sequence of jazz-funk songs based on Frank Herbert's novel as well as versions of the themes from *Star Wars* and *Silent Running*. He then threw in a faithful cover of "Space Oddity," making *Dune* one of the most comprehensive yet overlooked sci-fi albums in a year rife with them. Others simply followed in Meco's footsteps by tweaking the *Star Wars* theme for a disco crowd, like the one-off groups Graffiti Orchestra, Bang Bang Robot, and Galaxy 42. The ensemble Geoff Love's Big Disco Sound issued *Close Encounters of the Third Kind and Other Disco Galactic Themes* in 1978, likely hoping someone would confuse it for the better-selling *Close Encounters of Every Kind* by Meco.

Spielberg's *Close Encounters of the Third Kind* wasn't quite as big a sensation as *Star Wars*, but it reinforced sci-fi's box office ascendancy. The film hit theaters in November of 1977, after the summertime fervor of *Star Wars* had cooled off; accordingly, it's a more self-serious movie, a masterpiece of contemporary speculation that drew on J. Allen Hynek's popular ufology books while dramatizing the psychological impact of extraterrestrial contact. If *Star Wars* was escapist, *Close Encounters* returned sci-fi to the domain of everyday life. But unlike so many of the message-heavy sci-fi films of the early '70s, *Close Encounters* blended a profound statement about human identity in the Space Age—one on par with *2001*—with *Star Wars'* big-screen spectacle and awe. It even did so with music as a central premise. A haunting, five-note melody—played in the movie by a scientist on an ARP 2500 synthesizer—is used to communicate with the aliens. As *Inside the Actors Studio's* James Lipton pointed out, it's telling that Spielberg's father was a computer engineer and his mother was a concert pianist.

Despite its musical theme, *Close Encounters* didn't inspire anywhere near the quantity of musical homages as did *Star Wars*. Many artists, though, chose to use the sudden upswing in sci-fi to make more original sci-fi disco and funk—bolstered, no doubt, by P-Funk's recent Mothership christening. Earth, Wind & Fire, whose leader, Maurice White, had already expressed an interest in futuristic topics and stage costumes, released "Jupiter" in 1977, a song that crystallized the group's previously nebulous association with sci-fi. As in *Close Encounters*, the lyrics detail a visit from an alien traveler with a message of harmony rather than conquest, singing the praises of "a distant planet from where I come."

In the early '70s, a keyboardist named Andre Lewis of the funk group Maxayn visited Stevie Wonder. The Motown superstar had begun using a room-sized bank of synthesizers called TONTO, an acronym for The Original New Timbral Orchestra. It had been built by Malcolm Cecil of the electronic duo Tonto's Expanding Head Band, whose 1971 instrumental "Cybernaut" conveyed both robotic mechanicalness and interstellar grandeur. Looking around at the massive amounts of wires, components, and controls that comprised TONTO, Lewis was less than impressed. "In a couple years," he predicted, "this will be in a little box you can carry around. It doesn't need to be this big."

Lewis—a little cocky, perhaps in an effort to overcome his shyness—was, of course, right. Synthesizers were on the cusp of becoming relatively miniaturized and innovatively portable. The future was something that transfixed him. He'd played in the studio with the like-minded souls of Labelle, adding synthesizer to their 1972 album *Moon Shadow*. While in Maxayn, which was led by his wife, Maxayn Lewis, he contributed a flurry of spacey sounds to 1974's "Moonfunk," a synth-drenched instrumental that was just a touch ahead of its time. The unsuccessful single was the band's swan song, but Lewis had a backup plan. After signing to Motown as a solo artist—and becoming Wonder's labelmate in the process—he followed in the footsteps of David Bowie and George Clinton by adopting a sci-fi alter ego.

Mandré, as Lewis became known, released his self-titled debut album in 1977 along with his first single, "Solar Flight (Opus I)." The album featured a cover illustration of a robot—his mirrored face smooth, inscrutable, and reflecting the image of a keyboard—dressed in a tuxedo. The synth-driven music contained therein, "Solar Flight (Opus I)" being a prime example, portrayed funk as an interplay between supple cosmic forces and harsh advanced technology. With *Star Wars* going nova, P-Funk on the rise, and sci-fi disco filling dance floors, Mandré's timing couldn't have been better. Yet his music was just a little too ambitious, just a little too mad-scientist, to catch on with the masses. It didn't help that Lewis, who preferred tinkering in his studio, was averse to publicity and live performances; when he did venture out into public as Mandré, he started doing so wearing a custom-made mask that resembled the robotic character he'd created for himself.

After two more albums of a similar sound and concept in the '70s, *Mandré Two* and *M3000*, he left Motown to focus on working behind the scenes in the music industry. But he left behind a body of work that reverberated—and that his contemporaries were surely paying attention to. The long-running funk band War released "Galaxy" in 1977, a song with the familiar sci-fi theme of escaping Earth's troubles via space travel, and it opened with an epic synthesizer intro. The same year, long before having their hugest hit, "Word Up," a then-unknown band named Cameo released "Funk Funk"; it included a spoken-word intro involving the crew of a spaceship about to land on an alien planet, clearly a nod to *Star Trek*, right down to the overly logical science officer. The group Tropea converted spaceflight into jazz-funk with "Short Trip to Space," again laden with synthesizers, while Space Project's song "Conquest of the Stars" from 1977 presaged their *Disco from Another Galaxy* album a year later. And Laurie Marshall pulled no sci-fi punches on his 1977 single "The Disco Spaceship."

Sci-fi disco—a hybrid that would have been laughably noncommercial even a year prior—was suddenly unstoppable. The collective of groups Cloud One,

Universal Robot Band, and Bumblebee Unlimited—which revolved around producers Patrick Adams and Greg Carmichael—released cosmic dance singles like 1977's "Spaced Out" and 1979's "Space Shuttle Ride." In France, a band called Computer split the difference between Droids' android-like sounds and the star-spanning arrangements of Meco, resulting in "Nobody Loves a Computer Because a Computer Does Not Dance"—an endearingly weird song that came complete with lonely robot vocals rendered through voice modulation. The French electronic ensemble Space infused their 1977 single "Tango in Space" with jerky synthesizers and melodramatic sci-fi flourishes, topped off with astronaut costumes. The most formidable electro-disco song from France in 1977, however, came from a synthesizer-wielding studio whiz named Jean-Marc Cerrone. Building on the futuristic disco that Giorgio Moroder forged with his breakout hit for Donna Summer, "I Feel Love," that year, Cerrone crafted "Supernature," a monstrously catchy concoction of science-lab electronics with lyrics that presciently warned about genetically modified agriculture—surely the most danceable song ever to do so.

Parliament, on the other hand, wasn't quite so sold on disco. Playfully yet with a hint of true antipathy, the group's 1977 album *Funkentelechy vs. the Placebo Syndrome* railed against this rising tide of disco—which had been boosted immensely by an infusion of science fiction, P-Funk's not-so-secret weapon. The Placebo Syndrome in the record's title alluded to disco itself: it became the opposite of all that was right and pure in George Clinton's cosmic mythos, the Dark Side to the Force that was the Funk. Interestingly, Parliament member Fuzzy Haskins had released a dance-floor-friendly song in 1976 titled "Which Way Do I Disco," in which he laments his distance from the band. At the time, Haskins was embroiled in a financial dispute with Clinton that would lead to his acrimonious departure in 1977. "The Mothership just disconnected me," Haskins sang, "But the discotheque I know will protect me." To P-Funk purists, it was as if Haskins had gone over to the dark side.

JUST AS SCI-FI FUNK AND disco were erupting, David Bowie shed the last vestige of his brief soul era—and the last trace, for a while, of sci-fi lyrics. He released two albums in 1977, *Low* and *"Heroes."* Both were augmented by the electronics expertise and avant-garde tendencies of Brian Eno, and they veered into harsh realms of abstraction, minimalism, and sonic austerity. Rather than singing about outer space, as he had on *The Rise and Fall of*

Ziggy Stardust and the Spiders from Mars, or the apocalypse, as he had on *Diamond Dogs*, Bowie presented songs that seemed to tacitly, numbly assume the existence of both. Like his new friends in Kraftwerk, he had come to eschew singing about science fiction. Instead, he *was* science fiction—a character held stasis in some future-shock tableau.

"I received a phone call from David and Brian Eno, and they said, 'What can you bring to the table?'" producer Tony Visconti recalled about the technology that went into the making of *Low* and *"Heroes."* "I said, 'Well, I've got this new thing called a Harmonizer.' And they said, 'What does this thing do?' I said, 'It fucks with the fabric of time. This is science fiction.' And I could hear the two of them whooping on the other end. They just went like, 'Wooh, woah!'"

The Eventide H910 Harmonizer was introduced in 1975. It was a digital device, which were still novel in sound studios then, when magnetic tape still drove the recording process. It fucked with time, as Visconti put it, by shifting the pitch of signals, which were then delayed and layered back on top of the original sound. He was not exaggerating when he called it science fiction. The use of the Harmonizer on tracks like "Breaking Glass" from *Low*—combined with a multitude of synthesizers, not to mention "guitar treatments" and "synthetics," as they were credited to Eno on the album—untethered the music from the present. Like pop piped in from another dimension, it felt simultaneously too fast and too slow, a looping symphony of special relativity heightened by titles such as "Speed of Life" and "Always Crashing in the Same Car."

There may not have been concrete sci-fi themes to Bowie's 1977 output, but sci-fi still guided it. Six months after he finished filming *The Man Who Fell to Earth*, he sent a copy of *Low* to director Nicolas Roeg. Bowie included a note that read, "This is what I wanted to do for the soundtrack." Upon listening to the record, Roeg agreed, saying, "It would have been a wonderful score."

At the end of 1977, after *Low* and *"Heroes"* had come out, Eno released his fifth solo album. Titled *Before and After Science*, it employed many of the technological gadgets and avant-pop techniques he'd used on Bowie's albums. But the title hinted at traveling through space and time, as did many of the songs on *Before and After Science*. On "Here He Comes," Eno sang of "the boy who tried to vanish to the future or the past." "No One Receiving" alluded to a voyage through the cosmos. And on "Backwater," Eno straightforwardly states, "We're sailing at the edges of time." He employed a host of guest musi-

cians on the album, many of them practitioners of sci-fi music ther
Robert Fripp of King Crimson, who had worked with Eno on the ..
K. Dick–influenced album *(No Pussyfooting)*; Phil Manzanera of Roxy Music;
Phil Collins of Genesis; and Jaki Liebezeit of Can. It had been years since Eno
claimed he hailed from another planet, but a bit of the old visitor from Xenon
was still in him.

Before and After Science also featured keyboard contributions from Hans-
Joachim Roedelius and Dieter Moebius, members of the Krautrock group
Cluster. Earlier in 1977, they'd teamed up with Eno for the album *Cluster
& Eno*, a showcase for the duo's synthesizer wizardry and Eno's deep-space
ambience. That year, Cluster also performed in Metz, France, at the invitation
of the Festival International de la Science-Fiction; the resultant twenty-two-
minute synth-drone concert was released years later as the live track "Festival
International de la Science-Fiction." Apparently the organizers of the festival
deeply felt the cyborg-like connection between experimental synth duos and
science fiction. In 1978, they flew out the New York outfit Suicide—whose
confrontational, abrasive, yet hypnotic use of electronics was years ahead of
its time—to perform for hundreds of sci-fi fans and cognoscenti, including
guest of honor Frank Herbert.

Advancements in synthesizer technology were occurring constantly, all
part of the evolution from room-sized machines to those that fit "in a little
box," as foretold by Andre Lewis at the start of the decade. Numerous new
synth models by manufacturers like ARP, Korg, Roland, and Yamaha flooded
the market, each offering improvements—in terms of versatility, richness,
and user-friendliness—on what came before. The Roland GR-500, introduced
in 1977, was played using a guitar instead of a keyboard; a year earlier, the
Yamaha CS-80 set the bar for range, tone, and futuristic atmosphere, eventually being used on the soundtracks to '80s sci-fi films such as *Blade Runner*—
composed by Vangelis—and *Dune*. The synths used on *Machines*, the sole
album by the mysterious electronic group known as Lem, were pushed to
inhuman prominence. The band likely took their name from sci-fi author
Stanislaw Lem of *Solaris* fame, and their 1977 demonstration of funky synth
weirdness came complete with songs titled like "Cyborgs" and "Robots in
Heat."

Meanwhile, the Spanish band Neuronium launched *Quasar 2C361*,
an album whose twenty-six-minute centerpiece was a synthesizer-based,
trance-inducing voyage through the void toward a remote celestial object.

In England, 1977 saw the release of *Motivation Radio* by Steve Hillage. The veteran of the Canterbury-associated sci-fi bands Arzachel, Khan, and Gong included a song named "Octave Doctors" on the album, a reference to the alien operatives dreamed up by his Gong comrade Daevid Allen. "Saucer Surfing" also appeared on *Motivation Radio*; an exhilarating cross-pollination of prog and funk produced by Malcolm Cecil of Tonto's Expanding Head Band, it promoted the familiar ideas of human enlightenment through alien contact, facilitated through the manipulation of cosmic forces. "We're reality gypsies," Hillage sang, "Learning how to shift the phase of time." The following year, Hillage's next album, *Green*, took on an experimental, electronic mien that mirrored Bowie's approach at the time. But where Bowie retreated from sci-fi lyrics, Hillage ventured further into space on tracks such as "Unidentified (Flying Being)," "U.F.O. Over Paris," and "Crystal City," in which Hillage robotically enthuses that he's "waiting for our hearts to build the new future in earth and sky."

Other Gong alumni were slipping back into sci-fi as Hillage was releasing *Motivation Radio* and *Green*. Keyboardist Dave Stewart and drummer Pip Pyle formed a new band called National Health, and their self-titled debut in 1978 offered an account of an ancient civilization on Mercury titled "Tenemos Roads." Bassist Mike Howlett left Gong in 1977 to put together the short-lived group Strontium 90 along with guitarist Andy Summers, drummer Stewart Copeland, and a talented fellow bassist who oddly went by the name Sting. Howlett's three new bandmates would soon leave him to form the Police, but not before recording "Electron Romance," a funky jazz-prog workout with lyrics about futuristic lust and "phaser flicks in a phaser flood."

Spelled slightly different, "phasors" factored into 1978's *Black Noise*, the inaugural album by the Canadian prog band FM. The more dignified sci-fi term for rayguns had been popularized by *Star Trek* a decade earlier, and FM's song "Phasors on Stun" was a direct reference to the show, while the minute-long intro to the *Black Noise* track "Slaughter in Robot Village" comprised an array of laser blasts and droid beeps that sounded like they could have been swiped directly from *Star Wars*. FM had an abiding affection for science fiction; on their 1979 song "Rocket Roll," frontman Cameron Hawkins chanted a chorus of "Sci-fi rocket roll!" before declaring his love of science fiction, one that surely resonated with fans who shared that love: "Imagination is my closest friend / I can turn it on, and I am free."

The news that Gene Roddenberry was resurrecting *Star Trek* for the big screen—a process fast-tracked by the success of *Star Wars*—brought a fresh wave of interest in the decade-old franchise. FM wasn't alone in their musical tribute to *Trek*: in 1977, Spirit released *Future Games*, an album that returned the sci-fi preoccupation of leader Randy California to the fore. Like Spirit's 1969 song "1984," *Future Games* drew inspiration from a specific work of science fiction—in this case, *Star Trek*. The songs "Gorn Attack" and "The Romulan Experience" made no secret of their source material, while "Star Trek Dreaming" sealed the deal. Some even used actual clips of audio taken from *Star Trek* episodes, spliced into California's unhinged, lo-fi psychedelia. Other tracks, such as "Stars Are Love," were more generic in their sci-fi adoration, but no less ardent. "Yeah yeah yeah / Our phaser's set on smile," California sang with evident elation on "Bionic Unit." Few sci-fi albums of the '70s, or any era, would be as gleeful in their devotion to the genre.

"Have you seen *Close Encounters* yet?" California said in a 1978 interview, more excited to geek out about sci-fi films than discuss the album he was supposed to be promoting. "Well, the main premise of that movie is that we're communicating with people up there, and they come down—and their means of communication is sound and color keyboards. It's beautiful. I think *Star Wars* is great. I've seen it three times. *Star Wars* is a happy, entertaining type of movie—*Close Encounters* is much more serious . . . They're both good in their own way."

Alan Parsons drew on the work of another famous sci-fi creation in 1977: Isaac Asimov's *I, Robot*. Riding his momentum as the studio engineer of Pink Floyd's *The Dark Side of the Moon*, the producer launched the Alan Parsons Project, and their second album, *I Robot*, was sparked by Asimov's beloved 1950 short story collection. One of those stories, "Runaround," laid out the author's Three Laws of Robotics, which governed the behavior of sentient machines throughout his fictionalized universe—except, of course, when it dramatically didn't. Parsons and his songwriting collaborator, Eric Woolfson, originally intended to faithfully adapt Asimov's stories. As Woolfson remembered, "I did have a very pleasant call with Dr. Asimov. He was quite enthusiastic about the idea of us making an album inspired by *I, Robot*. But . . . he had already previously done a deal which would have encompassed this. We had to drop that idea." Having discovered that the adaptation rights to *I, Robot* were tied up in television-production limbo, they decided to take Asimov's inspiration, drop the comma from the title, and veer in the opposite direction.

"It was basically," Parsons said, "to totally reverse the philosophy that

Isaac Asimov came up with in his book. Asimov implied that robotic creatures would have been designed to be totally safe and would never be able to harm human beings. Our philosophy was that that's not at all what will happen. We're already approaching the age where machines are more intelligent than we are, and I think there is a real danger that if we invent thinking machines, they might ultimately destroy us."

The album combined prog, pop, and a chilling, clinically applied palette of electronic sounds, making extensive use of the new Yamaha CS-80 synthesizer. It reflected the dystopian dread of the album's theme, the threat of dehumanization through artificial intelligence. As excellent and innovative as it was, it was the type of album that should have become just another slice of '70s sci-fi music with a cult follow. Parsons was no star, and the group's rotating cast of musicians and singers wasn't even able to tour. But it was released in June of 1977, as the droid-heavy *Star Wars* was conquering every corner of pop culture. *I Robot* rocketed to the Billboard Top Ten. It remained on the charts for a year, and in 1978 it was certified platinum.

The tipping point had been reached. Two sci-fi albums, *I Robot* and Meco's *Star Wars and Other Galactic Funk*, were selling in the millions. Styx's epic prog-pop single "Come Sail Away" hit the Top Ten in the fall of 1977—and although it seemed at first to be a song about a sailor visited by angels, the narrator ultimately realizes, "I thought they were angels, but to my surprise / They climbed aboard their starship and headed for the skies." Judas Priest had not yet reached superstar status, but their 1977 alien-attack song "Invader" set the tone for sci-fi heavy metal as deftly as the Scorpion's "Robot Man" had two years prior. In 1980, Judas Priest's "Metal Gods" would exemplify the group's sci-fi influences. In lead singer Rob Halford's words, "I'm a bit of a science fiction fan, and I think I got the lyrics from that world, robots and sci-fi and metal gods, just by word association. It's a statement against Big Brother or something, about these metal gods that were taking over."

Queen had followed the sci-fi storytelling of "'39" with their multiplatinum 1978 album *News of the World*. It wasn't sci-fi in content, but its featured cover art depicting a giant robot. The band had been captivated by an issue of *Astounding Science Fiction* from 1953, so they contacted the cover artist, legendary sci-fi artist Frank Kelly Freas, and commissioned him to re-create the magazine cover—only instead of holding one dead man in its hand, the robot held the bloody bodies of the members of Queen. Parsons, apparently, wasn't the only musician trafficking in the fear of robots.

Despite Queen's flirtation with sci-fi in the '70s—mostly due to astrophysicist-slash-guitarist Brian May—lead singer Freddie Mercury declared in their 1978 hit song "Bicycle Race" that "I don't like *Star Wars*." Whether that was true or just a case of contrarian cheekiness, *Star Wars* had insinuated its way onto million-selling albums numerous times over. In any case, if Mercury did indeed dislike sci-fi movies, it was something he would have to get over by the time 1980 rolled around, when Queen would soundtrack one of that year's biggest sci-fi blockbusters.

Sci-fi wasn't the only revolution happening in rock music. Punk exploded in 1977 with the release of the Sex Pistols' *Never Mind the Bollocks, Here's the Sex Pistols*, the Clash's self-titled debut, and dozens of other impactful albums that helped define the movement's raw, defiant sound. Punk was, among other things, a reaction against the extravagance of prog—and sci-fi became guilty by association. No self-respecting punk band would sing about space-ships any sooner than they'd sing about hobbits.

The British punk group Alternative TV had a song in 1977 called "How Much Longer," in which Michael Moorcock is explicitly lumped in with hippie culture: "They grow their hair long and stringy and wear Jesus boots / . . . Talk about Moorcock, Floyd down the Reading Festival?" Punk was all about gritty social realism and pugnacious confrontation; anything perceived as escapist, sci-fi included, was deemed obsolete.

Yet the Sex Pistols loved the Bostonian proto-punk singer-songwriter Jonathan Richman and even covered his music—and Richman sang about aliens in his own boyish way in his 1976 song "Here Come the Martian Martians," a twangy, lighthearted tune that harkened back to the novelty invasion songs of previous decades. Even the Clash made allusions to *Doctor Who* on their 1977 song "Complete Control." "Gonna be a Dalek / I am a robot / I obey," growled Joe Strummer of the show's extraterrestrial race of robots. Guitarist Mick Jones was the resident sci-fi fan of the Clash. In his pre-punk days, he religiously attended every screening of a sci-fi movie he could, and he was an avid reader of Ballard—gravitating toward the author's view of urban spaces as mechanisms of conformism, a theme that bubbled up often in the Clash's songs. Robots were all the rage in 1977, but it's the last thing a punk would ever want to be called.

A glaring exception was the noise-rock outfit Chrome. Formed in San Francisco in 1975 by a synthesizer-wielding former art student named Thomas Wisse—who took the stage name Damon Edge—Chrome released their second album, *Alien Soundtracks*, in 1977. As promised, it sounded like something from another world, and not a particularly pleasant one. Like some cobbled-together contraption of shattered diodes and discarded circuits, the album abounded with shrieking echoes, strangulated distortion from guitarist Helios Creed, and the serrated hum of Edge's synth. Songs such as "All Data Lost," "Nova Feedback," and "Slip It to the Android" reveled in the detritus of what was supposed to have been a utopian tomorrow. "We were both just into the same stuff, like UFOs, bad science-fiction movies," Creed said of Damon. Chrome had tapped into a new way of using sci-fi: neither as novelty nor as serious subject matter, but as a prankish, dark, postmodern celebration of its campy weirdness and failed futurism. It didn't sound anything like the glammy soundtrack of *The Rocky Horror Picture Show* from two years prior, but it emanated from a similar sensibility. Other punks beyond Chrome, in their own ways, would soon pick up that cue.

"PEOPLE SIMPLY CAN'T COPE WITH the rate of change in this world. It's all far too fast," David Bowie told *Melody Maker* in October of 1977. "Since the industrial revolution there's been this upward spiral with people desperately trying to hang on, and now everybody's started to fall off. And it'll get worse." Yet he had just released *Low* and *"Heroes,"* his most technologically advanced albums to date. That dichotomy defined 1977. The dire warnings of *Future Shock*, *A Clockwork Orange*, and *Soylent Green* still reverberated, but people embraced new technology at a frantic rate: consume it or be left behind, society seemed to say. Home computing, which had been more of a pastime for kit-building hobbyists, went mainstream in 1977 with the rollouts of the Apple II, the Commodore PET, and Radio Shack's TRS-80, which brought computers into the homes of millions—no longer figments of sci-fi, but everyday appliances alongside refrigerators and toasters. Atari introduced the VCS—later to be known as the 2600—in September of 1977, and now video games were available to play at the flick of a switch. Musicians like Bowie, Eno, Parsons, and Edge adopted new synthesizer and sound manipulation technology in different ways, tailoring it to their own aesthetics and sci-fi-fueled visions of the future.

In 1977, music was also launched toward the stars. In August and September, the Voyager 1 and 2 probes set sail beyond Earth's atmosphere. Their mission was to collect data on the solar system and relay it to NASA as they slowly headed toward interstellar space. But Voyager had another, more sublime purpose. Affixed to each probe was an LP. Within the grooves of each copy of what was called the Voyager Golden Record, a selection of sounds had been captured. Some were greetings in various tongues; some were maxims rendered in Morse code; some were music. That music ranged from classical to folk to blues, with one exception made for popular music: Chuck Berry's 1958 rock 'n' roll anthem "Johnny B. Goode." Timothy Ferris, an editor at *Rolling Stone*, was among those chosen to sit on the council that decided what music would be pressed onto the LP, but the Library of Congress folklorist Alan Lomax sniffed at the inclusion of "Johnny B. Goode," calling it too adolescent to be representative of the human race. Eminent astrophysicist and author Carl Sagan rebutted, "There are a lot of adolescents on the planet." Sagan also successfully argued for a dedication to be inscribed in the run-out grooves near the center of the gold-plated record. There it stated: "To the makers of music—all worlds, all times."

The idea behind the Golden Records was that they would serve as time capsules, and that some alien race might one day find them, figure out how to play them, decipher their strange languages, and use them to learn about human civilization—whether that civilization still existed or not. It was a noble and hopeful sentiment, but one underscored with apocalyptic inevitability. Homo sapiens—regardless of all its fancy gadgets and galactic aspirations—is likely to become extinct at some point. Here was a document of what we sounded like. And it should go without saying that when you get to Chuck Berry, crank it up.

Voyager even inspired a piece of music of its own; unsurprisingly, it was by Dexter Wansel of *Life on Mars* fame, who released an album of spacey funk in 1978 titled *Voyager*. Still, *Star Wars* made a far bigger splash in pop culture. The world of sci-fi literature, on the other hand, was split. Baird Searles of the magazine *Fantasy & Science Fiction* wrote in 1977, "George Lucas has here constructed a universe that seems not only to satisfy the science fiction reader, but the public at large, who, I would guess, are as sick of meaningful little movies as I am and want something that is big, splashy, innocent, 'mindless,' and fun."

The New Wave of Science Fiction—the writers who set off sci-fi's explosion at the end of the 1960s—was less appreciative. Michael Moorcock recalled, "When I saw the first *Star Wars* movie I was disappointed." His *New Worlds* comrade J. G. Ballard wrote in his 1977 review of *Star Wars* that the film was "totally unoriginal, feebly plotted, [and] instantly forgettable." Their reactions weren't surprising. They had devoted their careers toward evolving sci-fi into something more complex, nuanced, antiheroic, and morally challenging. *Star Wars* was, in many ways, a throwback to the kind of big, bold, black-and-white adventure yarn that the New Wave had hoped to render obsolete.

David Crosby, one of the first musicians to tackle sci-fi in a serious way during his time with the Byrds, had his own way of enjoying Lucas's triumph, one that fully resonated with the remnants of the '60s counterculture he'd helped create. "It didn't hurt to smoke a joint and watch *Star Wars*," he confessed. Neil Young, his bandmate in Crosby, Stills, Nash & Young, wound up paying tribute to the film in a different way. Rather than writing a new sci-fi song full of droids and lightsabers to rival his cosmic folktale from 1970, "After the Gold Rush," he put Jawas onstage during his 1978 tour. The string of Neil Young and Crazy Horse concerts—which would wind up on the albums *Rust Never Sleeps* and *Live Rust*—featured roadies costumed in the recognizable brown hooded robes and glowing eyes of the diminutive scrap-dealers of the planet Tatooine, home of Luke Skywalker. Lucas threatened legal action for the unauthorized use of his creations, but it was settled out of court. In the film version of *Live Rust*, the Jawas remained.

Presciently, Alice Cooper had recorded his sci-fi song "Space Pirates" in 1975—two years before Han Solo became the most infamous space pirate in history. Following the release of *Star Wars*, he raved, "It's like a comic book. It was four years in the making and has ten times the special effects of *2001*. You just sit there in awe. Kids, fifty-year-old men, thirty-year-old women, all acting like little kids, screaming, 'Watch out behind you' in certain sections. It's got every element of fun stuff." *Star Wars* became a gateway into science fiction for millions who had never ventured there before, in the process normalizing the idea of space aliens and starships—much in the same way rock and funk pioneers had helped make everything from drug use to political protest to androgyny part of the mainstream in the '70s. As Bob Welch, the former frontman of Fleetwood Mac, said in 1978, "Of course these days you can talk about *Star Wars* and *Close Encounters*, too—you know, sort of ease into talking about the wacko stuff without seeming like an out-and-out kook."

Marc Bolan also adored *Star Wars*. It was a glittering space fantasy full of brightness and darkness, heroes and villains, magic and romance—everything Bolan loved. Sadly, his continuing efforts with T. Rex to combine sci-fi and fantasy in song had ceased to bear fruit. The band's 1977 song "Universe" was his final attempt, an upbeat and infectious tune that nonetheless failed to revive his stature. "We'll romance on Jupiter / Make love among the stars," he sang. Bolan's fairytale spaceboy innocence masked a deep malaise.

The former teen idol had been battling a dependence on drugs and alcohol, and allegedly making progress to clean himself up, when he went to the cinema in the summer of 1977 to see *Star Wars*. "It's as good as everyone's saying," he gushed soon after in his weekly column for the music paper *Record Mirror*. "Alec Guinness is superb, but the whole sci-fi thing has been put together so well, with so much skillful attention to detail, that it's a classic."

Bolan's column was published on September 10, 1977. Six days later he died in a car crash at the age of twenty-nine, never again to sing about planets, dragons, or stars. In his review of *Star Wars*, he penned a sentence that could have served as his own epitaph: "Now perhaps more people will pay more attention to the science fiction field, where so many great poets, writers, and musicians are lurking unsung."

HIT BY SPACE JUNK: *1978*

"THERE'S ONE BAND THAT I CAN MENTION. I LIKE THEM VERY MUCH indeed," David Bowie said in early 1978 when asked if he was fishing around for any new collaborators. "They're an unrecorded band in America called Devo. I've been listening to them for a long time since they sent me their tapes, and I hope if I have the time at the end of the year to record them."

Bowie was already busy enough without taking a new, unknown group under his wing. He was in the midst of making his second feature film as the star attraction, the ill-fated World War I period piece *Just a Gigolo*. He didn't release an album in 1978, but he had just come off the frenzy of activity with Eno that had yielded *Low* and *"Heroes."* Basking in the buzz of a revitalized career, both critically and commercially, he had pushed pop music to the bleeding edge of emerging technology and avant-garde futurism and not only survived, but thrived.

No wonder he noticed kindred spirits in Devo. The group came together in 1973 around core members Gerald Casale and Mark Mothersbaugh, former students at Kent State University in Ohio; both had been protesting the Vietnam War on the morning of May 4, 1970, when the National Guard opened fire and killed four young demonstrators. Soured on the peace-and-love ideal, Mothersbaugh began playing in a prog cover band that specialized in the sci-fi rock of Yes and Emerson, Lake & Palmer. "He had long hair down to his waist and a stack of keyboards," Casale recalled.

Devo, though, were a sharp departure from that. Rather than luxuriate in the ornate arrangements and pomp of prog, Devo forged a kind of future primitivism. Picking through pop culture like postapocalyptic scavengers in a junkyard, they cobbled together electronic equipment and a rudimentary palette of inhuman sounds. Mothersbaugh's brothers, Jim and Bob—as well as Casale's brother, also named Bob—soon joined, turning the band into a clannish kind of experimental hive. Jim soon left to become an inventor; before he did, he created his own electronic drum kit with pieces of an acoustic set, guitar pickups, and effects pedals. "It sounded really amazing, like a walking, broken-down robot," Mothersbaugh said.

"You must use technology or else it uses you," vowed an unspecified member of the band in a 1978 profile. They were interviewed collectively, as if plugged into a single brain. "It's a hippie, kind of asshole mentality to be afraid of technology as if it's some kind of separate entity. You see, technology allows you to be more primitive." As Casale summed up, "We wanted to make outer-space caveman music"—paralleling David Brock's claim that he wanted his role in Hawkwind to be that of "a barbarian with the machines." But unlike Hawkwind—admired by Michael Moorcock for being neither self-conscious nor pseudo-intellectual—Devo were acutely and conceptually aware. They drew from the reality-warping sci-fi of William S. Burroughs and Philip K. Dick and coined a loose theory dubbed de-evolution. According to the theory, humanity had reached the pinnacle of its possible evolution; from there, it was all downhill. But unlike the hordes of sci-fi alarmists in pop music throughout the decade, Devo didn't flinch in the face of humankind's catastrophic decline in the technological age. With bleak humor, they cheered it on—and sought to be its personification.

"De-evolution was a combination of a Wonder Woman comic book and the movie *Island of Lost Souls*," Casale said, citing the 1932 adaptation of H. G. Wells's 1896 sci-fi novel *The Island of Doctor Moreau*. In it, the titular doctor performs genetic experiments on his victims, fusing them with animals. Devo's pop-culture scavenging reflected their yen for kitsch—which was what most sci-fi circa 1978 was considered. *Star Wars* had made sci-fi immeasurably popular, but it hadn't changed the widespread view that most of the existing sci-fi canon was trash watched by weirdoes and marked by cheap production values, corny dialogue, and passé predictions. Sci-fi literature barely registered with the public at large, except as pulp. For Devo—as with their contemporaries in Chrome—sci-fi was the richest mulch from which to grow their mutant music, a brave new noise in the ruins of tomorrow.

One of Devo's first songs was "Mechanical Man." First recorded as a demo in 1974, it sounded like nothing else at the time. As raw, crude, and awkward as a malfunctioning hunk of clockwork, the track shambled along with jerky, disjointed locomotion. "I'm a mechanical man / Two mechanical arms, two mechanical legs," go the lyrics, filtered emotionlessly through dehumanizing electronic modulation.

It's likely that "Mechanical Man" was on the demo tape Devo sent to David Bowie. It was also released on the *Mechanical Man* EP in 1978, which included the unlisted song "Space Girl Blues"—an android-like plea for satisfaction that went, "I want your mechanism / Give me your mechanism." Not that Devo had been waiting around to be plucked from obscurity by some superstar. Headquartered in Akron, Ohio, the group chugged along under its own power, playing whatever odd shows they could muster and confounding audiences along the way. Akron was "in the center of the most highly industrialized part of the United States. It's hilly, gray, like culturally stripped," Casale said, as if to justify their equally colorless and industrial sound.

They weren't the only Ohio band mining a similar vein at the time; in nearby Cleveland, Pere Ubu were using synthesizers and atonality in a distressing exhibition of technological unease. But it was Devo who were chosen to open for the no less a luminary than Sun Ra at a venue called the Crypt in Akron in 1975. This meeting of two titans of '70s sci-fi music was less than auspicious. Although both existed on the fringes of pop culture, they fell on opposite ends of the spectrum. Where Sun Ra was lush and exultant, Devo were minimalist and hermetic. Sun Ra's province was the cosmos; Devo's was the atom. Inevitably, Devo alienated Sun Ra's audience, who cleared the club during their robotic, apocalyptic performance.

Casale, also an aspiring filmmaker, wanted to direct "an anti-capitalist science-fiction movie" in 1975. Instead, they wound up making a short film titled *The Truth About De-Evolution* that year. Although not sci-fi, it drove home Devo's theoretical points in an utterly surreal way—including bizarre masks and costumes, a hallmark of their stage act that would come to define them. Casale described it as "a sort of collage indoctrination to de-evolution. It is self-referential. In other words, it doesn't depend on anything outside of itself to exist. It's logical within itself." *Melody Maker* referred to it as "a mutated hybrid of *Planet of the Apes* and *Doctor Strangelove* filtered through a sort of Mekon chromosome," invoking Dan Dare's alien nemesis.

By the time Bowie started trumpeting Devo's merits in 1978—calling them "the band of the future" and describing them glowingly as "sort of like three Enos and a couple of Edgar Froeses [of Tangerine Dream] in one band"—their debut album was on the way. The group's first single "Jocko Homo," came out in England early that year, and it cribbed some of Bela Lugosi's lines from *Island of Lost Souls*. Those paraphrased lines became the title of the album: *Q: Are We Not Men? A: We Are Devo!* Released in the summer of 1978, it was a tense, choppy spasm of stinging guitar, stabbing ARP synthesizer, geometrical beats, and monotone bleats of lust, angst, doubt, humor, ire, and sci-fi disillusionment cloaked in fun.

The most telling song was "Space Junk." It's about a torrential downpour of metal from artificial satellites whose orbits have decayed over Earth, randomly hitting and killing people—including the narrator's beloved Sally: "She never saw it / When she was hit by space junk." At least, they're presumably satellites. For all the listener knew, those chunks of debris could have been the spacecraft of Major Tom, Thomas Jerome Newton, or any other doomed space traveler. Devo had made no secret of their affinity for sci-fi trash in the kitsch sense; here they openly sang of sci-fi trash in the literal sense.

Catchy in a way that grated against such morbid subject matter, "Space Junk" also exemplified Devo's shift from an abrasive, experimental group to a pop band, albeit a bizarre one. Their onstage uniforms grew stranger, eventually reaching an apex with their signature yellow jumpsuits—almost resembling biohazard gear—topped with their iconic red helmets, mysterious ziggurats that accentuated the band's plastic, prefab aesthetic. "Space Junk" was also the one song on the album that Brian Eno played on, contributing synthesizer and distorted vocals—he, along with Bowie, coproduced *Q: Are We Not Men?*, with Eno doing the lion's share of the duties. It was recorded in Germany at the studio of Conny Plank, where so many landmark Krautrock albums had been produced, not to mention Kraftwerk's *Autobahn*.

Devo possessed none of the trademark ethereality of the Eno and Bowie collaboration. But neither were they truly in line with the movement they were most often lumped into: punk. Instead, they existed in some phantom dimension between the two, a place where jagged, aggressive blasts of sound coexisted with pop hooks, and where highbrow sci-fi and lowbrow sci-fi became one. And they found yet another celebrity fan, one not as obvious as Bowie: Neil Young. The tattered, flannel-wearing folk-rocker—who, incidentally, had written the definitive song about the Kent State shootings, "Ohio" by Crosby, Stills, Nash & Young—became enamored of Devo. In 1978, he tapped them to costar and provide part of the score for his film *Human Highway*, a shaggy comedy about the imminent nuclear apocalypse. It wasn't to see the light of day, or the darkness of theaters, until 1982, by which point Devo had become as iconic as Young himself.

"We were all basically aliens—alienated aliens—who happened to be in Akron through accidents of birth," Casale said in 1978. "Devo is like the science of music or the science of creativity. Any information can be plugged into, mutated, or spit out. Which is all our songs are. At this point we're merely punk scientists, doing our research."

Two months before Devo released *Q: Are We Not Men?*, Kraftwerk rolled out their sci-fi masterpiece, *The Man-Machine*. "We're charging our battery / And now we're full of energy," went the album's portentous opening lines; that first song, "The Robots," set the tenor for the entire record. Kraftwerk had brushed against robotic themes before, most notably on "Showroom Dummies" from 1977's *Autobahn*. And "The Model," the most famous track off *The Man-Machine*, similarly deals with the visual artifice of humanity. But "The Robots" took the leap that always seemed inevitable with Kraftwerk: After growing increasingly automaton-like in look and sound over the course of the '70s, they'd finally converted. Their batteries were now charged. They were now full of energy. The future they'd foretold had arrived.

Like Devo, Kraftwerk presented themselves in uniform; the cover of *The Man-Machine* shows off the group's four members in matching red shirts, skinny black ties, cleanly slicked-back hair, and lipstick to match their shirts.

Rather than signify sensuality, as it did with the glam artists like Bowie, makeup became a way to accentuate bloodless pallor on the visages of Kraftwerk. Glam had been androgynous; Kraftwerk were asexual.

The tracks "Spacelab" and "Metropolis" are of a piece. Each is almost instrumental; the only concession to speech is the one-word title of each song, chanted as if the syllables were being mass-produced as you listened. Built of blips and beats, they felt like theme songs to sci-fi shows that existed only in the minds of Kraftwerk—although "Metropolis" was very possibly a reference to the groundbreaking robot film. Indeed, the band screened the Fritz Lang classic during the premiere of *The Man-Machine* album in Paris.

The record is bookended by "The Robots" at one end and "The Man-Machine" at the other. The latter track is more severe and less inviting than the former; there's still a trace of humanity discernable in "The Robots," whereas "The Man-Machine" feels colder and more metallic. "Man-Machine / Pseudo human being," Hütter intones, his voice now completely shorn of any biological signs. Yet the shell is still there.

Unlike so many gloomy sci-fi prognosticators of the era, Kraftwerk saw man and machine merging symbiotically. They mirrored Funkadelic's glorification of technology in the service of human evolution, an idea that would become known in science fiction—not to mention philosophy and science itself—as posthumanism. Kraftwerk's cool optimism was a fascinating stance, but not a popular one. At the time, the fear of automatons overtaking flesh-and-blood workers was rampant. Throughout the economically recessed '70s, a series of models such as the Stanford Arm, the Silver Arm, the IRB-6, and the ominously named Tomorrow Tool increased the viability of robotics as part of the industrial business model. The microchip was also coming into greater use, which was seen as the brain of this new beast; the IRB-6 was controlled by the revolutionary Intel 4004 microchip, which had been introduced in 1971 and revolutionized the central processing unit.

In 1978, computer scientist James Martin published his Pulitzer-nominated book *The Wired Society*. "Imagine yourself transported to a city ten or twenty years in the future," the dust jacket read. "Industry is run to a major extent by machines . . . the work week is three and a half days." That might have sounded utopian to an academic, but it could also be read as a case of workers being given fewer hours in the name of mechanized efficiency. *Westworld*, the 1973 sci-fi film based on the novel by Michael Crichton, and its sequel, 1976's *Futureworld*, posited exactly such a tomorrow. In theme parks in the far-off future of the 1980s, lifelike androids had taken the place of human employees—even prostitutes. The dramatic scenes where androids' faces were peeled back to reveal wiring struck a horrific chord.

Robotics professor Masahiro Mori identified the concept of the uncanny valley in 1970. It's since become commonly known, but it had just been translated and introduced to the English-speaking public in Jasia Reichardt's book *Robots: Fact, Fiction, and Prediction* in 1978. It was a radical notion to wrap one's head around, yet one that made instant sense: the closer an artificial construct comes to accurately mimicking human life, the more profoundly uneasy and revolted it makes real humans. As if by instinct, Kraftwerk toyed with this boundary—creating the pop-music equivalent of the uncanny valley for a civilization transitioning from meat to metal.

✴ **HER CHEEKS ROUND AND HER** teeth gleaming with braces, Poly Styrene sat in front of a television set, staring raptly at the flickering screen. At the age of twenty-one, she easily looked five years younger. She was also one of the most bold, unique, and electrifying new pop stars in England. Styrene's band, X-Ray Spex, had been launched into the limelight thanks to their 1978 debut album, *Germfree Adolescents*. Technically speaking, it was punk rock. But it also incorporated saxophone, synthesizers, and Styrene's buoyant yelp, a voice that was as bubbly as it was piercing.

Styrene was being filmed for the BBC's *Arena* documentary series, an hour-long episode titled, aptly enough, *Who Is Poly Styrene?* As she was being captured on TV, she was gazing at a TV, forming a weird recursion. Playing on that screen within a screen was a documentary about John Maynard Smith, the eminent geneticist and author of the canonical scientific text *The Theory of Evolution*. In it, Smith explained how genetic engineering—the deliberate manipulation of the human genome in order to effect a desired result in newborns—may come to play a large part in the evolution of the human species in the coming centuries.

Styrene's eyes were wide, but she wasn't buying it. In response to Smith's pronouncement that human beings will one day be engineered in the womb to grow up more qualified to work certain jobs, she said, "In the wrong hands and used the wrong way, [genetic engineering] is terrible. I mean, I find that quite frightening that actually we won't have much control." Her thinking merges the skepticism of a punk priestess with the dystopian clarity of a sci-fi prophet.

Styrene was born Marianne Joan Elliott-Said in 1957, the daughter of a Scottish-Irish mother and a Somali father. After a bout of teenage rebellion in the mid-'70s—including a stint as a hippie, not to mention one failed record as a reggae singer, titled "Silly Billy," that was released in 1976 under the name Mari Elliott—Styrene renamed herself upon becoming baptized by punk.

She was nineteen when she assumed her new persona. Her new band X-Ray Spex had been inspired by the shocking phenomenon of the Sex Pistols, whose sneering, blasphemous mouthpiece Johnny Rotten had become Britain's public enemy number one. For all its infamy, though, punk had broken down doors. Hordes of kids who had previously never thought themselves motivated or talented enough to start a band—especially in the age of prog, where virtuosity and expensive synthesizers were requisite—were now picking up guitars, drums, and microphones. As crude as the music was, this generation at last had a voice. And a loud one, at that.

X-Ray Spex were part of the second wave of English punk directly inspired by the Sex Pistols, but they were a different kind of punk band. Instead of chopping and spiking her hair, Styrene kept its natural curl. And rather than donning leather, safety pins, bondage pants, and other garb meant to evoke an image of nihilistic sadomasochism, Styrene wrapped herself in vivid pastels and kitschy old clothes from secondhand shops. Her pop-art style carried over to the name of the band, which was taken from a Cold War–era toy called X-ray specs—allegedly able to imbue the wearer with the ability to see through skin and clothing—which was advertised primarily in comic books.

It's telling that X-Ray Spex took their moniker from a cheap, frivolous, fraudulent bauble. Styrene, after all, named herself after a plastic. On *Germfree Adolescents,* the song "Art-I-Ficial" addressed that plastic nature, the slick and vacuum-sealed falseness that had come to envelope consumer society. In it, Styrene called her existence, "The kind that is supported / By mechanical resources"—as if she's enslaved in a state of frightening yet blissful cybernetic stasis. The feeling wasn't a rare one. By the late '70s, technophobia had established itself as one of the staple themes of science fiction, after the generally optimistic Golden Age of Science Fiction had given way to the more cynical New Wave. Oppressive techno-dystopias continued to grip the popular imagination, from *The Twilight Zone* episode "A Thing About Machines"—in which everyday appliances turned against their unappreciative owner—to Walter M. Miller, Jr.'s classic sci-fi novel *A Canticle for Leibowitz,* which prophesized a postapocalyptic future that shuns science.

Rather than recoil from technology, Styrene embraced it, however iron-ically. Her gleeful capitulation to mass-marketed inhumanity made it all the more chilling when she claimed, "I wanna be Instamatic / I wanna be a frozen pea / I wanna be dehydrated / In a consumer society," in the X-Ray Spex song "Art-I-Ficial." Consumerism in its most rampant form is another sci-fi theme that dominated *Germfree Adolescents*. Amid its serrated guitars, squawking sax, and barbed pop hooks, the album wove a sophisticated sub-text that mocked its own commercial aspirations while undeniably emblem-izing them. It envisioned an insidiously euphoric future where a gleaming sheen of homogenous art cocoons society like so much shrink wrap. Whether we like it or not, Styrene posited, that future had arrived. "My thing was more like consumerism, plastic artificial living," she said. "There was so much junk then. The idea was to send it all up. Screaming about it, saying: 'Look, this is what you have done to me, turned me into a piece of Styrofoam, I am your product. And this is what you created: Do you like her?'" Rather than made of gleaming steel, she was an automaton self-constructed from rubbish. Her sentiments resemble Devo's fetish for space junk, sci-fi trash, and kitsch in all its forms.

The record-buying public in England did indeed like her. Styrene, for a brief time, became a star in England, thanks to infectious punk anthems like "The Day the World Turned Day-Glo," a propulsive song with halluci-natory couplets such as "X-rays were penetrating through the latex breeze / Synthetic fiber, see-through leaves fell from nylon trees," which might have come straight out of one of J. G. Ballard's dreamlike catastrophe novels—especially 1966's *The Crystal World*, in which everything on Earth, organic and inorganic alike, inexplicably begins to morph into crystal. Her exultation in a state of pure plastic-ness set the tone for much of the post-punk music of the '80s, which was already coming to be called "new wave"—reminiscent of Moorcock's New Wave of Science Fiction.

"I wanted to write something using all kinds of plastic words and arti-ficial things, make kind of a fantasy style around it," Styrene said of "The Day the World Turned Day-Glo." "It means something too. In an indirect way it's about the modern world, and maybe you could say it's futuristic." Styrene never spoke openly about any sci-fi influences on her antiseptic yet kaleidoscopic view of art and society, but it had many precedents in the genre. The relation between consumerism and conformity is at the core of Aldous Huxley's 1932 milestone *Brave New World*, and these ideas also pop up in the works of Golden Age sci-fi authors Frederik Pohl and Cyril M. Kornbluth, both separately and as collaborators. In the 1950s, Pohl and Kornbluth each published short stories—"The Midas Plague" and "The Marching Morons," respectively—that projected the growing trend of consumerist obsession into a nightmarish tomorrow. They also cowrote the novels *The Space Merchants*, a favorite of Steely Dan's Donald Fagen, and *Search the Sky*. Satirical and scathing, these books served as cautionary tales against the herd mentality that Pohl and Kornbluth saw American society all too eager to adopt. Capitalist society purported to exalt the individual—as Ayn Rand alleged in *Anthem*, an idea filtered through Rush's *2112*—but given nearly infinite choice, most people chose to conform anyway. They even identified themselves by packages, brands, and consumer choices as much as anything that's unique and intrinsic to themselves. It's the same unsettling paradox that Styrene embodied, from her name to her music.

Befitting X-Ray Spex's worship of pop art, the only outright reference to sci-fi in Styrene's lyrics comes from one of the most popular television shows of the time. "Bionic Man is jumping / Through the television set," she sang in "Genetic Engineering," referencing the titular hero of *The Six Million Dollar Man*, which was canceled in 1978 after a successful five-season run. Granted, actor Lee Majors's character wasn't genetically engineered; he's a cyborg, half man and half machine, something more in the province of Kraftwerk. If anything, though, Styrene's cheerful disregard for scientific rigor only made her slapdash repurposing of sci-fi seem that much more fitting. And more punk.

Her knack for blurring the boundaries between fact and science fiction took on a devastating turn in 1979. Her then-undiagnosed mental illness contributed to a startling vision she saw while on tour with X-Ray Spex. As she remembered, "All of a sudden I looked out of the hotel window. And I saw this sort of energy. It was bright, bright, luminous pink, and it had a disc shape. It was faster than the speed of light. I was inside a window, but the radiation effect hit my body. I was suffering afterwards, and my body kept going hot and cold." This wasn't the drug-induced, apocryphal UFO sightings of David Bowie and George Clinton, but a psychotic break caused by bipolar disorder—the same disease that afflicted Robert Calvert of Hawkwind and ultimately caused his departure from that group.

X-Ray Spex disbanded soon after Styrene's breakdown. On the time capsule that was *Germfree Adolescents*, she came across as a citizen of some deceptively utopian future digging up the remnants of late-twentieth-century culture. Through the language of song, she attempted to make sense of our fossils.

The Scottish band the Rezillos were able to distill X-Ray Spex's profundity into something more splashy and cartoonish. Their 1978 album *Can't Stand the Rezillos* was catchy and bouncy, and it sported the songs "Destination Venus" and "Flying Saucer Attack," which sounded like schlocky B movies translated into music. Slightly deeper was "2000 AD." Guitarist Luke Warm said the song was "about this awful comic that I still in fact get every week." The comic in question, *2000 AD*, had debuted in 1977 and it featured numerous sci-fi characters—its most famous being the antihero Judge Dredd, a *Dirty Harry*–style executioner in the dystopian streets of Mega-City One. Brimming with manic visuals and ultraviolence straight out of *A Clockwork Orange*, it meshed perfectly with the emerging punk and metal scenes. Continued Warm, "I've always been a great Dan Dare fan, and this comic came out advertising 'The Return of Dan Dare.' Great. I got the comic, and I open it up, and there's a picture of Dan Dare looking like a cross between Luke Skywalker and Gary Glitter. But the song didn't turn out to be about Dan Dare."

Indeed it didn't. Instead, "2000 AD" is a thoughtful, even pensive glimpse into how retroactivity, futurism, and sci-fi had combined to leave the narrator feeling adrift in time. Being a punk song, it needed a dash of doommongering, which was delivered in the lines "It's easy to see / That 2000 AD / Will never appear."

A few other punks skimmed from sci-fi. The English band the Stranglers—a little older and less concerned with image than most other punk groups—issued two sci-fi songs in 1978, "Hey! (Rise of the Robots)" and "Rok It to the Moon," both of which were cheeky, frantic takes on the genre. "I'm looking forward to the year of '88 / We'll be eating each other, I fear, before that date," sang frontman Hugh Cornwell, agreeing with the Rezillos' lightheartedly dire prediction. Meanwhile, in the United States, a New Jersey outfit called the Misfits were howling about horror and sci-fi, most notably on songs like "Teenagers from Mars"—mining the same love of bygone kitsch shared by a handful of their contemporaries. Nearby in New York, UFO enthusiast Patti Smith went on record to say that if she were asked to make movies, "There ain't that much I'd really be interested in. A Muslim *Star Wars*, maybe." And in Georgia, the similarly kitsch-obsessed group the B-52's were readying their self-titled 1979 debut album, which contained "Planet Claire" and "There's a Moon in the Sky (Called the Moon)," a pair of songs that longed for the halcyon days of B-movie sci-fi. Thanks to punk, post-punk, and new wave, futurism had come full circle.

When asked in 1977 about the name of his new band Ultravox, leader John Foxx remarked, "It sounds like an electrical device, and that's what we are." Ultravox's music overlapped with punk, but there was clearly something more icy and sculptural going on in sci-fi songs such as "Artificial Life," and "Frozen Ones," both released in 1977 as the Sex Pistols spit and the Clash raged. Brian Eno produced their self-titled debut that year, and its standout track "I Want to Be a Machine" was pivotal. Liberally borrowing from the sound and tone of "Space Oddity," it took Bowie's forlorn astronaut fable and transferred it to robotics. Foxx even slips into German to utter the phrase *die mensch-maschine*—that is, the title of Kraftwerk's *The Man-Machine* in their native language, forespoken a year before that album came out.

Ultravox recorded their 1978 album, *Systems of Romance*, at Conny Plank's studio in Germany. Consequently, it felt of a piece with Kraftwerk's *Autobahn* and Devo's *Q: Are We Not Men?*, both captured in the same facility. But *Systems of Romance* colonized its own emotional void; with it, Ultravox shifted away from their guitar-based, punk-influenced approach and toward a minimalist assemblage of glassy synths. On the album's haunting final song, "Just for a Moment," Foxx sang, "Listening to the music the machines make / I let my heart break." But he defied the preconception that electronic music was inherently cold and inexpressive. Said Foxx, "It sounds very programmed and computerized, and it is—but only because we feel that's a more elegant and efficient way of getting whatever we feel into the music." A horde of like-minded groups in England were hot on their heels: programmed, computerized, elegant, and efficient. At the start of the '70s, outer space was the sci-fi songwriter's frontier. Toward the end of the decade, it had shifted to what was soon to become known as cyberspace, that intangible reality conjured among microprocessors. One Ultravox fan in particular—a musician barely out of his teens named Gary Numan, who fronted the little-known punk band Tubeway Army and who also happened to be obsessed with science fiction—was taking copious notes.

Within a few years of punk's Big Bang, a new subgenre of sci-fi literature coopted the movement's very name: cyberpunk, which was popularized in 1984 by *Neuromancer*, a novel that dealt with urban dystopia and computer technology—written by William Gibson who, in 1982, coined the phrase "cyberspace." Eventually that suffix would be used for an array of speculative-fiction subgenres, from steampunk to clockpunk to dieselpunk. Punk may have had little more than a glancing relationship with sci-fi, but sci-fi didn't hold any grudges.

✴ DISCO, ON THE OTHER HAND, intensified its tryst with sci-fi. Meco had held a lifelong fondness for the genre before *Star Wars* sparked his greatest triumph, but for the many imitators and opportunists who sprang up in his wake, the impetus was almost entirely commercial. Yet the range and ambition of sci-fi disco in 1978 transcended its superficiality. In fact, that superficiality became its means of propulsion. In the years prior, sci-fi music had been something to sit and contemplate the universe to; now it was something you could dance and have sex to.

Sometimes that sex was with a robot. Dee D. Jackson's "Automatic Lover" opened with a mechanized voice stating, "I am your automatic lover," which is repeated throughout the song; in the accompanying video, an actual robot makes an appearance to voice that refrain. Meanwhile Jackson—clad in a high-collared silver space-cape that might have made LaBelle envious— details an antiseptic future of "cold and unappealing" love. What may have begun as a metaphor for a romance grown frigid became a jaw-dropping pageant of sci-fi miscegenation. Sylvia Robinson, an impresario of Sugar Hill Records, which was soon to introduce rap to the world, released her own faithful version of the song later in 1978 under her monomymous stage name Sylvia. But the Jackson album that "Automatic Lover" appeared on, *Cosmic Curves*, was a stem-to-stern sci-fi record, packed with tracks like "Galaxy Police," "Meteor Man," and "Falling into Space."

The group Boney M.—based in Germany but made up of Caribbean singers—enjoyed a dance floor smash with "Nightflight to Venus." "Ladies and gentlemen, welcome to the starship Boney M. for our first passenger flight to Venus," went the song's vocoder-altered intro, sounding similar to the automaton-like opening of "Automatic Lover." Dressed in space helmets and antennae, the band brought a high level of theatricality to sci-fi disco, which was swiftly becoming the norm. It wasn't enough to sound like you were from outer space; you needed to look and act the part, a precedent Bowie had set half a decade earlier. Only now that glittery aesthetic was amped up, commodified, and familiar rather than disorienting—a form of packaging, albeit a gorgeous one.

The apotheosis of sci-fi disco was delivered by a teenaged English singer and dancer named Sarah Brightman. Her dance troupe Hot Gossip crossed over onto the pop charts with the 1978 single "I Lost My Heart to a Starship Trooper." With Brightman singing lead, the track threw just about every available sci-fi reference into a pot and stirred vigorously. *Star Wars, Star Trek, Close Encounters of the Third Kind, 2001: A Space Odyssey,* and *Flash Gordon* are among the sci-fi touchstones mentioned in the song—and the title itself alluded to Robert A. Heinlein's canonical novel *Starship Troopers.* Like the Yes song "Starship Trooper" from 1971, though, "I Lost My Heart to a Starship Trooper" didn't bear any outright Heinlein influence. The song reveled in its breathless barrage of science fiction, a mash-up that encapsulated the giddy, desperate energy of sci-fi disco as a whole.

Brightman returned to sci-fi the following year for less successful songs such as "Love Clone" and "Love in a UFO" before abandoning that sinking spaceship. Decades later—having become one of the biggest stage stars in the world—she announced she was going to pay fifty-two million dollars for a private flight to the International Space Station, where she intended to be the first professional singer to perform beyond Earth's atmosphere. She canceled those plans before the launch, but not before setting off speculation that "I Lost My Heart to a Starship Trooper" might make history in an entirely different way—by becoming the first song about space actually sung by a pop star in space.

Even Motown got in on the sci-fi disco craze, rushing *Space Dance*—an album credited to a faceless studio project called Motown Sounds—to market in 1978. The venerable record label redeemed itself that year, however, with one of sci-fi funk's most fascinating songs. The legendary Motown artist Marvin Gaye released "A Funky Space Reincarnation" that year. Over eight minutes long, it takes place in 2093 and details conquests both romantic and astronomical, referencing *Star Wars* by name in the process. It also dips into Afrofuturism, imagining a hopeful tomorrow where "Music won't have no race / Only space." Leave it to Gaye to perfect the pairing of sensuality with science fiction, in essence turning all of outer space into a single, infinite erogenous zone.

While most sci-fi musicians had switched to the vocoder by 1978, the funk band Slave stuck with the more organic-sounding talk box in its opus "Stellar Fungk." It depicted a dance across the galaxy urged on by android commands and laser noises, appearing the same year the sci-fi show *Battlestar Galactica* hit TV screens and made popular villains of its sinister, cybernetic Cylons. The show, which chronicled the journey of a fleet of starships adrift through the cosmos after the destruction of their home colonies, used the more expensive vocoder to transform actors' voices. But talk-box funk like "Stellar Fungk" just as effectively used robotic vocals to simultaneously mock and celebrate humanity's growing intersection with technology.

Although not quite as marketable as sci-fi disco, the flow of sci-fi funk continued. The Kay-Gees, previously a dressed-down band, put on space-man costumes for the cover of their 1978 album *Kilowatt*, which featured the sci-fi songs such as "Kilowatt Invasion." On a similar wavelength, drummer and bandleader Lenny White—who had worked in sci-fi jazz on his 1975 song "Venusian Summer," dialed up the funk for his 1978 concept album *Lenny White Presents the Adventures of Astral Pirates*. It's a gem of '70s sci-fi funk: intricately constructed, full of brilliant interludes, ranging from rock to jazz to disco to funk, and wrapped up in one of the decade's greatest sci-fi album covers—a painting of a vaguely skull-shaped spaceship topped by eye-popping movie-poster lettering.

White was rare in writing original sci-fi funk or disco in 1978. Most artists in those genres, spurred by Meco, interpreted others' sci-fi ideas into music. The group Mankind had a minor hit with a disco-friendly version of the synth-based *Doctor Who* theme song, and a handful of songs—among them Santiago's "Bionic Funk" and Norwich Street Extension's "Bionic Boogie Get Down"—sought to capitalize on *The Six Million Dollar Man* around that time. But *Star Wars* still dominated: "Can You Feel the Force" by Real Thing, "In a Galaxy Far Away" by Third Stream, "Cantina Band" by Gaz, and parts of the *Spaced Out Disco* album by the Galactic Force Band, which also featured disco renditions of music from *Star Trek*, *Close Encounters of the Third Kind*, and *2001*. A few *Star Wars*–inspired funk songs from 1978 stood out: "The Force" by the female trio Stargard borrowed the central philosophical concept of *Star Wars*, right down to the film's mantra of "May the Force be with you." At the same time, the lyrics carry a deeper resonance, equating the Force with spiritualism, inner strength, and empowerment. Unsurprisingly, it was written by Norman Whitfield, the architect of the Undisputed Truth.

The Jimmy Castor Bunch chased its 1977 song "Space Age" with a single that—like Neil Young's Jawa-filled stage show—flirted with copyright infringement. "Bertha Butt Encounters Vadar" pitted Bertha Butt, a character from an earlier Castor song, against a space-villain whose name was a misspelling of Darth Vader's. "It has to get right to the top," Castor insisted at the time. "That's why I have made it so commercial. It's so topical with the *Star Wars* thing." If the intention of the misspelling was to keep George Lucas from suing, it worked. The fact that the song was a flop might have helped. That said, "Bertha Butt Encounters Vadar" is a mega-funky blast of sci-fi lunacy, proving that even *Star Wars* cash-ins could provide fantastic entertainment on their own merits.

Even Mick Farren—the pioneer of gonzo sci-fi rock with the Deviants who had turned his talents to writing sci-fi novels—talked of hopping on the bandwagon. "After I'd seen *Star Wars* last year, I wanted to do a Darth Vader record with this peculiar voice on it. To do it almost as a disco record with lots of weird electronics on it," he said in 1978. The mind reels at what that might have sounded like.

The masters of high-concept sci-funk remained P-Funk. But *Star Wars* touched even them. "Like *Star Wars* but underwater!" is how George Clinton described Parliament's 1978 album, *Motor Booty Affair*, the latest installment of their Mothership saga. Funkadelic's album from that year, *One Nation Under a Groove*, came with liner notes summarizing "The Funk Wars" that took place "Once upon a time . . . in a faraway parallel universe." A nefarious figure named Barft Vada is named, as well as a weapon called the Blight Saber. Not that *Star Wars* was the only sci-fi movie P-Funk had on its mind in 1978. The spin-off group the Brides of Funkenstein issued the sci-fi funk song "War Ship Touchante"; a close listen reveals a piano line quoting the five-note alien message from *Close Encounters*. Not even the Mothership could escape Hollywood's gravitational field.

COMPARED TO DEVO, KRAFTWERK, X-RAY Spex, Ultravox, and the laser-guided rhythm of galactic disco, the previous wave of '70s sci-fi rock seemed suddenly old hat. The crisp iciness of electronic innovation had caught up with the science fiction that informed it. The cyborg and the computer now ruled. German synthesizer maestro Edgar Froese—to whom Bowie had recently equated Devo—released his latest solo album apart from Tangerine Dream. Titled *Ages*, it bore a song called "Metropolis"—and as if to counteract the ambiguity of "Metropolis" from Kraftwerk's *The Man-Machine*, Froese's song was explicitly subtitled "Inspired by Fritz Lang's Movie." "Nights of the Automatic Women" also graced the album, a track that served as an unconscious gender-flip of Dee D. Jackson's "Automatic Lover." Mating with technology was in the air. Circuits had been made sensuous.

Froese's fellow explorer on the event horizon of electronic music, France's Richard Pinhas, was involved in no fewer than three classic sci-fi albums in 1978. His group Heldon—who had established their credentials with 1974's *Electronique Guerilla*, dedicated to sci-fi author Norman Spinrad—reemerged with *Interface* and tracks such as "Les Soucoupes Volantes Vertes," or "Green Flying Saucers," and its sequel, "Le Retour des Soucoupes Volantes." It was harsher than Kraftwerk, but shared the elder group's clattering passion for industrialized repetition. "The main German band I loved was, of course, Kraftwerk," Pinhas recalled. "And later I would meet them when they came to Paris, lots of times from 1976 to 1981."

Pinhas relied on the work of Frank Herbert, whom he had written about in his PhD dissertation at the Sorbonne, for his 1978 solo album *Chronolyse*. The pinging, droning, majestic record is entirely based on *Dune*, with song titles that mention specific characters from the novel, including Paul Atreides and Duncan Idaho. It wasn't the first time Pinhas had drawn on *Dune*; his 1977 solo debut *Rhizosphere* contained the track "A Piece for Duncan." *Chronolyse*'s title, however, was not taken from Dune. It came from *Chronolysis*, the 1973 novel by the French sci-fi author Michael Jeury, a book that dealt with time travel through the intake of drugs. The third sci-fi album Pinhas was part of that year was *Adonia*, a more conventionally melodic synth-prog album by the project known as Ose. Instrumental and hypnotic, it took place on an extraterrestrial colony with twin suns.

After taking a prolonged sabbatical from making music throughout much of the '80s, Pinhas returned to sci-fi music in the '90s—and wound up collaborating on musical projects with Norman Spinrad, whose 1972 novel, *The Iron Dream*, had been the source of Heldon's name. He also came to meet another literary hero and profound influence on his music. "I spent thirty-six hours with Philip K. Dick in Orange County once," he recounted. During their meeting, the author "was really paranoid. He said the FBI had burned all his manuscripts. He was really incredible." Added Pinhas, "He was the last prophet we got."

One of sci-fi's first prophets, H. G. Wells, was getting his own musical tribute in 1978. Jeff Wayne, a jingle writer from Queens who also had a background in TV themes and stage composing, audaciously produced his debut album, *Jeff Wayne's Musical Version of the War of the Worlds*. At the time, he was all but unknown to the record-buying public. Regardless, the album wound up selling millions. With *Star Wars*, *Battlestar Galactica*, and even a new sci-fi comedy on TV called *Mork & Mindy*—starring Robin Williams as Mork, an alien he'd previously played on *Happy Days*—having whetted listeners' appetites for science fiction, *War of the Worlds* soared up the charts thanks to its subject matter as well as Wayne's opulent production. Rick Wakeman had opened the door for such projects with 1974's *Journey to the Centre of the Earth*, and Wayne followed through with a flourish.

Spaceships were now appearing on so many album covers, it was impossible to keep up. ELO's *Out of the Blue* from 1977 featured cover art typical of the time: a shuttlecraft docking with a giant space station that was designed to look like the ELO logo. The LP came with a cardboard insert of the same station. Leader Jeff Lynne, no stranger to sci-fi music, carried that theme over to the group's *Out of the Blue* world tour in 1978. Onstage, the band exited a giant fiberglass UFO, and the concerts boasted a laser light show of a scale never seen before. It became the highest grossing concert tour of the year, and *Out of the Blue*—space station and all—went on to sell ten million copies.

A member of sci-fi rock's old guard clung to the decade's darkness. Alex Harvey—forty-three years old and practically forgotten by his former sci-fi protégé, David Bowie, who was now enamored of Kraftwerk and Devo—released a song called "Nightmare City" in 1978. It couldn't have been more out of step in a world of *Star Wars* and synthesizers. Like a long-lost, hard-edged glam song from years earlier, it slunk through the same apocalyptic shadows that Bowie's Halloween Jack had haunted in *Diamond Dogs*. On it, Harvey imagined a human race reduced to savagery and cannibalism, adding poignantly, "I wish it was the way it used to be / Open shirt on a long, hot summer night." Four years later, on the eve of his forty-seventh birthday, he died of a heart attack while on his way to a gig, never to wonder about the future again. The man who had introduced the young Bowie to the work of Arthur C. Clarke in the late '60s—and in doing so helped to pave the way for the creation of Major Tom—passed into eternal obscurity, eclipsed by his former satellite.

ON NOVEMBER 17, 1978, THE United States got its second taste of *Star Wars*. For many, it was less than sweet. *The Star Wars Holiday Special* aired that night on CBS, and Lucas had signed off on it without demanding any direct involvement. The result was a self-parody of *Star Wars*, scattered between comedy, music, a cartoon, and a bizarre Wookiee family drama involving Chewbacca's father, Itchy, and his son, Lumpy.

The music, however, stood out. At one point in the special, a holographic band appears on a video music box. They perform a rock song about UFOs called "Light the Sky on Fire," although the working title had been "Cigar-Shaped Object (Vanished Without a Trace)." The band was not named during the segment, but astute music fans didn't need to scan the show's credits to recognize them. It was Jefferson Starship.

Paul Kantner had never given up on his sci-fi rock imperative. Granted, his output of sci-fi songs after *Blows Against the Empire* had amounted to little more than a trickle—but he was also balancing his own passions against the songwriting contributions of other band members, not to mention the need to keep the group commercially viable. Despite its planetary title, Jefferson Starship's 1978 album, *Earth*, didn't contain any sci-fi songs. But it's plausible that the band's appearance on *The Star Wars Holiday Special*—based on the creations of Lucas, who had filmed Jefferson Airplane all those years ago at Altamont—reignited Kantner's desire to tell science fiction through song. In 1979, Jefferson Starship released *Freedom at Point Zero*, and embedded in its playlist was the seed of a new sci-fi concept.

The song "Lightning Rose (Carry the Fire)" was, according to Kantner, "basically about people in an outlaw camp outside a domed city with nuclear reactors." Rather than projecting the '60s counterculture into outer space, as *Blows Against the Empire* had done, "Lightning Rose" introduced a young female savior in a dystopian future—a sort of Joan of Arc for the nuclear age. His attempts to smuggle in more of the Lightning Rose song cycle in bits and pieces, all the way through Jefferson Starship's 1984 album *Nuclear Furniture*, took their toll. Disillusioned with the radio-friendly direction the band was barreling toward, he left that year; the remaining members regrouped as Starship and had the biggest hit of their career, 1985's "We Built This City." For the remainder of his life, Kantner doubled down on sci-fi music, never selling many records but maintaining his greatest creative love. Eventually he even published the sci-fi novel he'd been writing, on and off, for years. Its title: *The Empire Blows Back*.

Three weeks before *The Stars Wars Holiday Special*, another musical, made-for-TV sci-fi movie was broadcast on a network in the United States. This one, however, wasn't meant to coincide with Thanksgiving and Christmas, but with Halloween. *Kiss Meets the Phantom of the Park* was shown on

NBC on October 28, 1978, and its premise matched the campy nature of Kiss itself. The group's four members, wielding superpowers, take on a mad scientist and his battalion of evil cyborgs in an amusement park. It did share one thing with *The Star Wars Holiday Special*: it disappointed many hard-core fans. But it also showed off the sci-fi side of Kiss, a revelation that was no accident. The costumed, makeup-masked personas of Paul "Starchild" Stanley and Ace "Space Ace" Frehley were the first clue, but additional hints of sci-fi had been sneaking into their music all along.

Frehley cowrote the band's 1977 song "Rocket Ride," which equated sex with astronautics using the crudest, most Kiss-esque metaphor conceivable: the rocket as a phallus. But he played his part to the hilt, claiming as so many rock stars of the '70s had that he hailed from another planet. "I was always fascinated with science fiction and space travel," said Frehley, whose taste in sci-fi cinema leaned toward classics like *The Day the Earth Stood Still*, *Forbidden Planet*, *The Silent Earth*, and *Invaders from Mars*. "It was a natural extension of my personality."

Two years after "Rocket Ride," Kiss covered the Rolling Stones' sci-fi song "2000 Man." And their own 1979 song "X-Ray Eyes" takes one of Superman's abilities—granted to him by his status as an immigrant from another planet—and twists it into a weapon of jealousy. Richard Donner's big-screen adaptation of *Superman* had been a blockbuster in 1978—and *The Man With the X-Ray Eyes* was the title of a 1963 sci-fi horror film by Roger Corman, of which Simmons, "an avowed horror and science-fiction fan," was surely aware. He counted everything from *Metropolis* to *2001* to *Star Wars* among his favorites, not to mention *Island of Lost Souls*, the film so beloved by Devo that they coopted it for the name of their debut album. When asked by *Creem* in 1979 how he felt about Devo—a group that, like Kiss, wore costumes and devoured sci-fi—Simmons was less than impressed. "I think [Devo's music] is real class, sophisticated kind of rock 'n' roll," he remarked. In Kiss's world, that's an insult. "I don't know what those costumes mean. The name is very ambiguous."

He did, however, instantly recognize the source of the "Are we not men?" part of *Q: Are We Not Men? A: We Are Devo!*—and he was happy to geek out about it at length. "It comes from an H. G. Wells paragraph in *Island of Lost Souls*, with Dr. Moreau," Simmons went on. "He's raised these animal men; he's transformed these animals into half men. And he always tries to keep them from going too far overboard and attacking each other. He snaps his whip and says, 'What ees the law?', and they go, 'Dee law ees, we shall not eat flesh, for are we not men?', and they all go, 'Are we not men?" and he goes, 'What ees the law?' 'Dee law ees, we shall not drink blood, for are we not men?', then they all go, 'Are we not men?' That's where they go, 'No, we are Devo.' Nice. Cute. But if I'm fifteen years old, and I'm from Davenport, Iowa, I could give a shit. I mean, give me Van Halen."

While it's not obvious from the context of Simmons's interview, Van Halen's frontman David Lee Roth was also a huge fan of *Island of Lost Souls*—something Simmons likely knew, being an early champion of Van Halen and the producer of their 1976 demo. In the mid-'70s, the up-and-coming California band regularly performed an early version of their song "House of Pain," which appeared on the Simmons demo—and whose sci-fi lyrics were based on *Island of Lost Souls*. "It's about a doctor who takes his people to a house of pain," Roth said by way of introducing the song during a concert at the Starwood in West Hollywood in 1976. A revised version of the song was recorded years later—minus any trace of science fiction—for Van Halen's multiplatinum triumph *1984*, a consummate party album that was not based in any way on the George Orwell novel.

Roth and Simmons belonged to a certain school of sci-fi rock that had emerged—one that paid straightforward homage to the works of sci-fi they uncomplicatedly enjoyed. Devo, as Simmons sensed, were on the other side of the divide. The Akron band's appropriation of sci-fi was complicated, conflicted, and—while this term surely never fell from Simmons's lips—postmodern. Highbrow clashed with lowbrow. Ten years after Kirk and Uhura's interracial kiss on *Star Trek* had brought the culture war to sci-fi, Kiss brought the culture war to sci-fi music.

WHEN THE MACHINES ROCK: *1979*

QUEENS HALL IN LEEDS, ENGLAND, WAS NOT A PLACE ANYONE WOULD have called futuristic. The circular, concrete exhibition hall was, by one account, "an oversized tram shed reeking of beer and glue." But on the weekend of September 8 and 9, 1979, hundreds of music fans and sci-fi aficionados filled the hall for what was being billed as "The World's First Science Fiction Music Festival"—otherwise known as the Futurama Festival.

The event was organized to showcase a handful of exciting bands of the burgeoning post-punk movement. Artsy, angst-ridden, and angular, these bands had been channeling the energy and do-it-yourself ethos of punk while forgoing most of its nihilism and wanton simplemindedness. In that vacuum, a fractured explosion of strange noise occurred. The more popular groups who played at the Futurama Festival embodied this new approach, each in a unique way: Joy Division, Echo and the Bunnymen, Orchestral Manoeuvres in the Dark, Soft Cell, Simple Minds, the Fall, the Mekons, the Teardrop Explodes, Cabaret Voltaire, Scritti Politti, and Public Image Ltd.—led by former Sex Pistols frontman Johnny Rotten, who was now going by his real name John Lydon and forging a distinctly abrasive form of experimental rock. Not all of them were influenced by sci-fi, but they all seemed like citizens of tomorrow—the kinds of bands sci-fi writers might have imagined composing the soundtrack of the future. Still, a curious holdover from a previous era headlined the second night of the festival: Hawkwind, a band that predated punk but had foreshadowed in the early '70s much of what was now happening.

"This one's a love song . . . to Einstein." So said the singer of one of Sunday's opening acts, an unknown group called Gotham City Teenage Werewolves that was never to be heard from again. In a sense, every song played by every band that weekend was a love song to Einstein—to the age of light speed, spacetime, and relativity. Orchestral Manoeuvres in the Dark, a duo of electronic musicians, used a reel-to-reel tape machine onstage, playing along with prerecorded tracks of their own synthetic sound. Cabaret Voltaire manipulated synthesizers while projecting eerie film clips. The group Punishment of Luxury—who specialized in a disjointed mix of post-punk and prog—somehow managed to play their tricky music while wearing glow-in-the-dark tentacle-fingered gloves. Their 1979 sci-fi song "Radar Bug"—which was about "life in a pleasure dome with a solar ceiling," a far cry from Queens Hall—included the telling lines, "There's music from the song machine / But I still feel out of place."

Along with music, the Futurama Festival offered laser light shows, movie screenings, and "other sci-fi attractions." One of those attractions was people dressed as robots, who wandered the hall, brought along by Roger Ruskin Spear, a prior member of the Bonzo Dog Doo-Dah Band—the group that helped usher in a decade of sci-fi music with their 1968 song "I'm the Urban Spaceman." Cabaret Voltaire's Richard H. Kirk called the festival "grim," "bleak," and "with gray dust everywhere"; a concertgoer remembered, "the Queens Hall venue floor came off on your clothing. By the end of Saturday, everyone was a uniform bleak gray." Come Sunday, those in attendance looked a little like robots themselves.

Joy Division certainly had a touch of the robotic about them. Lead singer Ian Curtis was prone to bouts of impromptu onstage choreography that was stiff and inhumanly choppy, like an android in the throes of malfunction, and his voice was a ghostly baritone. He loved Bowie, right down to swiping "Warszawa"—the title of a song from *Low*—and changing it to Warsaw for the name of an early incarnation of Joy Division. And like Bowie, Curtis was a sci-fi fan. His reading favored the work of William S. Burroughs and J. G. Ballard; the Joy Division songs "Interzone" and "The Atrocity Exhibition" were taken from the work of each author, respectively. Their songs dealt with emotional and existential devastation, but they also sometimes strayed into dystopia. On "Ice Age," Curtis sang of a frigid time when "We'll live in holes and disused shafts / Hopes for little more."

Curtis was also a fan of Michael Moorcock. They became acquainted after the singer had been seen buying back issues of Moorcock's sci-fi magazine *New Worlds* at a counterculture bookshop called Savoy, in Manchester. "Ian Curtis and [Joy Division drummer] Stephen Morris enthused about Moorcock [and] Ballard," said Savoy owner David Britton. At one point, that acquaintance between Curtis and Moorcock turned into the prospect of a collaboration. "There was some talk of us working together," Moorcock said. "Shame it never came off. Poor lad. I liked Joy Division a fair bit . . . At one point we discussed Joy Division doing a version of *The Brothel in Rosenstrasse*." It isn't clear if Moorcock meant his book—a period piece set in nineteenth-century Germany—or his song with the Deep Fix, both of which shared that title. In any case, both were released in 1982, which means Moorcock would have been discussing teaming up with Joy Division on one of his works in progress. Tragically, it never came to be; eight months after the Futurama Festival, Curtis committed suicide at the age of twenty-three, hanging himself the night before Joy Division was scheduled to embark on their first American tour.

Curtis's chief rival as the spokesman of Mancunian post-punk was Mark E. Smith. The vitriolic frontman of the jagged post-punk band the Fall, he seemed to brook little patience for sci-fi. One Futurama attendee saw Smith "hassling the Hawkwind fans about their 'cosmic crap,'" In the Fall's 1979 song "It's the New Thing," which they very well may have played at Futurama, Smith sang with acid in his voice, "Looks like science fiction films or revival gothic pigswill." Yet Smith, a voracious reader like Curtis, later admitted that he enjoyed the work of at least one sci-fi author, Philip K. Dick. Cabaret Voltaire—an even more sonically challenging band whose electronic attack anticipated the mechanistic clang of what would become known as industrial music—said they drew inspiration from the sci-fi shows of their youth, *Doctor Who* and *Quatermass*. It's evident in "Nag Nag Nag," Cabaret Voltaire's 1979 single, which features distorted and filtered vocals resembling those of the Daleks of *Doctor Who*. Orchestral Manoeuvres in the Dark, better known as OMD after they'd become pop stars in the '80s, were a more pop-oriented electronic band—and while they weren't singing about sci-fi in 1979, singer Andy McCluskey had spent time in the clearly *Doctor Who*–loving band Dalek I Love You the previous year. And Soft Cell, years before finding fame with their '80s synth-pop anthem "Tainted Love," likely performed their early song "Science Fiction Stories" at Futurama.

Not every band at Futurama was experimental. The Only Ones were a more conventional outfit who favored classic pop-rock songwriting with a twist of punk. Their 1978 hit single "Another Girl, Another Planet," used sci-fi as a metaphor for drug use. The spiky, spastic band Spizzenergi, on the other hand, surely graced the audience of Futurama with "Where's Captain Kirk?," a 1979 single that unapologetically celebrated *Star Trek* as kitsch, much the same way the Rezillos had treated sci-fi a year earlier. In 1980, after changing their name to Athletico Spizz 80, the group issued the sequel to "Where's Captain Kirk?," a single titled "Spock's Missing."

The Mekons were also listed on the Futurama Festival's initial lineup. The joyously ramshackle post-punk band took their name from the alien nemesis of the Dan Dare comics, and they even released a song in 1979 titled "Dan Dare." But their sci-fi pedigree went deeper. Leader Jon Langford was the younger brother of David Langford, a critic and author who was one of the leading lights of the British sci-fi community. At the 1979 World Science Fiction Convention, held in Brighton, England, two weeks before the Futurama Festival, David won his first Hugo Award. He would go on to win twenty-one Hugos, the most of any person in history, lending his brother's band a formidable sci-fi pedigree by association.

A CONSPICUOUS ABSENCE COULD BE felt among the robots and synthesizers of the Futurama Festival: Gary Numan. He could be excused, though. His second album of 1979, *The Pleasure Principle*, had been released on September 7, the day before the festival, so he was understandably occupied. The album followed *Replicas*, which had come out in April. Both records hit the number-one spot on the British charts, thrusting the twenty-one-year-old former forklift driver into the upper echelon of stardom practically overnight. He was, however, as unlikely a pop icon as Bowie had been earlier in the decade. Numan wasn't about connecting with people. His automaton-like persona and songs—sleek, shiny, and shiver-inducing—did precisely the opposite.

"Me! I Disconnect from You" was the opening track of *Replicas*. Punctuated with blips and pops of computerized punctuation and skeletal melody, it laid bare Numan's acute emotional alienation, something viewed as both a curse and a comfort; he would later be diagnosed with Asperger syndrome, to which he's credited at least some of his sympathy with androids and cyborgs. But he was also an avid consumer of sci-fi. The entirety of *Replicas* is steeped in the technological estrangement and psychological dystopianism of Dick and Ballard, post-punk's favorite sci-fi writers. The album "was very loosely about what I thought London might become in fifty to a hundred years because of computers and violence and ways there might be to deal with that kind of thing,"

His earliest sci-fi fascinations included *Fireball XL5*, the British children's show from the early '60s, as well as *Star Trek*. But revelation came in 1970. "I read *Do Androids Dream of Electric Sheep?* when I was twelve," he said, "and I got loads of things from that." The 1968 Dick novel, about a mercenary who hunts rogue androids passing as human, became his most treasured tome, along with Isaac Asimov's *I, Robot*. This source code is everywhere in *Replicas*. From "Are 'Friends' Electric?" to "I Nearly Married a Human" to the instrumental "When the Machines Rock"—the last of which might as well have been Numan's slogan—the songs on the album picture a future where robots have to be factored into an increasingly nightmarish social equation. *Friends Come in Boxes*, a 1973 novel by Michael G. Coney, also exerted a pull on Numan's music. The obvious nod is in "Are 'Friends' Electric?," which dwells on the same big questions as Coney's novel: How can empathy be maintained in a world where the line between human and machine becomes blurred?

Numan never undertook a direct adaptation of the works of Dick, Coney, or any other writer. "Influences, when used wisely, should be a series of little sparks that just ignite your own ideas," he said. Instead, he absorbed his favorite sci-fi books and movies, converting them into raw material to be molded into new yet hauntingly familiar shapes. In that sense, Numan exemplified pop music's relationship with sci-fi throughout the '70s: science fiction could be a direct source of subject matter, but it could also be a catalyst for one's own concepts and narratives. In addition to being indebted to his readily confessed inspirations, *Replicas* was largely drawn from a sci-fi novel Numan had been working on, one that never wound up being finished—at least not in prose form. After the artistic and commercial triumph of *Replicas*, there seemed to be little point. Why labor on prose in quietude and seclusion when an entire book's worth of sci-fi spectacle, fear, and wonder could be pressed onto a record then performed at head-spinning volume in the theatrical setting of a concert stage? The story Numan wanted to tell had already been consummately told—in song.

Just as consummate was Numan's appearance. Crisply attired in a black tie over a black shirt, which glaringly offset his powder-white skin and hair, he looms on the cover of *Replicas* like an android straight out of his own songs. Bowie was the most blatant reference, but there was just as much Kraftwerk in his buttoned-up clothes and mannequin pose. It all combined to project an image of fiction brought to life—as complete and tightly sealed as the sci-fi personas of Kiss or Devo. Just as Kiss fans called themselves the Kiss Army and Devo fans called themselves Spudboys, Numan fans called themselves Numanoids, a portmanteau of "Numan" and "humanoids." With dehumanization the newest paranoia in the encroaching digital age, the posthuman sight and sound of Numan—his name even hinted at "new man"—struck a chord not even Bowie could match circa 1979.

The Numanoid-in-Chief didn't roll off the assembly line fully built. A year before *Replicas*, he released a self-titled debut album under the name Tubeway Army. It was more punk in nature, and several songs were about the routine topics of sex and drugs. But his sci-fi proclivities were already beginning to show. Early on he had billed himself on record as Valerian, which caused rumors that he was a devotee of the long-running French space-opera comic series *Valérian and Laureline*. But Numan insists he got the name from some graffiti he saw scrawled on a wall, much in the way he picked the name Numan—he was born Gary Webb—not because it sounded like "new man," but because it came up when he flipped through the phone book looking for a pseudonym. *Tubeway Army* wasn't as synthesizer-centered as *Replicas*; still, its sci-fi themes were obvious in the first line of the first song, "Listen to the Sirens," which went, "Flow my tears, the new police song"—a nod to Dick's 1974 novel *Flow My Tears, The Policeman Said*, a book about, interestingly enough, a genetically engineered pop star. And in "Steel and You,"

Numan sings, "Do you know that friends come in boxes?," citing Coney's *Friends Come in Boxes* as if to test a prototype of "Are 'Friends' Electric?"

Numan's second album of 1979, *The Pleasure Principle*, did away with the already minimal guitars of *Replicas*. The synthesizer took over. Even Bowie's *Low* and *"Heroes,"* as innovative as they were, felt like careful compromises between organic and inorganic tones. Numan felt no such need. Songs like "Metal" and "Engineers" exalted a new mechanical reality. In the former, an android yearns to be taken as a sentient being; on the latter, Numan sings, "All that we know / Is you and machinery." But the album's biggest song wasn't as openly concerned with sci-fi. Existing in the overlap of isolation and technology, "Cars" rendered our apprehension of an increasingly complex world as a retreat into a new kind of steel womb—that is, the automobile. The resemblance to Ballard's 1973 novel *Crash* is pronounced; although *Crash* isn't sci-fi per se, it probes the intersection of flesh and machine in a hallucinatory way that made even Ballard's own sci-fi seem quaint. It also mirrored a song from Bowie's *Low*, "Always Crashing in the Same Car," which could have been a cousin of "Cars."

As much as he patterned himself after Bowie and Kraftwerk, Numan was enamored of someone more contemporary: John Foxx, who had left Ultravox in 1978 to launch a solo career. But where Foxx delicately layered traces of android coldness in his music and image, Numan moved them front and center. Despite the enormous space-music trend kicked up by *Star Wars*, Numan cared little about that segment of sci-fi. Aliens make an appearance in *Replicas*—there's even a song called "Praying to the Aliens"—but they seem thrown in as an afterthought. "I'm not particularly interested in Martians and strange aliens, although that has its moments," he remarked. "My big interest for a while, when I started to write music seriously, was really about the development of technology and how that was going to affect us." In doing so, he went down as the first bona fide synth-pop star—proving that after decades of being considered oddballs tinkering with gizmos on the fringes of music, the worshippers of pop futurism could go mainstream. He also anticipated the imminent tide of cyberpunk and posthuman sci-fi, which would transform the literature of the '80s, not to mention our view of the future itself.

Another forward-reaching act that would have fit the bill at Futurama was the Human League. Formed in 1977 under the auspicious name the Future, the synthesizer-based outfit played their first show in 1978, at which they performed a version of the *Doctor Who* theme song. A profile of the band published in 1979 noted that the home of member Adrian Wright prominently displayed "a row of little Daleks by the door." They took their name the Human League from the designation of a galactic federation in StarForce, a sci-fi board game they liked to play. Later in 1978, Bowie caught a show of theirs and exclaimed that he "had seen the future of pop music." Of course, he had just sung the praises of Devo as well. It was as though his sci-fi progeny had left the nest, and he was sending them off with his blessing.

As with so many of their synth-slinging, post-punk comrades, the Human League voraciously read the fiction of Ballard and Dick. By frontman Philip Oakey's admission, their 1978 song "Circus of Death" was influenced by *Ubik*, Dick's 1969 novel about the existential pitfalls of a psychically enhanced human populace. Oakey had previously worked in a bookstore, and he considered Dick his favorite author. He held Moorcock in such high regard that he had considered taking the writer's Jerry Cornelius character and adopting it as his own stage persona. His subsequent androgynous look, complete with a severely geometrical haircut, was "a crafted touch directly influenced by . . . Jerry Cornelius, who combined both sexes." In that regard, he was following in Bowie's footsteps, as Cornelius was one of the many characters the elder artist folded into his composite identity of Ziggy Stardust.

"Circus of Death" was just the beginning. "Almost Medieval," released in 1979, was obsessed with century-hopping and jumbled timelines—a premise straight out of *Doctor Who*. The same year, the group released *The Dignity of Labour*; it wasn't sci-fi, but it was a concept EP about cosmonaut Yuri Gagarin's historic Vostok 1 mission in 1961, when he became the first human in space. The cover of the record featured a photo of Gagarin receiving a Soviet medal. The Human League, along with Cabaret Voltaire, were from Sheffield. Two other bands, lesser known, hailed from the same city and created their own synth-driven, sci-fi post-punk: Vice Versa, who in 1979 released songs such as "Science Fact" and "New Girls Neutrons," and Clock DVA, who purloined their name from *A Clockwork Orange* and who, unlike the Human League, actually did manage to play the Futurama Festival.

Not all of the post-punk bands with sci-fi sympathies preferred the synthesizer. Joy Division didn't start using the instrument until the very end of their existence. Less famous groups like the Comsat Angels—neighbors of the Human League in Sheffield and whose name came from a Ballard short story—barely used the machine on their 1979 song "Red Planet," despite its futuristic depiction of a trip to Mars. Meanwhile, Doll by Doll—whose song "The Palace of Love" from the same year was based on Jack Vance's 1967 space-opera novel—weren't very experimental at all. But much of post-punk was spreading the synthesizer like a virus in 1979, a means by which to bypass rock guitars, music theory, and the very notion of orthodox songwriting—all clichés to the post-punks—through advanced technology.

A single from 1978 had helped catalyze this idea. Naturally, it was sci-fi. Daniel Miller assumed the name the Normal and released a single bearing two songs, "Warm Leatherette" and "T.V.O.D.," each carving out of blocks of electronic noise. Like Bowie's "Always Crashing in the Same Car" and Numan's "Cars," it thrummed along on the same wavelength as Ballard's *Crash*. Only, in Miller's case, he was explicit about the influence. He was compelled to launch the Normal after a friend urged him to read *Crash* the year before. To him, the book "wasn't like science fiction in the sense that it was outer space and stuff like that. It felt like it was five minutes into the future."

Visage ventured further out. In 1978, the newly minted studio project recorded a demo in hopes of getting a record deal, and included was a cover of Zager and Evans' 1969 hit "In the Year 2525." Unlike the original, it wasn't rendered as folk rock. It was played on synthesizers in the strange new style that was sweeping across England, a seminal sci-fi song updated for the ears and needs of tomorrow. The group featured Billy Currie of Ultravox, who had also made a guest appearance on *The Pleasure Principle* by Ultravox disciple Gary Numan. Quite conversant with sci-fi post-punk, Currie and crew issued a debut single in 1979 that featured the song "Frequency 7." It delivered a definitive statement on the state of both sci-fi music and real-life technology at the close of the '70s: "Video screens, tape machines, electric cars, radios, life in Mars," chanted singer Steve Strange over a growingly familiar demonstration of clattering synths. He knew you couldn't fight the future. His own future had a surprise in store; he had no way of knowing it at the time, but he was a year away from playing a role in the resurrection of sci-fi music's most iconic character.

Some of the post-punk bands that appeared at Futurama—or should have—in 1979 would become massive, decade-defining acts of the '80s: the Human League, OMD, Soft Cell, and New Order, the group once known as Joy Division that had soldiered on after Curtis's death. Sci-fi, though, became

ce rather than the substance. These bands were only able to score
͜͜͜ when they retained their futuristic sound and appearance but sang
simple love songs. To someone other than Einstein, that is.

✷ **THE BAND RED NOISE WAS** originally slated to appear at Futurama
but pulled out due to studio commitments. Their presence would have
been entirely appropriate. Red Noise was the latest project from Bill Nelson
of Be-Bop Deluxe, whose 1975 album was titled *Futurama*. Be-Bop Deluxe's
final album, *Drastic Plastic*, had been released in 1978; like most of the band's
output, it was awash in sci-fi. Not only did it feature songs such as "Electrical
Language"—in which Nelson sang, "I speak to you through electrical language / Sometimes you hear me when our frequencies meet"—it took a turn
toward the synthesizer-laden severity of the emerging post-punk, synth-pop,
and new wave artists.

Sound-on-Sound, the first and only album by Red Noise, continued that
trajectory. Nelson, with Be-Bop Deluxe keyboardist Andy Clark and a cast of
fresh musicians, made clipped, jerky, sparkling songs with sci-fi themes like
"Substitute Flesh" and "Radar in My Heart." The cover art was a photograph
of a robot with a wig, lying in bed and reaching for a phone, yet another
expression of how the primitive human needs of sex and communication had
become subsumed by technology. Although Red Noise was made up of veterans of the sci-fi music scene, *Sound-on-Sound* was far more in line with what the
younger generation of artists was up to, including Gary Numan, the Human
League, and Visage. The title of the album's opening track, "Don't Touch Me
(I'm Electric)," even sounded like it could have belonged to a Numan song.
And like Visage's Steve Strange, Red Noise's Andy Clark was about to play a
small part in a great sci-fi-music resurrection.

Hawkwind's appearance at Futurama may have drawn ridicule from the
Fall's Mark E. Smith, but the unrepentant space-barbarians from the hippie
era weren't as out of place at the festival as they might have seemed on paper.
Like Bill Nelson, Hawkwind had recently upgraded their approach to sci-fi
rock. The band's three albums in the late '70s—*Astounding Sounds, Amazing
Music* from 1976; *Quark, Strangeness and Charm* from 1977; and *PXR5* from
1979—extended their involvement with the works of Ballard, Asimov, Zelazny, and Spinrad. The track "High-Rise" on *PXR5* was just the latest Hawkwind song to be based on a specific work of sci-fi. In this case, it was Ballard's
1975 novel of the same name, which posited the social breakdown in a luxury

condominium structure that suddenly finds itself closed off from the outside world. Like Daniel Miller's assessment of *Crash*, *High-Rise* felt as though it took place five minutes in the future.

So did the music on *Quark, Strangeness, and Charm* and *PXR5*. Since *Astounding Sounds*—the first album made without Lemmy on bass—the group had been gradually cranking down the once earth-shattering volume of their distorted guitars and relying on a more manicured, keyboard-reliant template. *Quark, Strangeness, and Charm* and *PXR5* took an even bigger leap, picking up cues from punk rock and post-punk. Although he didn't appear on these albums, Hawkwind's newest recruit, keyboardist Tim Blake, helped revivify their sound. A former member of Gong who had played on their classic sci-fi albums of the early '70s, Blake had gone solo in 1977, delivering the synthesizer workout *Crystal Machine* and becoming one of the pioneers of the use of lasers in rock concerts—something that had become widespread by 1979. His solo album from 1978, *Blake's New Jerusalem*, added a more overt dose of sci-fi, as heard on the tracks "Song for a New Age"—a cosmic folk anthem that combined space colonization with pagan mysticism—and "Generator (Laserbeam)," a pulsating song that split the difference between old Krautrock and new synth-pop.

Further abetting the idea that Hawkwind wasn't a relic, a host of spin-offs, side projects, and alter egos possessing sci-fi lyrics and synthesizer leanings released records in 1978 and 1979, including Hawklords, Nik Turner's Sphynx, Disco Dream and the Androids, and Melodic Energy Commission. Even Motörhead, the bulldozing hard-rock band formed by the ousted Lemmy, clocked in with a sci-fi song in 1979 titled "Metropolis"—making him the latest in a long line of musicians to have taken inspiration from the Fritz Lang film.

Nik Turner joined Hawkwind onstage at Futurama to perform two songs with his old band, including their sci-fi anthem "Master of the Universe." But upon leaving the group in 1976, soon after the release of *Astounding Sounds*, he had felt the squeeze of being pigeonholed. "You can't say there is a stereotype of what Hawkwind music should be, that it should be space rock or it should be all about science fiction or magic and sorcery," he said, in flagrant contradiction of the album Hawkwind had just put out. He wasn't the only one. Robert Calvert, who had rejoined the band in 1975 after a brief break to treat his bipolar disorder, said in 1978, "I don't like sci-fi that much. Nobody in this band is particularly a sci-fi fanatic." He then added, "Most sci-fi is trash, actually." At the start of the '70s, Hawkwind had been one of the undisputed leaders of sci-fi music; as the decade neared its end, they were just another group out of hundreds trying to make a living at it. Not that it would keep them from sci-fi. The band persevered through music trends, lineup changes, and the deaths of members, always keeping science fiction at the forefront of their imagery and lyrics.

There was a slight hiccup, though. In the spring of 1979, Hawkwind temporarily broke up when violinist and keyboardist Simon House abruptly quit the band. He had good reason. Calvert's mental illness was again becoming an issue, to the point where he also left Hawkwind in 1979, this time for good; he would die nine years later of a heart attack at the age forty-three. But House had received an offer he couldn't refuse: to play in Bowie's band.

Throughout Hawkwind's trials and transformations of the late '70s, Moorcock remained associated with them. He continued to appear live with the group and contributed occasional concepts, lyrics, and vocals in the studio. A sci-fi novel starring Hawkwind was even published with Moorcock's name on the cover: *The Time of the Hawklords* appeared in 1977, and it chronicled the astral adventures of the members of the group, with the author himself showing up as Moorlock the Acid Sorcerer. The book was cocredited to Michael Butterworth, a friend of Moorcock's; however, Moorcock disowned the book entirely, saying he had no part in its writing, similar to the claim he'd make in 1978 with the publication of a sequel, *Queens of Deliria*.

Moorcock struck up a new rock 'n' roll friendship as well. Blue Öyster Cult's immersion in sci-fi—like Hawkwind's—had only grown as the '70s progressed. The New York outfit had gone from 1974's "Astronomy" and "Flaming Telepaths" to 1976's "E.T.I. (Extra Terrestrial Intelligence)," a song that incorporated a host of UFO terminology, including "daylight discs"—flying saucers seen during the daylight, according to J. Allen Hynek's *The UFO Experience*—and the mysterious "men in black" who appear at contact sights in order to facilitate the cover-up of the existence of extraterrestrials, an idea popularized by Kurt Glemser in his 1974 book, *The Men in Black Report*.

The lyrics to "E.T.I. (Extra Terrestrial Intelligence)" had been written by Sandy Pearlman, but by 1979, BÖC had soured on being the instruments of Pearlman's elaborate Imaginos story line. Cutting off ties with him, they turned to a known sci-fi author with whom to collaborate: Moorcock. The result was 1979's "The Great Sun Jester," a song based on Moorcock's sci-fi novel *The Fireclown*—the same novel that had likely inspired Syd Barrett to write Pink Floyd's "Set the Controls for the Heart of the Sun." BÖC teamed up with Moorcock again over the next couple years, most famously for the song "Veteran of the Psychic Wars," which appeared on the soundtrack to the 1981 science-fantasy film *Heavy Metal*. Moorcock had first used the phrase "veteran of the psychic wars" in Hawkwind's 1975 song "Standing at the Edge," but it originates with Jim Morrison of the Doors, who used it in a 1970 poem titled "Far Arden."

In the early '80s, BÖC would begin a working relationship with another sci-fi writer, John Shirley, one of the architects of cyberpunk. And eventually, they reunited with Pearlman, finally wrapping up his sprawling, piecemeal story in their 1988 album *Imaginos*—a sci-fi rock saga of aliens, conspiracies, and the secret forces ruling the universe that wound up being over twenty years in the making.

Another well-known sci-fi author collaborated with some familiar musicians in 1979. Robert Sheckley loaned out his novella "In a Land of Clear Colors"—a meditation on Buddhist philosophy as filtered through science fiction, similar in that regard to the novel *Lord of Light* by Sheckley's friend Roger Zelazny—to Brian Eno and Peter Sinfield. Eno had just finished working on the final installment of Bowie's Berlin Trilogy, the 1979 album *Lodger*; Sinfield was best known as a former lyricist for Emerson, Lake & Palmer and King Crimson, even writing the lyrics to the latter group's "21st Century Schizoid Man." Together they recorded a limited-edition, album-plus-book set on which Eno supplied ambient instrumentals while Sinfield read Sheckley's text.

Meanwhile, keyboardist Tony Banks of Genesis released his debut solo album, *A Curious Feeling*, which was loosely patterned after *Flowers for Algernon*, Daniel Keyes's 1966 sci-fi novel about a mentally disabled man who undergoes an experiment to increase his intelligence. Billy Thorpe's "Children of the Sun," a fluke 1979 hit by the Australian rocker, detailed the salvation of the human race after an alien visitation; in the '80s, Thorpe wound up scoring television shows, including *Star Trek: The Next Generation*. The title track of *Dream Police*, the 1979 album by the power-pop band Cheap Trick, painted an Orwellian scenario where telepathic authorities pursue those with illegal thoughts. Meanwhile, the rising star Pat Benatar confounded fans with an album track titled "My Clone Sleeps Alone," a hard-rock meditation on future sexuality and genetic engineering. In Japan, a young electronic composer named Ryuichi Sakamoto led his group Yellow Magic Orchestra, whose 1979 instrumental "Technopolis" portrayed a bright, kinetic, utopian tomorrow through synthesizers and drum machines. Like a funky, upbeat Kraftwerk, Yellow Magic Orchestra presaged a new style of sci-fi music—electro—that was set to morph the sound of the next decade.

EVER SINCE ALEJANDRO JODOROWSKY'S FAILED film adaptation of *Dune*, rumors had been rife about how and when Frank Herbert's beloved novel would make it to the big screen. It wasn't a matter of if. After the *Star Wars* phenomenon, studios were snatching up established sci-fi properties in the hopes of capitalizing on the next big space-opera blockbuster. Original sci-fi shows like *Space: 1999*, launched in 1975, and *Blake's 7*, introduced in 1978, had their merits and fans, but the safer bet was to give a *Star Wars* makeover to a name people already knew. The venerable sci-fi character Buck Rogers—a man from the twentieth century who awakens in the far future—made a comeback in cinemas with *Buck Rogers in the 25th Century*, a feature film released in March of 1979. It also served as the pilot for a subsequent TV show on NBC, which helped fill the void left by *Battlestar Galactica*'s cancelation by ABC in spring of that year. It must have been a thrill for the Georges Clinton and Lucas, whose budding young brains had been illuminated by earlier incarnations of Buck Rogers. With that crossed off the checklist, *Dune* became the next big hope for sci-fi cinema.

Dune, however, was very different from *Star Wars*. Apart from the surface similarities of the book's desert planet, Arrakis, and the movie's desert planet, Tatooine—not to mention the fact that their respective heroes, Paul Atreides and Luke Skywalker, embodied the Chosen One trope, where a young hero seems handpicked by fate to fulfill a powerful destiny—the two couldn't have been more different. Where *Star Wars* was swift and fun, *Dune* was contemplative and complex. And apart from a couple scenes, *Dune* didn't take place in space at all, but on the barren surface of Arrakis.

In 1979, the British filmmaker Ridley Scott took the reins of the film adaptation of *Dune* following Jodorowsky's aborted attempt earlier in the decade, which had collapsed under its massive financial burden. Scott's breakout movie, *Alien*, opened in the United States in May, and it served as the antidote to sci-fi's rising tide of dashing heroes in the *Star Wars* vein; in their place were morally challenged, working-class crewmembers of a space freighter fighting for their lives against a bloodcurdling alien stowaway. Ridley left *Dune* after working on it for a few months due to the huge commitment it would take to complete the project, which was planned to comprise three films. Still, it seemed inevitable that Frank Herbert's towering epic would make it to the silver screen soon, which whipped up great anticipation among fans—some of them being, naturally, musicians.

Krautrock progenitor Klaus Schulze was among the artists who released *Dune*-related music in 1979, hot on the heels of Richard Pinhas's *Chronolyse* from the year before. Schulze wasn't coy about it. His solo album, *Dune*, comprised two lengthy, evocative tracks—with Arthur Brown, whose résumé of sci-fi music continued to grow, supplying guest vocals. If the album was intended to be an audition of sorts, with the hopes that Schulze might be chosen to score the film when it finally came to fruition, it was unsuccessful. When David Lynch's *Dune* hit theaters in 1984, it did not feature Schulze. But the album stood as a breathtaking sonic interpretation of one of sci-fi's most beloved texts. Schulze made another sci-fi album in 1979: *Time Actor*, released under the alias Richard Wahnfried, again with vocal assistance from Brown. Rather than cinematic in feel, it fell closer to a Kraftwerk-inspired mix of motorik beats and synth-pop; the lyrics, as delivered in a heavily effect-laden voice by Brown, sketched out a tale of intrepid invention and time travel.

Following in the footsteps of his fellow Frenchman Pinhas, the electronic musician Bernard Szajner issued *Visions of Dune* under the name Zed in 1979. The album was broken into songs of conventional length, each titled after a character, group, or object from Herbert's novel. Where Schulze's *Dune* leaned toward an electronic version of classical music, *Visions of Dune* was more pop in nature, with simpler, tighter arrangements—not to mention vocoder-altered vocals that added the requisite futuristic touch.

In 1979, sci-fi proliferated in media of all shapes and sizes. *Mad Max*, a film set in a dystopian Australia, launched one of the genre's most successful franchises. Among its fans was Gary Numan, who would go on to pattern his 1983 album, *Warriors*, after it. And a BBC radio show, *The Hitchhiker's Guide to the Galaxy*, appeared as a novel. The author of both, Douglas Adams, envisioned a satirical scenario where a man named Arthur Dent is whisked haplessly around the cosmos after Earth is summarily destroyed to make way for an intergalactic hyperspace bypass. The book's big catchphrase, "Don't panic," echoed Hawkwind's "Do not panic!" line from their early song "Sonic Attack." Witty and irreverent, *The Hitchhiker's Guide* became a sensation, deflating the seriousness of sci-fi while playing up its most outrageous elements. In a way, it was the punk rock of sci-fi. It also engaged to a degree with pop culture—music included. In an episode of the 1978 radio program, Arthur and his companions land on a dead planet. One of the crew, a depressed android named Marvin, begins playing an atmospheric instrumental on his built-in sound system. Arthur quips, "Did you know your robot can hum Pink Floyd?"

The biggest sci-fi event of 1979, however, was the release of *Star Trek: The Motion Picture*. After a decade in the Hollywood wilderness, Gene Roddenberry had triumphed in bringing back *Star Trek* in live-action form—and on a bigger canvas than it had ever existed before. The film, beset by writing and production problems, had been fast-tracked by Paramount in 1978 following the success of *Star Wars*. Instead of playing it safe and tailoring *Star Trek* for a more action-oriented audience, Roddenberry, who produced the film, guided it toward something more slow, stately, and subtle. It was, in essence, *Star Trek* the show meets *2001: A Space Odyssey*—the problem being, that kind of sci-fi movie was no longer in vogue. Simpler, swifter, more clear-cut storytelling was the space-opera order of the day. Since the early '70s, the moviegoing public had shaken off the brooding preoccupation with future-shock topics. They wanted vivid, lively escapism. *Star Trek: The Motion Picture* did not provide it. It did well at the box office—the pent-up demand ensured that—but it wasn't a major success.

Accordingly, the movie didn't spawn the same number of musical tributes as *Star Wars*. Spizzenergi's "Where's Captain Kirk?" aside, only a handful of *Star Trek* records appeared in 1979. Disco versions of the theme song predictably came out, by faceless groups such as Cosmo Wave and the Space Cadets. One *Star Trek*–related record of 1979, though, was more legitimate. Nichelle "Uhura" Nichols released a single that year with a sci-fi song titled "Beyond Antares." It was no milestone of sci-fi music, but its breezy, space age–disco sound was enjoyable enough—and it was heartening to hear at least one member of *Star Trek*'s cast having fun.

Star Wars music, on the other hand, continued to trickle out. Sheila and B. Devotion, a space-disco outfit whose singer Sheila was cut from the same cloth as Sarah Brightman and Dee D. Jackson, released a single called "Spacer" in 1979. At first glance, it didn't seem to have a connection to *Star Wars*—but Han Solo is a Corellian spacer, and the song catalogs the virtues of a roguish starship hero. "In his own special way, he is gentle and kind," Sheila sang, and she might as well have been singing about Solo.

A more full-blooded *Star Wars* song from that year came courtesy of the group Instant Funk. They were dabbling in disco at the time, but they returned to the territory of hard, stomping funk for their 1979 single "Dark Vader." Like Jimmy Castor's "Bertha Butt Encounters Vadar" before it, "Dark Vader" seemed to be intentionally misspelling Darth Vader's name in an attempt to dodge a copyright-infringement suit from the litigious Lucas. That may have been part of the reason—but in full, "Dark Vader" is an impressive piece of *Star Wars* lore and Afrofuturist music. Unlike the many shallow appropriations of *Star Wars* set to music in the late '70s, the song recasts Darth Vader— played in the film by the white actor David Prowse yet voiced by James Earl Jones in his basso profundo—as Dark Vader, an explicitly black character. In doing so, the song reclaims Darth Vader, casting him as a kind of interstellar blaxploitation antihero—or as the lyrics describe, "a tall black man, entirely fearless." It's less a tribute to *Star Wars* and more a retelling of the story from a point of view that's sympathetic to the villain. In essence, "Dark Vader" is to Darth Vader as *Wicked* is to the Wicked Witch of the West—at a time when Vader's true identity as the somewhat sympathetic Anakin Skywalker had yet to be revealed.

MICHAEL JACKSON MAY OR MAY not have made the bestselling *Star Wars* song of 1979. His breakout solo album, *Off the Wall*, was released that year, finally turning the Jackson 5 singer into a superstar in his own right. On it was the chart-topping, Grammy-winning single "Don't Stop 'Til You Get Enough"—a song in which Jackson chants the refrain, "Keep on with the force, don't stop / Don't stop 'til you get enough." Nothing else in the song even hints at *Star Wars* or sci-fi, but it's caused speculation for years about whether "the force" in Jackson's lyrics is indeed the Force from *Star Wars*. The director of the song's video was Nick Saxton, who had been a production assistant on Lucas's *THX 1138*—and Jackson had proven his facility with sci-fi years earlier with the Jackson 5's "Dancing Machine." Jackson never made it clear what he meant by "the force." Listeners for decades have made their own assumptions, including David Byrne of Talking Heads, who remarked, "It had these bizarre lyrics, to me, that were quoting *Star Wars*."

Jackson's robotic stage moves from "Dancing Machine" earlier in the decade had been the peak of the Funk Robot dance craze, which had dropped off entirely by 1974. A straggler entered in 1979, though: "Robot Dance" by Marvin Wright, a disco song that sought in vain to resurrect some form of the Funky Robot for the C-3PO age.

Another trend in sci-fi music that had gone by the wayside was basing songs on space missions. Although the Space Shuttle program was raising public interest in space exploration to its highest point in years, science fiction had once again surpassed science fact in the imaginations of musicians. Sadly, it took a disaster to muster someone in 1979 to write songs about the space program again. The disco project the Astronuts released a single in 1979 bearing two songs: "Skylab Is Falling" and "Skylab Has Fallen." It was a novelty record aspiring to ride the latest space spectacle: not a launch or an appearance of a comet, but a crash. The Skylab space station had been launched by NASA in 1973, and over the course of the next few years, it became a beacon of humankind's presence in space—a toehold in the beyond, after NASA all but abandoned the prospect of future Moon missions. But after numerous history-making visits to Skylab by astronauts in the '70s, the station's orbit decayed. The crew of the Space Shuttle was supposed to dock with and refurbish Skylab, but that plan had been delayed. So NASA made the decision to let Skylab descend to Earth, burning up on reentry and disintegrating in a scattering of debris across Western Australia in July of 1979.

The Astronuts' song has been forgotten, but the crash of Skylab marked a pivotal point in the space program. It was a symbolic burning of the old to make way for the new, just as the '70s were giving way to the '80s and the Space Shuttle promised an exhilarating new era in exploration beyond our planet. Some disco songs from 1979, like Atmosfear's "Dancing in Outer Space," banked on that feeling of weightless hope and renewal. "Future World" by the Austrian group Ganymed followed their 1978 sci-fi concept album, *Takes You Higher*, and the song offered yet another positive, glittering depiction of humanity's space-bound, technologically compatible tomorrow. The funk group Splendor, on the other hand, brought back the idea of alien abduction—only in the case of their 1979 single "Take Me to Your Disco," they played with the sci-fi cliché "Take me to your leader," uttered by aliens to the nearest human upon landing on Earth.

When it came to funk, sci-fi had also begun to dry up. Apart from Instant Funk's intriguing but otherwise minor contribution to the canon, only a smattering of sci-fi funk songs appeared in 1979. "Radiation Level" by Sun began with a countdown to a blastoff into outer space—in much the same way one of the first sci-fi funk songs, "Escape from Planet Earth" by the Continent Four, had done seven years prior. "Radiation Level" appeared on *Destination: Sun*, which flaunted an incredible piece of cover art depicting a spaceship on the front and a space-villain on the back that resembled a cross between Darth Vader and a Cylon from *Battlestar Galactica*. It was just one of hundreds of records released in 1979 with sci-fi artwork on the cover, most of which had little or nothing to do with sci-fi in a musical sense. The precedent set by Boston with their self-titled album in 1976 held: Putting a spaceship on the cover of an album was a great way to draw attention to it. Inside that album, though, you didn't have to follow through. It had become a look—one that made it increasingly difficult for actual sci-fi musicians to cut through and be noticed as such.

"The Alien Succumbs to the Macho Intergalactic Funkativity of the Funk Blasters" was not, despite all appearances, the name of a P-Funk song. Instead, it was a track released by jazz-funk keyboardist George Duke on his 1979 album, *Master of the Game*. The spread of sci-fi funk at the end of the '70s left the subgenre ripe for self-parody. In 1979, P-Funk's cosmic mythology and tongue-twisting technobabble had become widespread—to the point where Duke spoofed it. The song's title would have been at home on any number of Parliament or Funkadelic records in the '70s, and musically, Duke was just as playful as Clinton and crew. "Underwater intergalactic jam / With folks from another space and time" he sings while coaxing disco-on-Neptune sounds from his synthesizers. "The Alien Succumbs" is the best P-Funk song that P-Funk never made—a testament to how thoroughly Clinton's futuristic vision, and sci-fi funk as a whole, had saturated the music scene. Another Duke song from 1979, "I Am for Real (May the Funk Be with You)," made the inevitable leap of sprinkling *Star Wars* into the Clintonian stew.

For their part, Parliament released their final full sci-fi concept album in 1979. *Gloryhallastoopid*. "There are eight billion tales in the naked universe / This is just one of them," states the album's "Prologue." From there, Clinton and company traverse the galaxy, seeking its origins in the Funk while circling that most ominous of astral metaphors: "We are deep in the black hole," goes "(Gloryhallastoopid) Pin the Tail on the Funky." The Mothership rematerializes, as do boilerplate P-Funk lines like "By the time you get to Venus / You should be funky." On the track "Theme from the Black Hole"—no relation to the theme from *The Black Hole*, the Disney sci-fi film released in 1979—Sir Nose D'Voidoffunk taunts Clinton's Star Child as if he were Darth Vader taunting Luke Skywalker in *The Empire Strikes Back*, a film that was still a year away.

Parliament's final studio album, *Trombipulation*, came out in 1980. Only a remnant of their mythos remained. As if exhausted by the weight of the world he held up, Clinton—the Atlas of sci-fi funk—laid down his burden. He still dipped into the mythos from time to time in his solo work, and on tour, P-Funk kept their Afrofuturist legacy vital and alive. But the last page of the story had been written, and the book had been closed. It would be up to a new generation of P-Funk acolytes—practitioners primarily of electro and hip-hop—to take up Clinton's funky folklore of the future and race to the stars with it.

✴ **ELFIN AND DELICATE, THE ANDROID** named Klaus Nomi danced across the screen. His blank, factory-installed astonishment appeared to be programmed onto his face, sculpted into the makeup that glared bone-white beneath his geometric hairdo—a variation of the look shared that year by everyone from Gary Numan to the Human League's Philip Oakey. Nomi's movements were clenched and calibrated, as though servos and circuits had been installed beneath his taut layer of artificial skin. Staring unblinkingly at the camera, he approached a microphone, opened his bow-shaped mouth, and sang.

Nomi stood on a soundstage in a television studio in his adopted city of New York. He was filming an appearance on a popular comedy show that had debuted four years earlier: *Saturday Night Live*. Before him, looking almost as otherworldly, stood his bandleader and benefactor, David Bowie.

Nomi was born in Bavaria in 1944. But rather than becoming a Krautrock artist, as he might have in a parallel universe, he moved to New York in 1972 to seek his fortune. He was a pastry chef by trade; his passion, though, was opera. After a few years of making very few inroads in that competitive world, he took to the thriving art scene in downtown Manhattan. There he concocted a stage persona: a fey plastic-covered creature surrounded by twinkling lights who sang in an unearthly countertenor. Nomi used his real name, which only served to erase the distinction between his true identity and his fictionalized self. By the end of the '70s, his performances had grown popular, and he fine-tuned his persona into an immaculate, impossibly dapper alloy of alien and automaton.

Bowie—who spent much time in New York and had already proven himself to have an excellent ear for up-and-coming sci-fi-music talent—caught wind of Nomi. He met with him and his friend Joey Arias at the Mudd Club, one of Manhattan's hippest venues, and made the relatively unknown duo a once-in-a-lifetime proposition: to be his backup singers and dancers for his upcoming appearance on *Saturday Night Live*.

Sci-fi had not been high on Bowie's list of priorities in 1979. Aside from championing the likes of Kraftwerk, Devo, and the Human League, he had spent the late '70s sounding futuristic but doing almost everything he could to avoid singing about the future. On *Lodger*, his 1979 album, only one song came anywhere near sci-fi. "Fantastic Voyage" ruminated on the threat of nuclear war, but it didn't speculate about any kind of apocalypse or dystopia beyond that, as Bowie had in the past. His fear of nuclear obliteration was no longer shrouded in myth and metaphor, but rendered as a straightforward, sentimental plea for peace, full of platitudinous lines like "Our lives are valuable too."

For *Saturday Night Live*, Bowie played three songs with Nomi. One of them, "Boys Keep Swinging," was from *Lodger*. The other two were drawn from the sci-fi end of his repertoire: 1977's "TVC15," with its playful theme of telecommunication as an interdimensional portal, and 1970's "The Man Who Sold the World," a song whose title seemed to wink at *The Man Who Sold the Moon*, the sci-fi novel by one of Bowie's early favorites, Robert A. Heinlein. As arresting as Bowie is on those *Saturday Night Live* performances, Nomi is downright riveting. A clockwork Pinocchio for the digital age, he pouts and putters and whirrs behind Bowie—a shadow, an understudy, a new model. On *Replicas*, Numan had included the song "When the Machines Rock." If he'd been watching *Saturday Night Live* that night, he would have seen a machine rock—and not just any machine, but his long-lost android brother.

After securing a record deal and experiencing modest success as a cult act singing operatic new wave pop, Nomi died in in 1983. He was only thirty-nine. Like Jobriath, that other gay, tragically underrated, sci-fi-music figure of the '70s, Nomi was an early victim of AIDS; in fact, they passed away just two days apart. Both had been influenced by Bowie—the artist who had first blended science fiction, popular music, and sexuality into an irreducible whole. After the *Saturday Night Live* performance—which took place on December 15, 1979—Bowie's first decade as a world-famous performer and songwriter came to a close.

"Space Oddity" had ushered that decade in ten years earlier, and "Space Oddity" also ushered it out. On December 31, 1979, a new version of "Space Oddity" debuted in England on *Kenny Everett's New Year's Eve Show*, along with a new promotional video. In it, a neatly styled Bowie—dressed conservatively in a plain long-sleeve button-down shirt—played an acoustic guitar and peered intently into the camera as he sang. His performance was interspersed with shots of Bowie as Major Tom, clad in a silvery jumpsuit and sitting in the futuristic control chair of a spaceship that was installed, surreally, in a kitchen. He calmly flipped through a newspaper as appliances exploded around him. In a brief scene, bizarrely colored with some strange visual effect, a pair of outlandishly costumed humanoids—perhaps one is a clown—walked along a beach. The video ended with Bowie-as-Tom dangling lifelessly from a strange wall of seemingly alien design, attached by tubes that fed into his spacesuit. Whether they were infusing him with life or draining it from him was not clear.

Although Bowie had wandered from sci-fi over the course of the decade, he had never fully left. During his explorations, other sci-fi musicians had rushed in to fill the vacuum. Now he was returning to the source, the genre that had launched him into the orbit of superstardom. Bowie, at last, had come home. Maybe it was time Major Tom did the same.

THE PLANET IS GLOWING: THE START *OF THE* *'80*s

"WHEN I ORIGINALLY WROTE ABOUT MAJOR TOM, I WAS A VERY PRAG-
matic and self-opinionated lad that thought he knew all about the great
American dream and where it started and where it should stop," David Bowie
said in 1980, looking back at "Space Oddity" and discussing its sequel—his
new single "Ashes to Ashes." He went on, "Here we had the great blast of
American technological know-how shoving this guy up into space, but once
he gets there he's not quite sure why he's there. And that's where I left him.
Now we've found out that he's under some kind of realization that the whole
process that had got him up there had decayed, was born out of decay; it has

decayed him, and he's in the process of decaying. But he wishes to return to the nice, round womb, the Earth, from whence he started."

"Ashes to Ashes" came out on August 8, 1980. Eleven years had passed since "Space Oddity." In that time, much had changed for Major Tom. Left adrift in space, he'd grown paranoid and addicted to drugs, his consciousness fractured. The first verse of the song points directly back to "Space Oddity": "Do you remember a guy that's been / In such an early song?" Major Tom then runs through a litany of memories, regrets, and hallucinations, along with a desperate desire to get better: "I'm hoping to kick / But the planet is glowing."

The song ended with the chant, "My mama said, to get things done / You'd better not mess with Major Tom." In singing those lines, Bowie was disobeying them. He was messing with Major Tom again after having left him to his cosmic rest over a decade earlier.

Bowie recorded the song in early 1980 as the lead single for his upcoming album *Scary Monsters (and Super Creeps)*. The contrast between "Space Oddity" and "Ashes to Ashes" illustrated everything Bowie had gone through in the '70s. His voice was now deeper and more profound. The music was jagged, jarring, and richly textured in a completely different way than "Space Oddity" had been. Rather than psychedelically spacious, it sounded compressed, a tight mix of computers, androids, and off-kilter motorization. Guitarist Chuck Hammer conveyed this feeling with layers of effects-heavy guitar. Flangers gave it an alien quality. The drums were stuttering yet mathematical, accented in unusual places, a rhythmic metaphor for disorientation—a disco beat from another dimension. Andy Clark, formerly of Be-Bop Deluxe and Red Noise, had been recruited to play synthesizer; his symphonic swells at the end of the song were like the waves of an interstellar ocean.

"Ashes to Ashes," as peculiar as it was, became Bowie's second number-one single in England—the first being his reissue of "Space Oddity" in 1975. Much of that had to do with the anticipatory buzz surrounding Major Tom's return—part of an overall lust for sequels that had grown in the age of *Star Wars*, whose sequel *The Empire Strikes Back*, released in 1980, changed the way filmmakers made and marketed sequels. Rather than being mostly self-contained—like the installments of sci-fi's last major film series, *Planet of the Apes*, which were nonlinear and complicated in their chronology—movies in a series could now be part of a single, longer narrative, with one picking up where the other left off. Thanks to "Ashes to Ashes," Major Tom had become, in essence, a sci-fi franchise.

To underscore this phenomenon, RCA Records released a promotional single in 1980 titled "The Continuing Story of Major Tom." On it, "Space Oddity" was mixed smoothly into "Ashes to Ashes," creating a single nine-minute epic. The ending of the first song meshed uncannily well with the start of the second: the beeping at the end of "Space Oddity" bled into the high-pitched, pizzicato-like melody at the start of "Ashes to Ashes."

The video for "Ashes to Ashes" aided immensely in its popularity. Although the inauguration of MTV was still a year away, the music video format—which had existed to a lesser extent for decades—was becoming ubiquitous in 1980. Without a network dedicated to music videos, record companies had nonetheless started investing more money into videos for their artists, hoping for whatever exposure they might bring. As such, they were often produced on the cheap and with little attention paid to concept and story, thanks largely to the fact that they were shown only occasionally on television variety shows, without any dedicated network to air them.

"Ashes to Ashes" changed that. Bowie's label sank a sizeable chunk of resources into it; at the time, it was the most expensive pop video ever made. Director David Mallet had also filmed the video for the new, acoustic version of "Space Oddity" that had been broadcast on British television on New Year's Eve of 1979. When he tackled "Ashes to Ashes," he used some of the same sets and footage of Bowie in a spacesuit—including shots of the singer hooked up to the innards of a spaceship. The images were inspired by *Alien*, particularly the grotesquely beautiful production designs of Swiss artist H. R. Giger. Said Bowie, "It was supposed to be the archetypal 1980s ideal of the futuristic colony that has been founded by an earthling, and in that particular sequence, the idea was for the earthling to be pumping out himself and to be having pumped into him something organic. So there was a very strong Giger influence there: the organic meets hi-tech."

Bowie had storyboarded the video himself. The story involved a bizarre group of clown-like beings, Bowie among them, walking along a beach. One of those figures was Steve Strange, leader of Visage, whom Bowie had met at a nightclub called the Blitz, where Strange and other members of a new, Bowie-influenced music scene had begun to congregate. Strange became the latest in a long line of sci-fi musicians—from Brian Eno to Kraftwerk to Devo to the Human League to Klaus Nomi—that Bowie had championed in the previous decade. Even his touring and recording bands of the late '70s and early '80s reflected his affinity for his fellow veterans of the sci-fi music scene:

not only had he hired Hawkwind's Simon House and Be-Bop Deluxe's Andy Clark, he'd tapped Aynsley Dunbar of Jefferson Airplane, Robert Powell of Utopia, and Robert Fripp of King Crimson.

Along with the high-concept sets and story line of the "Ashes to Ashes" video, it was rendered even more futuristic by a startling video effect. Quantel Paintbox, a new computer graphics workstation, wasn't launched commercially until 1981, but it was used in the video to turn the skies black and the seas pink, lending a chromatic otherworldliness. Bowie had spent the eleven years since "Space Oddity" honing his use of sonic technology; now he was at the forefront of video technology. The video for "Ashes to Ashes" conveyed "some feeling of nostalgia for the future. I've always been hung up on that. It creeps into everything I do, however far away I try to keep from it," he said. "Now I tend to go with it rather than escape from it because it's obviously an area that, even if I refuse to face it, does interest me. The idea of having seen the future of somewhere we've already been keeps coming back to me."

Apart from "Ashes to Ashes," the lyrics of *Scary Monsters* contained no overtly sci-fi content. But a song called "Crystal Japan"—tucked away on the B side of the album's final single, "Up the Hill Backwards"—carried a sci-fi reference in code. The track was instrumental, so there were no lyrics to decipher. But amid its droning, spaceship-hum ambience, a synthesizer melody rose to the surface. As with the Brides of Funkenstein's "War Ship Touchante" from two years prior, Bowie's "Crystal Japan" borrowed that delicate five-note sequence that aliens used to communicate with humanity in *Close Encounters of the Third Kind*.

BOWIE HAD RECEIVED A JOLT of inspiration from Steve Strange and his entourage at the Blitz as he was making *Scary Monsters*, but it went both ways. Visage led a rising tide of groups strongly influenced by Bowie, who combined elements of almost every Bowie incarnation into a synth-spiked, mascara-lined, future-glam whole. The movement was dubbed New Romantic, and it hit its peak of global popularity in the early '80s—thanks largely to a band who were recording their debut single in 1980. A London quintet named Duran Duran, who took their name from a character in the sci-fi film *Barbarella*, released "Planet Earth" in February of 1981, and its lux, picture-perfect reimagining of synth-pop not only made Duran Duran stars, it heralded a kind of cool, plastic futurism that would define the decade. The term "New Romantic" came from a line in "Planet Earth," a song that spoke vaguely of outer space, viewing Earth from orbit, and "coming down to land."

Despite these elements, Duran Duran can hardly be considered a sci-fi band. They're emblematic of one of the '80s greatest ironies: skimming the surface of the sound and imagery of the sci-fi music of the '70s, bands with shiny outfits and android makeup looked the part, but they largely refrained from committing wholeheartedly to songs about aliens, spaceships, robots, or the postapocalypse. The geeks had won—but what exactly was the prize? With sci-fi now one of the most dominant aesthetics in pop music, it no longer mattered if the lyrical content was hollow at its heart, as long as the neon glowed and the chrome gleamed. To Duran Duran's credit, their 1984 song "The Wild Boys" was sparked by William S. Burroughs's surreal, sexual sci-fi novel of the same name—the one that Bowie had drawn from to create Ziggy Stardust. The postapocalyptic video for the song, directed by Russell Mulcahy, later of *Highlander* fame, was even intended by the director to be a kind of sales pitch for a feature-film adaptation of the book.

That movie never came to fruition, but it underscored the complicated interplay of style, substance, and sci-fi that had risen since the early '70s. Back then, it was a commercial risk to perform and release sci-fi music, and people mostly did it out of a love of the genre, usually one stretching back to childhood. Such earnestness was passé in the postmodern '80s. It's just as likely that Duran Duran wrote a song about *The Wild Boys* because they'd heard Bowie mention the title in an interview than from having any prior knowledge of the book itself. It didn't matter. By the mid-'80s, artists as utterly un-futuristic as Tom Petty would be making sci-fi videos. It had become a style, a way to grab attention, and a lucrative one at that.

Some members of the emerging New Romantic groups hailed from the punk scene. Classix Nouveaux came about after the remains of X-Ray Spex solicited a new singer following Poly Styrene's breakdown and departure in 1979. Styrene was gone, and the sound had changed, but sci-fi remained: the first two Classix Nouveaux singles, "The Robots Dance" and "Nasty Little Green Men," were released in 1980, and both were unmistakably sci-fi in theme. Styrene reemerged in 1980 with a solo album titled *Translucence*, a restrained yet sublime record that vibrated on the same blissed-out plane of cosmic mysticism as *Germfree Adolescents*—that is, as much as a synth-heavy new wave album could. The same year, an obscure group from Scotland called Dreamboys released what would be their only record, a single with a song titled "Outer Limits," a reference to the '60s sci-fi TV show. The band's young singer-guitarist, Peter Capaldi, would make a different kind of name for himself in sci-fi decades later; in 2013, he became the twelfth actor to play Doctor Who. His interpretation of the character came with a fondness for shredding solos on an electric guitar.

The Human League remained solidly in the synth-pop camp in the early '80s, but they adopted a more New Romantic–tinged image—along with a more crowd-pleasing sound, which resulted in global hits like 1981's "Don't You Want Me." Funny enough, it took the arrival of a member of another sci-fi band to facilitate the Human League's turn away from sci-fi. Jo Callis of the Rezillos joined the Human League in 1981, and his songwriting skills led the band toward more conventional love songs. By 1986, the Human League was releasing hits like "Human," in which Philip Oakey tenderly sings, "I'm only human / Of flesh and blood I'm made." It was the opposite of the group's origins, where robotic noises were the ideal and Daleks loomed in the background.

OMD, meanwhile, went in the other direction. After criticized for being the most lightweight of the synth-pop bands, they reacted in 1983 with *Dazzle Ships*, a staggeringly inventive and immersive album that combined elements of sci-fi, retrofuturism, and experimental pop. *Dazzle Ship*'s lead single was "Genetic Engineering"—no relation to the X-Ray Spex song—which spliced together utopia and dystopia into a disquietingly catchy exhibition of synth-pop songcraft. The album, challenging and abstract, was met with critical hostility and poor sales before eventually being regarded as a classic. Another sci-fi album from 1983 enjoyed a far better reception on its release. Styx, whose earlier song "Come Sail Away" had established their fascination with sci-fi, delivered *Kilroy Was Here*—a synth-driven, dystopian rock opera crowned by "Mr. Roboto," a hit single whose famous refrain of "Domo arigato, Mr. Roboto" is rendered through the familiar electronic filter of the vocoder.

Duran Duran was not alone in recording a song called "Planet Earth." So did Devo. Their "Planet Earth" concluded their 1980 album *Freedom of Choice*, which was Devo's commercial breakthrough thanks to the smash "Whip It." But "Planet Earth," written by Gerald Casale, didn't present a glamorous view of space travel. Instead, it imagined a time when life beyond Earth was possible—but the narrator chooses to stay here, with all its mundane conflicts and tedium, because "it's a place to live your life." *Freedom of Choice* was preceded by *Duty Now for the Future* in 1979—and although it wasn't produced by

Brian Eno, as was their debut album, it was helmed by another Bowie cohort, Ken Scott, who had coproduced *The Rise and Fall of Ziggy Stardust and the Spiders from Mars*. On *Duty Now for the Future* was the bizarre "Devo Corporate Anthem," a call to capitalist conformity that was sarcastic and scary at the same time. The concept came from a sci-fi film: "We got that from *Rollerball*, a really good 1975 movie which had the corporate anthem idea," Casale said. "Smart Patrol/Mr. DNA" from *Duty Now for the Future* sported sci-fi lyrics that summarized Devo and their continuing mission more succinctly than anyone else ever could: "The Smart Patrol, nowhere to go / Suburban robots that monitor reality."

Music videos became instrumental in turning the sci-fi cult artists of the late '70s into the sci-fi stars of the early '80s. Bowie's groundbreaking "Ashes to Ashes" video helped see to that. MTV was launched in 1981, and its inaugural video—directed by Mulcahy, years before he worked on Duran Duran's "The Wild Boys"—was "Video Killed the Radio Star" by the Buggles. Comprising singer-bassist Trevor Horn and keyboardist Geoff Downes, they were a synth-pop project whose allegience to the new video medium reflected everything that was in flux in popular music at the time. It only made sense that they were also a sci-fi band. Their 1980 debut album *The Age of Plastic* contained songs such as "I Love You (Miss Robot)," "Astroboy," and "Kid Dynamo," all of which embedded sci-fi ideas into exquisitely wrought techno-pop. They were aided greatly by a new device that had come to market in 1979: the Fairlight CMI, a digital synthesizer and sampler that increased the ability to create, manipulate, and layer sound. "We call it futuristic science-fiction music. It's like modern psychedelic music. It's very futuristic," explained Downes. "There's [a] track on the album called 'Kid Dynamo' which is about a futuristic kid in the '80s who is exposed to all sorts of media and the effects this has on him."

At the start of the '70s, sci-fi usually meant spaceships; by the start of the '80s, it was just as much about technological advancements in mass media and the impact it might have on society. The centerpiece of *The Age of Plastic* was "Video Killed the Radio Star," which had first been released in 1979 as a single, two years before becoming an MTV hit. Explained Horn, "J. G. Ballard was a big inspiration at the time. 'Video Killed the Radio Star' came from a Ballard story called 'The Sound-Sweep' in which a boy goes around old buildings with a vacuum cleaner that sucks up sound. I had a feeling that we were reflecting an age in the same way that he was."

Another version of "Video Killed the Radio Star" came out in 1979. Bruce Woolley, the original singer of the Buggles, left the band that year to form a group called Camera Club. They recorded and released their own rendition of the song that year on their album *English Garden*. It faded to obscurity in the shadow of the Buggles' famous version. But an unknown young keyboardist with a knack for tech named Thomas Dolby was a member of Camera Club at the time—and he'd wind up making his own indelible mark on sci-fi music with his 1982 sci-fi album *The Golden Age of Wireless*, a work of retrofuturism that bore similarities in that regard to OMD's *Dazzle Ships*. It also contained his big hit "She Blinded Me with Science," on which the noted science writer Magnus Pyke delivered the famous exclamation of "Science!" Among Pyke's many books was 1962's *The Science Myth*, a cautionary text that warned of how industrialized society can lead to a dangerous conformity—a sentiment Devo was spoofing and subversively embodying. Among the musicians who appeared on *The Golden Age of Wireless* were Daniel Miller of the Normal as well as future Bowie guitarist Kevin Armstrong. And playing electric violin on "She Blinded Me with Science" was Simon House, the veteran of Hawkwind and Bowie's band.

Horn and Downes, prolific and hungry, joined another sci-fi band in 1980: no less established an act than Yes. The group had reconnected to its sci-fi roots in 1978 with the song "Arriving UFO" from the album *Tormato*, by which point Rick Wakeman had rejoined the lineup and lent his sci-fi synths to Jon Anderson's account of skepticism giving way to a profound belief in alien life. Still, prog had petered out in the face of punk and new wave by the start of the '80s—lying dormant to await an inevitable resurgence—while the Buggles represented the changing of the guard. But prog and synth-pop had more in common than it seemed: both worshipped synthesizers and sci-fi. With Anderson off to collaborate with Vangelis, Yes needed some fresh blood, and Horn became their new lead singer. Downes came along as the group's new keyboardist.

Drama, the only Yes album featuring this lineup, was unveiled in 1980. A streamlined amalgam of the Buggles and Yes that leaned far more toward the latter, it rejuvenated the elder group with sci-fi songs like "Machine Messiah," in which "Cables that carry life / To the cities we build" become harbingers of a more sinister technocracy. Curiously, one track on *Drama* is about Gary Numan. "White Car"—reminiscent of Numan's "Cars"—features the line "Move like a ghost on the skyline," which deliberately refers to the eerie paleness of Numan's android-like stage persona. The worlds of sci-fi prog and sci-fi synth-pop, for the span of an album, had converged.

Synth-pop was beginning to merge with an entirely different kind of sci-fi music in 1980: funk. Mobilized by George Clinton—and spurred by the demise of Parliament as a recording unit—a host of bands ran with P-Funk's futuristic sound and imagery, incorporating the harsh rhythms, android vocals, and seamless precision of synth-pop pioneers such as Kraftwerk and Gary Numan. Songs such as the Jonzun Crew's "Space Is the Place" in 1982; Midnight Star's "Freak-A-Zoid" and Warp 9's "Light Years Away," both in 1983; and Newcleus's "Computer Age (Push the Button)" in 1984 comprised a new movement called electro, in which Afrofuturist themes of outer-space exodus and posthuman liberation were converted into the robotic rhythms of the dance floor.

They weren't the first. Juan Atkins was an eighteen-year-old kid living in Detroit in 1980 when he put together a project called Cybotron. Likely unaware of the Australian electronic band of the same name from the '70s, Atkins took his own love of Kraftwerk, Numan, and P-Funk and crafted a skeletal, electronic sound based around the synthetic percussion of the Roland TR-808 drum machine. Introduced in 1980, the 808 was panned for its inability to create any sound resembling a real drum kit. Atkins was one of the many budding producers who embraced rather than shunned this sound. "I had a class called Future Studies, about the transition from an industrial society to a technological society," Atkins said. "I just applied a lot of those principles to my music-making." He also became a DJ, playing parties in abandoned warehouses in Detroit—much as John Brunner had predicted in his 1968 sci-fi novel *Stand on Zanzibar*, with its Detroit warehouse parties pumping a form of electronic music known as "zock." On his own label, Deep Space Records, Atkins began releasing Cybotron's music in 1981, songs with names like "Cosmic Car," "Industrial Lies," and "Techno City." They not only inspired electro, but other electronic-dance genres that would appear in the '80s such as techno and house.

In New York, a revolution of its own was taking place. Hip-hop, after bubbling in the underground for years, had finally gone mainstream with 1980's "Rapper's Delight" by the Sugar Hill Gang. One of the many hip-hop records released that year was "Zulu Nation Throw Down," the debut by a group from the Bronx called Afrika Bambaataa and the Cosmic Force. Along with Grandmaster Flash and Kool DJ Herc, Bambaataa had been one of the pioneering hip-hop DJs in the Bronx in the '70s. The group changed its name to the Soulsonic Force by the release of their 1982 single "Planet Rock"; built on the 808, which had become the robotic heartbeat of electro, it was another piece of the electro puzzle, a song that borrowed liberally from an international selection of sources, including Kraftwerk, Yellow Magic Orchestra, and Gary Numan. "Numan was doing that thing with 'Bombers,'" said Bambaataa, citing the Tubeway Army's 1978 single. "That was one of the early records we used to play when rappers was rapping. I don't know if Gary even knows there was so many black and Latino youth jamming to his music."

It took a less likely New York group to release the first song that blended sci-fi with rap. Blondie, the new wave band that dabbled in a plethora of styles, from punk to disco to reggae, put out their fifth album *Autoamerican* in 1980. One track, "Rapture," became a hit single the following year—thanks to its lengthy coda, a rap by lead singer Debbie Harry. In it, a Martian lands in a UFO and proceeds to eat people, cars, and even entire bars before departing the planet, "where he won't have a hassle with the human race." It was an odd beginning for sci-fi hip-hop—but the subgenre would evolve spectacularly from there in the coming decades.

The late-'70s boom in sci-fi funk and disco had all but dissipated by 1980. The energy of sci-fi funk had been diverted into hip-hop and electro; sci-fi disco was experiencing the same rabid backlash, often racist and homophobic in nature, that the rest of the genre was facing. Against those odds, Grace Jones thrived. A veritable sci-fi diva, the Jamaican supermodel had turned to music in 1977, coasting on disco before moving into weirder territory. With her shorn scalp, automaton stage moves, and imposing monotone, she released a cover of the Normal's Ballard-inspired song "Warm Leatherette" in 1980; also that year, she covered "She's Lost Control" by another Ballard-influenced post-punk group, Joy Division. In the same way that Kraftwerk symbolized science fiction rather than singing about it, so did Jones become a musical personification of Afrofuturism.

A strange and barely known song served as a fitting postscript to the golden age of sci-fi disco and funk. A singled titled "U.F.O." came out on a tiny independent label in 1980. Its cover is breathtakingly bizarre: Unlike the slick, ultra-detailed sci-fi artwork that had come to grace so many records by then, the cover of "U.F.O." was a rudimentary, almost childlike painting of a man with an Afro wearing a cross between a spacesuit and a superhero costume. Behind him were humans and crudely rendered aliens, dancing together with abandon. In the background, the green-and-blue curve of Earth could be seen through a set of large windows, beneath which is a bank of computers. This incredible scene is taking place on a spaceship in orbit, a fact confirmed by the song itself. Over a wobbly, funky beat, a man yelps, "I took a ride, and now I know / A UFO ain't nuthin' but a disco!"

The song was by Curtis Knight, the R & B bandleader who had given Jimi Hendrix—sci-fi rock's forefather—one of his first gigs as a professional touring musician in the '60s. Knight had not been hugely popular then, and he was less so now. "U.F.O." went nowhere; not only was Knight's career in the dumps in 1980, the record looked and sounded instantly obsolete upon its release. Yet heard today, it has a curiously timeless quality about it, a mix of innocence, desperation, goofy fun, cynical commercialism, and space-age wonder that sums up an era of sci-fi music as few songs can.

✴ **NEW GENRES OF MUSIC WERE** sprouting everywhere circa 1980, one of which bore the unwieldy moniker the New Wave of British Heavy Metal. Taking cues from Judas Priest, Motörhead, and the faster songs of Black Sabbath—all bands with sci-fi fixations—the NWOBHM pared down and intensified the loosely defined style known as heavy metal, which still exhibited bits of psychedelia and prog. NWOBHM groups mercilessly carved away all those vestigial trappings of early metal—except for sci-fi. The movement was led by Iron Maiden, whose self-titled debut album in 1980 made their sci-fi sympathies known. The song "Strange World" spoke of a "ship of white light in the sky" along with the offer, "Let's walk in deepest space." Lead singer Paul Di'Anno delivered those lines, but they were written by bassist Steve Harris, and they presaged the many sci-fi lyrics the group would write after Bruce Dickinson replaced Di'Anno in 1981—as well as setting the pace for the many metal bands of the '80s who would spike nightmares of the future among their riffs.

The shadow of authors like Ballard and Philip K. Dick continued to fall heavily across sci-fi music in 1980, but Michael Moorcock's grew faint. Inextricably linked to the hippie counterculture and then hard rock, he saw his involvement in the music scene wane. In fact, he barely wrote science fiction anymore; instead, he had begun to focus on his own mythic brand of historical fantasy. He continued to work with Hawkwind on occasion throughout the '80s, although his brief association with Blue Öyster Cult would end in 1981 with "Veteran of the Psychic Wars." He did, however, write a book in 1980 that forged one last, immortal link between his fiction and popular music. Commissioned by Virgin Books to write a novelization of *The Great Rock 'N' Roll Swindle*, a film about the Sex Pistols—a band he didn't even like—Moorcock penned the adaptation purely for a paycheck. It mirrored the film in its chaotic mix of the Pistols' self-mythology and music. Later in the decade, Moorcock wound up taking the raw material of *The Great Rock 'N' Roll Swindle* and rewriting the book as *Gold Diggers of 1977*, a swipe at the infamously money-hungry band. In the process, he changed the names of the real-life characters in *The Great Rock 'N' Roll Swindle*, turning *Gold Diggers* into a Jerry Cornelius novel. It was perversely appropriate: after seeing his books used as the basis for dozens of sci-fi songs, he took the real-life legend of the Sex Pistols and translated it into his own sci-fi mythos.

Moorcock drifted away from sci-fi at an opportune time. As a shining example of the New Wave of Science Fiction, he had championed a way of using technology as a gateway to explore the inherent ambiguity and weirdness of the universe. That had fallen out of vogue by 1980. That year, novels such as Robert L. Forward's *Dragon's Egg*—about a neutron star inhabited by a minute race of alien beings—helped consolidate the forces of hard science fiction. Unlike the New Wave, hard sci-fi favored rigorous scientific and mathematical principles, which were expressed in detail within the story itself. Its authors, many of them with backgrounds in science and technology, speculated about the future, but they did so using their current understanding of reality as a benchmark. Hard sci-fi couldn't have been further from the freewheeling, morally relative tales of Moorcock and company—and it, along with cyberpunk, became one of the dominant forms of sci-fi literature in the '80s.

Hand in hand with the rise of hard sci-fi was the introduction of Carl Sagan's *Cosmos*. The astronomer—who had argued for the inclusion of Chuck Berry's music on the Voyager probe's Golden Records in 1977—published his best-known book in 1980, becoming a runaway bestseller and the winner of numerous accolades, including a Hugo Award for Best Nonfiction Book. Covering everything from the origins of the universe to the possibility of extraterrestrial life from a grounded point of view, *Cosmos* rejected the fuzzy hypothesizing and fear-stoking that had defined so much pop-science writing of the '70s, from J. Allen Hynek to Alvin Toffler. The book's success was aided by its adaptation into a massively popular television show, hosted by Sagan on PBS that year. Together, the book and show made hard science hip.

It didn't hurt that the next phase of the United States' space program was imminent. A long countdown was underway to the launch of the maiden voyage of the Space Shuttle *Columbia*. The *Enterprise*, christened in 1977 after *Star Trek*'s iconic starship, had been the prototype; now it was *Columbia*'s turn. On April 14, 1981, it landed after a two-day mission in space, becoming the first successfully reusable spacecraft. It also marked the return of American astronauts to space after a six-year absence. Space travel was not only back, it was sustainable. It was just a matter of time, it seemed, before private citizens would be taking routine Space Shuttle flights to some grand space station—or beyond. After a decade of disillusionment, disaster, and doubt, the United States was wholeheartedly excited about space again. Not even the growing risk of a nuclear holocaust in the era of the newly elected Ronald Reagan—whose hard-line stance against the USSR seemed designed to provoke confrontation—could dull that.

Hard science was hot in 1980, but it hadn't carried over to the silver screen. Although *Alien* introduced a grim, stripped-down visual language to sci-fi cinema the year before, the fantastic side of the genre still reigned. *Flash Gordon*, a campy revamp of the venerable pulp character, thrilled millions upon its release during the 1980 holiday season—thanks in part to the soundtrack by Queen. It was still a new practice to have a rock band score a film, and Queen's electrifying theme song became a hit in its own right. Freddie Mercury—no stranger to camp himself—may have sung "I don't like *Star Wars*" in 1978's "Bicycle Race," but he and his band, including sci-fi enthusiast Brian May, couldn't have been a better fit.

Star Wars finally made its comeback in 1980. *The Empire Strikes Back* hit theaters in May, and proved that the success of the first film had not been a fluke. If anything, it was an improvement over the first film, and audiences responded with renewed zeal. The *Star Wars* franchise, however, had become a known quantity by then; although plot twists abounded in the film, gone was the shock of the new. *Star Wars* had revolutionized sci-fi, while *The Empire Strikes Back* was a reassuring return to form. As such, it didn't inspire anywhere near the amount of music that *Star Wars* did in 1977. Predictably, Meco—who had launched the entire space-disco craze—clocked in with his rendition of the theme to *The Empire Strikes Back* in 1980. But rather than warranting an entire album, it was released as a four-song EP, one that sold modestly in comparison to his *Star Wars* records. After his *Return of the Jedi*–themed *Ewok Celebration* album in 1983, he stopped releasing records, having been pigeonholed by his greatest success.

A new kind of sci-fi media began influencing music in 1980: video games. In particular, the arcade game *Space Invaders* was infiltrating the world. Introduced in Japan in 1978—after creator Tomohiro Nishikado had been inspired by *Star Wars*—*Space Invaders* became the template for the sci-fi shooting game. Hundreds of thousands of the machines had flooded American arcades by 1980, the same year it was introduced for home players on Atari. It sparked a new era in video games and set a new standard for the medium's music and sound production.

The game's electronic soundtrack, beeping and minimal, was absorbed and reflected by the nascent electro scene—and even led to records of its own. A 1979 single titled "Space Invaders" by a studio project called Player [1] enchantingly mimicked the game's digital bloops and effects, and it was sampled often by early electro and house producers. Then in 1980, the album *Space Invasion* appeared. It collected a wide variety of sci-fi songs of the previous decade, including "Galaxy" by War, "A Spaceman Came Travelling" by Chris de Burgh, "Calling Occupants of Interplanetary Craft" by the Carpenters, "Rocket Man" by Elton John, "Watcher of the Skies" by Genesis, "Spacer" by Sheila B. and Devotion, "Dancing in Outer Space" by Atmosfear, and "Silver Machine" by Hawkwind. Topping it off, Yellow Magic Orchestra delivered a synth-driven version of the *Space Invaders* theme. Long before sci-fi music became widely considered as such, an ostensibly cheap cash-in record was its first comprehensive document.

THE ENORMOUS SUCCESS OF "ASHES to Ashes" rekindled interest not only in Bowie's music but in Bowie as both a creator and a creature of science fiction. His career, and sci-fi music as a whole, would never be the same. In 1980, he admitted that his sequel to "Space Oddity" had been "long overdue," adding that it was "the end of something." By writing "Ashes to Ashes," he said, "I was wrapping up the '70s really for myself, and that seemed a good enough epitaph for it. We've lost [Major Tom], he's out there somewhere, we'll leave him be."

Despite his promise, Bowie did not leave Major Tom be. After others had borrowed him—most notably the German synth-pop star Peter Schilling, whose 1983 hit "Major Tom (Coming Home)" was fanfic in song form—Bowie revisited his famous character in his 1995 song "Hallo Spaceboy," cowritten with Eno. In the lyrics, Bowie bids farewell to Major Tom: "Spaceboy, you're sleepy now / Your silhouette is so stationary." Locked in stasis, like Sleeping

Beauty in outer space, Major Tom seems caught somewhere between suspended animation and death.

But Major Tom was not dead. On May 12, 2013, Canadian astronaut Chris Hadfield posted a YouTube video that featured him singing and playing an acoustic version of "Space Oddity" while in orbit on the International Space Station. It soon went viral, racking up tens of millions of views. In the video, Hadfield floats weightless, strumming and lamenting his isolation. With it, a circuit was completed, and mythology became fact.

One month later, Bowie was inducted into the Science Fiction and Fantasy Hall of Fame, the first musician to be awarded that honor. Near the end of 2013, he listed his favorite books of all time, showcasing a broad literary panorama that spotlighted speculative-fiction classics such as Mikhail Bulgakov's *The Master and Margarita* and Angela Carter's *Nights at the Circus* alongside his old fallbacks *Nineteen Eighty-Four* and *A Clockwork Orange*—not to mention Junot Díaz's 2007 novel, *The Brief Wondrous Life of Oscar Wao*, whose main character, a boy infatuated with science fiction, might have seemed familiar to Bowie.

David Bowie died on January 10, 2016. The cause was liver cancer, which he'd kept secret from the public. Two days earlier, his final album, *Blackstar*, had been released. The video for its ten-minute title song takes place on an unknown planet—or perhaps it's our planet, far in the future or far in the past. In the sky hangs an ominous sun that has either become eclipsed or burns with some insidious darkness. A girl with a tail comes across a humanoid figure in a NASA-style space suit reclining against a rock. As if reprising the helmet-donning gesture of Major Tom in the video for "Space Oddity," half a century prior, the astronaut's visor is raised. Behind it lies a skull encrusted with jewels and gold filigree—the ornamented corpse of a space traveler left to spin through eternity.

ACKNOWLEDGMENTS

A book about the overlap between science fiction and music had been percolating in the back of my brain for years, but it didn't really take shape until my editor, Ryan Harrington, got his hands on my rudimentary proposal. Without his input and guidance, I would have written an encyclopedia, not a story. I can't thank him enough for his patience, wisdom, and enthusiasm.

Many conversations with many smart and passionate people helped make *Strange Stars* what it is, but my chats with Marc Gascoigne of Angry

Robot Books were the most lengthy and profound. His knowledge of music is unsurpassed, and his feedback and suggestions during the early stages of *Strange Stars* were invaluable. Plus he once suffered a horrible plate of food-court fish and chips with me on an otherwise lovely afternoon in Seattle while I blabbed on and on about the merits of Pop Will Eat Itself, for which I'm eternally grateful.

My wife, Angie Sigg, provided moral and emotional support above and beyond the call of matrimonial duty while I worked on *Strange Stars*. I couldn't have done it without her. Likewise, my current agent, Eddie Schneider, and my former agent, Jennifer Jackson, have my gratitude for their great assistance and insight. Stephanie DeLuca has been an amazing publicist, and I can't rave enough about Butcher Billy and his dazzling cover art for the book, for which I feel blessed. The fact that he and I share a birthday only makes our partnership feel more preordained. Many thanks to Marina Drukman for her eye-catching art direction, Kaitlin Severini for her smart copy edit, and Susan Rella for pulling it all together.

I owe so much to the many editors who have allowed me to write about sci-fi music over the past few years, including Jonathan Wright of *Adventure Rocketship!*; Neil Clarke, Kate Baker, and Sean Wallace at *Clarkesworld*; Ryan Dombal, Mark Richardson, and Jillian Mapes at *Pitchfork*; Lenika Cruz at *The Atlantic*; David Haglund at *The New Yorker*; Hank Shteamer at *Rolling Stone*; Petra Mayer, Robin Hilton, and Jacob Ganz at NPR; and Bridget McGovern at Tor.com. I give special thanks to Ann and Jeff VanderMeer for letting me write about sci-fi music in their wonderful anthology *The Time Traveler's Almanac* and for their help overall. The platform these editors have given me made this book possible.

Speaking in public is not always my strong suit, but Eric Weisbard and everyone at PopCon at Seattle's Museum of Pop Culture made me comfortable and confident when I spoke there about sci-fi funk in the spring of 2017, and I appreciate it greatly. I also can't give enough thanks to Rose Beetem and her dedicated staff at MileHiCon, Denver's longest running science fiction convention, who let me inflict my musical taste and opinions on the con every year.

Finally, I'm eternally indebted to Duane Davis, Dave Stidman, and the rest of the crew at Denver's Wax Trax Records, my place of employ throughout my twenties. Working in an independent record store afforded me the chance to have lengthy, sometimes erudite, sometimes ludicrous conversations about music every day for years on end while being exposed to every manner of music under the sun. Wax Trax was my university, and I'm a proud alumnus.

NOTES

CHAPTER 1

3 **Bowie lived in a modest flat:** Paul Trynka, *David Bowie: Starman* (Boston: Little, Brown, 2011), 98.

3 **The aptly named Dandie:** Paul Morley, *The Age of Bowie* (New York: Gallery, 2016), 177.

4 **Including a flamboyant American:** Eve M. Kahn, "Hendrix and Handel but Mostly Hendrix," *The New York Times*, Aug. 19, 2010.

4 **That summer, Ray Davies:** Keith Altham, "The One-Up Kink: Raymond Douglas Davies," *New Musical Express*, Aug. 31, 1968.

4 ***The Hollywood Reporter* wrote:** John Mahoney, "Kubrick's 'Space Oddity' One of MGM's All-Time Hits," *Hollywood Reporter*, Apr., 1968.

4 **"I was out of my gourd":** Bill DeMain, "The Sound and Vision of David Bowie," *Performing Songwriter*, Sep. 2003.

4 In particular, he was transfixed: Christopher Sandford, *Bowie: Loving the Alien* (Boston: Da Capo, 1998), 50.

4 He and his friend Tony Visconti: David Buckley, *Strange Fascination: David Bowie: The Definitive Biography* (London: Virgin, 1993), 54.

5 Ray Bradbury, Theodore Sturgeon: Buckley, *Strange*, 138.

5 along with many of the increasingly: Chris O'Leary, *Rebel Rebel: All the Songs of David Bowie from '64 to '76* (Zero, 2015), 55.

5 As a teenager, Jones: O'Leary, *Rebel*, 55.

7 "We knew him around the time": Russell Leadbetter, "The Quieter Side of Rock's Flamboyant Singer Alex Harvey," *Herald*, Mar. 11, 2016.

7 "Alex recommended that David": Alistair McKay, "Alex Harvey—The Last of the Teenage Idols," *Uncut*, Apr. 4, 2016.

7 One of the flat's other residents: Paul Trynka, "The Older Sister/Lover," www .trynka.net/archive/Duncan.html.

9 The influential editor: Jeet Heer, "Science Fiction's White Boys' Club Strikes Back," *New Republic*, Apr. 16, 2015.

12 "ice ages, burning planets": Adam Mitchell, "Jimi Hendrix, Spaceships, and Science-Fiction," www.tor.com/2012/05/10/jimi-hendrix-spaceships-and-science-fiction/.

12 "The first one Jimi read": John McDermott, Eddie Kramer, and Billy Cox, *Ultimate Hendrix: An Illustrated Encyclopedia of Live Concerts and Sessions* (New York: Backbeat, 2009), 26.

12 Backstage before a concert: Steven Roby, *Black Gold: The Lost Archives of Jimi Hendrix* (New York: Billboard, 2002), 67.

13 It was Robert A. Heinlein's: "Video Interview with David Crosby and Spider Robinson," cameronknowlton, Nov. 15, 2006, video, 4:41, www.youtube.com /watch?v=clUviBkic2k.

13 latching on to the work: Bill Robinson, "David Crosby: A Certified, Anti-War, Folk/Rock Icon," www.huffingtonpost.com/billrobinson/david-crosby-a-certified -_b_8079334.html.

13 "Science fiction was so expansive: David Crosby, interview with Neil deGrasse Tyson, *StarTalk*, podcast audio, Jan. 15, 2016, www.startalkradio.net/show/science -and-social-justice-with-david-crosby/.

13 In *Crawdaddy*, an aspiring songwriter: Sandy Pearlman, "The Byrds—Younger Than Yesterday," *Crawdaddy*, June, 1967.

15 Swirling with lights: David Downing, *Future Rock* (New York: HarperCollins, 1976), 96.

16 He also came of age: Julian Palacios, *Syd Barrett and Pink Floyd: Dark Globe* (London: Plexus, 2015), Kindle edition.

17 Through a twist of synchronicity: Downing, *Future*, 96.

17 a sci-fi hobbyist in his own right: Russell Reising, *Speak to Me: The Legacy of Pink Floyd's The Dark Side of the Moon* (Abingdon: Routledge, 2017), 35.

17 Barrett was acquainted with: Jonathan Wright, *Adventure Rocketship!: Let's All Go to the Science Fiction Disco* (Bristol: Adventure Rocketship!, 2013), 16.

18 "There are actually people standing": David Gilmour, "My Moon-Landing Jam Session," *Guardian*, July 1, 2009, www.theguardian.com/science/2009/jul/02 /apollo-11-pink-floyd-session.

18 On the night of July 20, 1969: Gilmour, *Guardian*.

18 "a bit off the wall": Gilmour, *Guardian*.

18 "a nice, atmospheric, spacey, twelve-bar blues": Gilmour, *Guardian*.

18 "It was fantastic": Gilmour, *Guardian*.

19 "I think at the time": Gilmour, *Guardian*.

19 He'd recorded a demo: Nicholas Pegg, *The Complete David Bowie: New Edition* (London: Titan, 2016), 255.

19 rushed the release of "Space Oddity": Rob Young, *Electric Eden: Unearthing Britain's Visionary Music* (New York: Farrar, Straus and Giroux, 2011), 258.

20 "It was picked up": DeMain, *Performing*.

21 "At the end of the song": Mary Finnigan, *Psychedelic Suburbia: David Bowie and the Beckenham Arts Lab* (Portland: Jorvik, 2016), Kindle edition.

21 "I related to the sense": Peter Doggett, *The Man Who Sold the World: David Bowie and the 1970s* (New York: Harper Perennial, 2013), 59.

21 "seismic impact": Sandford, *Bowie*, 50.

21 "The publicity image of a spaceman": Finnigan, *Psychedelic*, Kindle edition.

22 the song wasn't played: "Bowie @ the Beeb," Jan. 8, 2001, www.bbc.co.uk/world service/arts/highlights/010108_bowie.shtml.

22 thanks largely to an appearance: Pegg, *Complete*, 225.

22 "I want it to be the first anthem": Doggett, *Man*, 57.

22 "It is probably not hyperbole": Philip H. Ennis, *Seventh Stream: The Emergence of Rocknroll in American Popular Music* (Middletown: Wesleyan, 1992), Google Books.

22 Camille Paglia said: Buckley, *Fascination*, 51.

23 "Bowie once said he considered: O'Leary, *Rebel*, 108.

23 that Neil Armstrong set foot: "Moody Blues at Red Rocks 5-7-11 Higher and Higher," JenneBreck, 2011, video, 5:53, www.vimeo.com/23652897.

CHAPTER 2

28 "I was an abandoned child": Jeff Tamarkin, *Got a Revolution!: The Turbulent Flight of Jefferson Airplane* (New York: Atria, 2005), 15.

28 Then one day, in third grade: Greg Gildersleeve, "Paul Kantner," www.jefferson airplane.com/the-band/paul-kantner/.

28 Robert A. Heinlein, Arthur C. Clarke: Ian Birch, "Jefferson Starship's Paul Kantner," *ZigZag*, Nov. 1976.

28 "went off into the cosmos": Tamarkin, *Got*, 19.

28 "alternate quantum universes": Tamarkin, *Got*, 15.

28 "our new parallel universe": Tamarkin, *Got*, xxi.

28 "a reflection of the quantum": Tamarkin, *Got*, xxi.

29 but he happily sought permission: Tamarkin, *Got*, 158.

29 "I have thousands of influences": Tamarkin, *Got*, 168.

29 "We were trying to make a living": Tamarkin, *Got*, 15.

30 "[We] imagined ourselves": David Crosby, liner notes to Crosby, Stills & Nash, *CSN*, Atlantic, 1991, compact disc.

31 "I met Ted Sturgeon": David Crosby, Introduction to Theodore Sturgeon, *Baby Is Three: Volume VI: The Complete Stories of Theodore Sturgeon* (Berkeley: North Atlantic, 1999), ix.

31 Said Stills, "It won't be": Richard Williams, "Stills and Young," *Melody Maker*, Jan. 10, 1970.

31 "It was a nightmare": Crosby, *Baby*, xi.

31 "We're gonna do kind of a science fiction story": "Wooden Ships—CSNY (Live at Woodstock '69)," Amer Djulbic, Apr. 22, 2010, video, 5:56, www.youtube.com /watch?v=vlg FVazSQHw.

31 "Definitely a science fiction song": Andy Greene, "Track by Track: Crosby, Stills & Nash on Their Self-Titled Debut," *Rolling Stone*, Aug. 18, 2008.

32 "It was sort of an end-of-the-world movie": Jimmy McDonough, *Shakey: Neil Young's Biography* (New York: Random House, 2002), 331.

32 "There's the future": McDonough, *Shakey*, 339.

33 "[Writing sci-fi music]": Crosby, *StarTalk*.

33 Robert Hunter, who, years later: Dean Budnick, "The Return of Robert Hunter," *Relix*, Sept., 2013.

35 "I used to write science fiction stories": Raymond Telford, "Julian's Treatment Cures All," *Melody Maker*, Apr. 17, 1970.

35 "Of course the music is strange": Telford, *Melody Maker*.

36 "The vocalist assumes the stance": Chrissie Hynde, "Magma: Walthamstow, London," *New Musical Express*, Mar. 9, 1974.

36 "We baptized that other world": Jason Gross, "Christian Vander Interview," http://www.furious.com/perfect/magma2.html.

37 "about a guy who invented a time machine": Richard Green, "Black Sabbath Win Struggle Against Black Magic Tag," *New Musical Express*, Sept. 26, 1970.

37 "a smoky, jazz club number": Green, *New Musical Express*.

37 "a very distant, *2001*-ish track": "Black Sabbath," *Beat Instrumental*, Nov. 1970.

38 Along with the standard authorial influences": Thom Jurek, "Peter Hammill Artist Biography," www.allmusic.com/artist/peter-hammill-mn0000843607/biography.

38 "The '70s, of course, were a great time": Jorge Luis Fernandez and Robin Cook, "Peter Hammill: Stumbler in the Dark," Aug. 2007, www.furious.com/perfect/peterhammill.html.

38 Much of the computer's chilling, inhuman intonation: Dave Tompkins, *How to Wreck a Nice Beach* (Chicago: Stop Smiling, 2010), 162.

40 "Taupin was going through a period": Charles Shaar Murray, "The Life and Times of Elton John," *New Musical Express*, Feb. 22, 1975.

40 "Fondness for a space story": Birch, *ZigZag*.

41 "A lot of what [the space program] does": Birch, *ZigZag*.

CHAPTER 3

42 The concert wasn't being held: Michael Moorcock, *London Peculiar and Other Nonfiction* (Oakland: PM, 2012), 169.

42 "I had a rotten childhood": Sam Jordison, *Adventure Rocketship!: Let's All Go to the Science Fiction Disco* (Bristol: Adventure Rocketship!, 2013), 22.

43 They'd even adopted their band name: *Hawkwind: Do Not Panic*, directed by Simon Chu, written by Tim Cumming, featuring Dave Brock, Robert Calvert, Simon House, Ian "Lemmy" Kilmister, Michael Moorcock, and Nik Turner, aired Aug. 10, 2007, on the British Broadcasting Corporation.

43 "I had become used to metamorphosis": Moorcock, London, 17.

44 "The metamorphosis of Blitzed London": Moorcock, London, 21.

45 he was even approached by a frustrated Stanley Kubrick: Michael Moorcock, "Close to Tears, He Left at the Intermission: How Stanley Kubrick Upset Arthur C. Clarke," *New Statesmen*, Jan. 8, 2017, www.newstatesman.com/culture/books/2017/01/close-tears-he-left-intermission-how-stanley-kubrick-upset-arthur-c-clarke.

45 "When Hendrix died": Ian Abrahams, *Hawkwind: Sonic Assassins* (self-pub., CreateSpace, 2017), Kindle edition.

45 "They were like the mad crew": Abrahams, *Hawkwind*.

45 "Moorcock endorsed Hawkwind publicly": Abrahams, *Hawkwind*.

46 "When I first saw them": Mike Davies, "The Hawklords Riddle," *New Musical Express*, Nov. 13, 1978.

46 "We really were trying to find": Abrahams, *Hawkwind*.

46 "I prefer to be a barbarian": Steve Newton, "Dave Brock Says Hawkwind's Space-Rock Wasn't Influenced By Anyone," *Georgia Straight*, Dec. 13, 1990.

46   His verse had been published in New Worlds: Abrahams, *Hawkwind*.

47   "This is music for the astral apocalypse": Lester Bangs, "Review: Hawkwind, *In Search of Space*," *Rolling Stone*, June 22, 1972.

47   An advertisement for the album": www.superseventies.com/sphawkwind.html.

48   "One of his most audacious: Abrahams, *Hawkwind*.

48   "It's not predicting what is going to happen": Abrahams, *Hawkwind*.

49   "At that time there were a lot of songs": Don Greenhalgh, "Sending Up Space," *Daily Mail*, Aug. 7, 2008.

49   "look out, the Earth is about to collide": Abrahams, *Hawkwind*.

49   "We were a black fucking nightmare": Abrahams, *Hawkwind*.

49   Its official title was African American Studies 198: Oliver Hall, "The Black Man in the Cosmos: Sun Ra Teaches at UC Berkeley, 1971," *Dangerous Minds*, July 18, 2014, www.dangerous minds.net/comments/the_black_man_in_the_cosmos_sun_ra _teaches_at_uc_berkeley_1971.

49   As sci-fi as that sounds: University of California, Berkeley, General Catalog, 1970–1971, www.digitalassets.lib.berkeley.edu/generalcatalog/text/1970_1971_courses .pdf.

49   "Music is a language": "Sun Ra Speaks: Berkeley Lecture Pt. 1," Sun Ra Music Channel, June 23, 2014, video, 28.50, www.youtube.com/watch?list=PLcmazi H9sW6ONBBh KaUxB NI44pr51vFcg&time_continue=1&v=Cfy2BpbkGe8.

50   "This planet is vulnerable": "Sun Ra Speaks: Berkeley Lecture Pt. 2," Sun Ra Music Channel, June 23, 2014, video, 23.57, www.youtube.com/watch?v=1LWEQmAGeRQ &list=PLc maziH9sW6ONBBhKaUxBNI44pr51vFcg&index=2.

50   "one little antenna on each ear": John Szwed, *Space Is the Place: The Lives and Times of Sun Ra* (New York: Pantheon, 1997), 28.

51   Months after Ra's 1971 Berkeley lectures: Rebecca Bengal, "The Interstellar Style of Sun Ra," *Pitchfork*, Apr. 18, 2006, www.pitchfork.com/features/from-the-pitch-fork-review/9866-the-interstellar-style-of-sun-ra/.

52   "It was literally meant": Chris Welch, *Yes: Close to the Edge* (London: Omnibus, 2008), Kindle edition.

52   "I thought about that very literally": Jeri Rowe, "Roger Dean: The Artist Behind the Music," *Greensboro News-Record*, Apr. 23, 2004.

52   "*Starship Troopers* was a great title": Carl Wiser, "Jon Anderson of Yes," *Song-facts*, May 17, 2013, http://www.songfacts.com/blog/interviews/jon_anderson_of _yes/.

53   "One day I walked into the studio": Malcolm Dome, "ELP's Tarkus: The Story Be-hind the Album," *Teamrock*, June 14, 2016, www.teamrock.com/feature/2016-06-14 /elp-s-tarkus-the-story-behind-the-album.

55   "That show opened a lot of doors": Joseph McBride, *Steven Spielberg: A Biography*, *Second Edition* (Jackson: University Press of Mississippi, 2011), 189.

58   "A sensitive young girl's reaction": Pegg, *Complete*, 162.

58   "Star Trek with long hair and drugs": Kilmister, *Hawkwind: Do Not Panic*.

58   "*Star Trek* in a leather jacket": Will Brooker, *Forever Stardust: David Bowie Across the Universe* (New York: I.B. Tauris, 2017), Kindle edition.

CHAPTER 4

59   "an ordinary function room": Stephen King, *The Ziggy Stardust Companion*, www .5years.com/stephenking.htm.

59   "A gaunt fortress of a pub": King, *Ziggy*.

60   Before Bowie took the stage: Michael Watts, "Oh, You Pretty Thing," *Melody Maker*, Jan. 22, 1972.

61 "a blurring of 'found' symbols": Buckley, *Strange*, 114.

62 "He was so vivid": Bono, "Bono Remembers David Bowie: 'He Is My Idea of a Rock Star,'" *Rolling Stone*, Feb. 11, 2016.

62 "It was like a creature falling": Rob Sheffield, *On Bowie* (New York: Dey Street, 2016), 70.

62 "*Vogue's* idea of what the well-dressed astronaut": Michael Watts, "Waiting for the Man," *Melody Maker*, July 1, 1972.

63 "staggeringly, awesomely trite": "Bowie at the Bijou," David Bowie: *The Last Interview* (New York: Melville House, 2016), 119.

63 "The whole thing was to try": O'Leary, *Rebel*, 227.

63 "It was a cross between [*The Wild Boys*]": Sean Egan, *Bowie on Bowie: Interviews and Encounters with David Bowie* (Chicago: Chicago Review Press, 2015), 238.

64 "trying to be George Orwell": Lester Bangs, *Psychotic Reactions and Carburetor Dung* (New York: Knopf, 1987), 164.

64 "deposited onstage after seemingly being dipped": Bangs, *Psychotic*, 162.

64 "decorated in a science-fiction mode": Craig Copetas, "Beat Godfather Meets Glitter Mainman: William Burroughs Interviews David Bowie," *Rolling Stone*, Feb. 28, 1974.

64 "The time is five years to go": Copetas, *Rolling Stone*.

65 He called the song "fabulous": Chris Norris, "Golden Years," *Spin*, Nov., 1999.

65 "a science-fiction fantasy of today": Copetas, *Rolling Stone*.

66 "It seemed a bit too flower-powery": Copetas, *Rolling Stone*.

66 "I was certain someone would call": Simon Reynolds, *Shock and Awe: Glam Rock and Its Legacy, from the Seventies to the Twenty-First Century* (New York: Dey Street, 2016), 253.

67 "Pied Pipers [. . .], transporting": Young, *Electric*, 474.

69 The grand ballroom of the Statler: Howard Smith and Sally Helgesen, "Scenes," *Village Voice*, Jan. 27, 1972.

69 Passersby gawked at moon rocks: "Star Trek Lives!—Convention," www.fanlore .org/wiki/Star_Trek_Lives!_(convention)#cite_note-4

69 "adult sci-fi freaks and show buffs": Smith and Helgesen, *Village Voice*.

71 "Future shock had arrived": Robert Hilburn, "David Bowie Rocks in Santa Monica," *Los Angeles Times*, Oct. 23, 1972.

71 "The flashing strobe lights": Hilburn, *Los Angeles Times*.

72 "was science fiction personified": Philip Auslander, *Performing Glam Rock: Gender and Theatricality in Popular Music* (Ann Arbor: University of Michigan Press, 2006), 134.

72 "Leonardo, Galileo, Newton, Gandhi": Sandford, *Bowie*, 70.

72 "You know, spirits from other places": Auslander, *Performing*, 127.

73 "the inevitability of the apocalypse": Egan, *Bowie on Bowie*, 17.

CHAPTER 5

76 "Yes. This would be fantastic": Lester Bangs, "Kraftwerk: The Final Solution to the Music Problem?," *New Musical Express*, Sep. 6, 1975.

76 "If Hawkwind are the Michael Moorcock": Barry Miles, "Krautwerk: This Is What Your Fathers Fought to Save You From," *New Musical Express*, Oct. 16, 1976.

77 "overpowering the listener": David Stubbs, *Future Days: Krautrock and the Birth of a Revolutionary New Music* (New York: Melville House, 2015), 101.

77 "cosmic music liberates the listener": Greg Shaw, "The Future Will Happen This Year: Space Rock," *Phonograph Record*, Mar. 1973.

78 "to all people who feel obliged": Ian McDonald, "Krautrock: Germany Calling #2," *New Musical Express*, Dec. 16, 1972.

78   "I was a huge fan": "Interview with Klaus Schulze," 2015, www.klaus-schulze
.com/interv/inb501.htm.

78   "a dialogue partner for the musician": "Interview with Klaus Schulze," 1976,
https://www.klaus-schulze.com/interv/in7606.htm.

79   "How these people, the Eloi": Menno von Brucken Fock, "Interview with Eloy's
Frank Bornemann," www.dprp.net/wp/interviews/?page_id=443.

79   "a start into an unknown future": "Beginn Unde Erste Fortschritte," www
.eloy-legacy.com/eloy.php?Area=history&Sub=epoch1.

80   he'd actually met Burroughs: David Weigel, *The Show That Never Ends: The Rise
and Fall of Prog Rock* (New York: W. W. Norton, 2017), 7.

80   "an invisible forcefield": "Gong," *Encyclopedia of Science Fiction*, Sept. 25, 2014,
www.sf-encyclopedia.com/entry/gong.

80   "meshed with Allen's belief": Philip Hayward, *Off the Planet: Music, Sound, and
Science Fiction Cinema* (Herts: John Libbey, 2004), 17.

80   "a Tolkien-scale history": Ian McDonald, "Daevid Allen," *New Musical Express*,
Sept. 6, 1975.

82   "shelves of sci-fi paperbacks": Richard Williams, "King Crimson: Robert Fripp . . .
Super Stud?", *Melody Maker*, Aug. 18, 1973.

82   He once confessed that he was a fan: Michael Bracewell, *Re-Make/Re-Model: Becoming Roxy Music* (Boston: Da Capo, 2008), 16.

82   The keyboardist suggested that one: David Sheppard, *On Some Faraway Beach*
(Chicago: Chicago Review Press, 2009), 140.

82   "Samuel Taylor Coleridge by way of Philip K. Dick": Sheppard, *On Some Faraway
Beach*, 203.

82   the fictional electronic-music composer Brent Mini: Philip K. Dick, *The Exegesis of
Philip K. Dick*, (New York: Houghton Mifflin Harcourt, 2011), 279.

82   "The album had a mood established": Ian McDonald, "Before and After Science:
Thinking About Music with Brian Eno," *New Musical Express*, Nov. 26, 1977.

83   Eno asserted that he'd traveled to Earth: Abrahams, *Hawkwind*.

84   It's entirely possible Bowie picked it up: Jackie Clark, "You Must Be Joking: In
Conversation with Roger Damon Price," Sept. 2005, www.effdee.demon.co.uk
/new%20TP%20site/Interviews/Roger.htm.

86   Jones stood on the set of his variety show: "Rufus Thomas—1973—The Funky
Robot—Black Omnibus," Historic Films Stock Footage Archive, Oct. 6, 2014,
video, 3:34, www.you tube.com/watch?v=ZpoEK58T-G4.

86   "I don't really know how these youngsters": "Rufus Thomas," blackomni74, Dec.
16, 2008, video, 1:08, www.youtube.com/watch?v=eNmCsgodjvg.

86   "The kids came up with another one": "Rufus Thomas—1973—The Funky
Robot—Black Omnibus."

87   By the late '60s, however, the dancer Charles "Robot" Washington: Lamont
Clark, *B-Boys; A Children's Guide to Hip-Hop* (self-pub., CreateSpace, 2013), Kindle
edition.

87   "Okay, let's have a look": "Rufus Thomas—1973—The Funky Robot—Black
Omnibus."

CHAPTER 6

92   Amid a cascade of unearthly electric piano: "Blue Öyster Cult—Astronomy—
Live 1976," Bruno S., Jan. 22, 2016, video, 7:26, www.youtube.com/watch?v=Nz
RVm65lNdU.

93   "very fascinated by the old druids": Martin Popoff, *Agents of Fortune: The Blue Öyster Cult Story* (London: Wymer, 2016), Kindle edition.

93 While living at the fabled Chelsea Hotel: Patti Smith, *Just Kids* (New York: Ecco, 2010), Kindle edition.

94 He published his first zine: "The Tattooed Dragon Meets the Wolfman: Lenny Kaye's Science Fiction Fanzines 1941-1970," www.boo-hooray.com/lenny-kaye -science-fiction-fanzines/.

94 "It's really what I call a gothic technology song": Popoff, *Agents*.

94 "very futuristic, definitely otherworldly": Popoff, *Agents*.

94 "These treaties founded a secret science": Popoff, *Agents*.

95 "in a scientific way": Popoff, *Agents*.

95 David Bowie darted around his conjoined: Pegg, *Complete*, 376.

96 he recalled that he wanted it set: Doggett, *Man*, 247.

96 "doom through science fiction": Chris Charlesworth, "David Bowie: Diamond Dogs," *Melody Maker*, May 11, 1974.

96 "He videoed his set for thirty minutes": Tony Visconti, *Tony Visconti: The Autobiography: Bowie, Bolan, and the Brooklyn Boy* (London: HarperCollins UK, 2007), 224.

96 Called it a work of "future shock": Tony Visconti, "Tony Visconti on Mixing *Diamond Dogs*," booklet to *David Bowie, Who Can I Be Now? [1974-1976]*, Parlophone, 2016, compact disc.

97 "Especially one of his favorite books": Pegg, *Complete*, 368.

97 "Now I'm doing Orwell's *Nineteen Eighty-Four*": Copetas, *Rolling Stone*.

97 "I found out that if I dared touch": Kurt Loder, "Stardust Memories: Reflections on a Life of Wit and Style," *Rolling Stone*, Apr. 23, 1987.

98 "At the end of 1973 George Orwell's widow": Pegg, *Complete*, 368.

98 "I had in my mind this kind of half": Pegg, *Complete*, 74.

98 "I know the impetus for *Diamond Dogs*": Loder, *Rolling Stone*.

98 On the resulting tour to support *Diamond Dogs*: Sandford, *Bowie*, 125.

99 During one show, the hydraulic arm: Sandford, *Bowie*, 125.

99 "David asked if I could capture": Visconti, "Tony Visconti on Mixing *Diamond Dogs*."

99 "desperate, almost panicked": Sandford, *Bowie*, 120.

99 "very English, apocalyptic kind of view": Pegg, *Complete*, 371.

99 because it was kind of *mine*: Laurie Tuffrey, "Pin Ups: A David Bowie Baker's Dozen Compilation," *Quietus*, Jan. 12, 2016, www.thequietus.com/articles/19525 -david-bowie-bakers-dozen-musicians-writers-favourite-albums?page=18.

101 "a science fiction writer who sings": Steve Turner, "Marc Bolan," *Beat Instrumental*, Feb. 1971.

101 "I'd long had an interest in sci-fi": David Quantick, *Adventure Rocketship!: Let's All Go to the Science Fiction Disco* (Bristol: Adventure Rocketship!, 2013), 42.

101 Be-Bop Deluxe would sometimes perform: Sylvie Simmons, "Ol' Bill: Be-Bop Deluxe's Bill Nelson," *Record Mirror*, Feb. 25, 1978.

102 Nelson considered himself equally influenced: Simmons, *Record Mirror*.

104 "The time ship floats through the galaxy": Stubbs, *Future*, 390.

106 "an alien from the other world": Ashley Heath, "Jesus Is a Soul Man," *Face*, Apr. 1997.

106 "Lee Perry's productions and theory fictions": Kodwo Eshun, *More Brilliant Than the Sun* (Northampton. Interlink, 1999), 62.

CHAPTER 7

109 "the Space Limousine": Thomas Dolby, *The Speed of Sound: Breaking the Barriers Between Music and Technology: A Memoir* (New York: Flatiron, 2016), 110.

109 "suddenly a beam of light from a UFO": Rob Fitzpatrick, "Space: George Clinton's Final Frontier," *Guardian*, June 15, 2011, www.theguardian.com/music/2011/jun/15/space-george-clinton-final-frontier.

109 "We had just went into the border": Lindsey Sullivan, "The One Time George Clinton and Bootsy Collins Almost Got Abducted by Aliens," *SiriusXM*, Nov. 6, 2014, www.blog.siriusxm.com/that-one-time-george-clinton-and-bootsy-collins-almost-got-abducted-by-aliens/.

111 "we had imagined a black man": George Clinton, *Brothas Be, Yo Like George, Ain't That Funkin' Kinda Hard on You?: A Memoir* (New York: Atria, 2014), 139.

111 "they were almost speaking in code": Ytasha L. Womack, *Afrofuturism: The World of Black Sci-Fi and Fantasy Culture* (Chicago: Chicago Review, 2013), Kindle edition.

112 Afrofuturists such as Clinton: Womack, *Afrofuturism*.

112 "*Buck Rogers* was the beginning": Amelia Mason, "George Clinton, Sun Ra, and the Sci-Fi Funk of Afrofuturism," *ARTery*, Mar. 2, 2014, www.wbur.org/artery/2014/03/02/george-clinton-afrofuturism.

112 *The Outer Limits* and *Star Trek*: Kris Needs, *George Clinton and the Cosmic Odyssey of the P-Funk Empire* (New York: Overlook, 2014), Kindle edition.

112 "I did love science fiction, of course": Clinton, *Brothas*, 140.

112 "I kind of grew up with it on TV": Charlie Jane Anders, "Bootsy Collins Tells Us How to Get a Seat on the Mothership," *io9*, Apr. 29, 2011, www.io9.gizmodo.com/5797067/bootsy-collins-tells-us-how-to-get-a-seat-on-the-mothership.

113 "When *A Clockwork Orange* brought the codpiece": Scott Hacker (Pagan Kennedy, ed.), *Platforms: A Microwaved Cultural Chronicle of the '70s* (New York: St. Martin's, 1994), 147.

113 "Afronauts capable of funkitizing galaxies": Mason, *ARTery*.

113 "took funkateers out of the disco-dominated dance scene": Kennedy, *Platforms*.

115 "the cosmic thing": Nelson George, *Where Did Our Love Go?: The Rise and Fall of the Motown Sound* (New York: St. Martin's, 1986), 172.

115 "We've been into the cosmic thing": John Abbey, "The Undisputed Truth: Their Aim Is Higher Than High," *Blues & Soul*, Nov. 1975.

116 they would sometimes glide down: Ian Ravendale, "Labelle's Nona Hendryx," *Rock's Backpages*, 1979, mp3, 19:42, www.rocksbackpages.com/Library/Article/labelles-nona-hendryx-1979.

117 "Nona's working clothes are futuristic": Clayton Riley, "Pop: Labelle Has the Sound and the Power," *The New York Times*, Feb. 17, 1974.

117 "I'm always finding myself": Caterine Milinaire and Carol Troy, *Cheap Chic: Hundreds of Money-Saving Hints to Create Your Own Great Look* (New York: Harmony, 1975), Kindle edition.

117 "a kind of feminist 'Rocket Man'": Wayne Robins, "Labelle: Phoenix," *Creem*, Dec. 1975.

117 She avidly read: Riley, *The New York Times*.

117 But it wasn't until the twenty-first century: Dan MacIntosh, "Nona Hendryx," *Songfacts*, Aug. 7, 2012, www.songfacts.com/blog/interviews/nona_hendryx/.

119 "looked like an alien being's idea": Abrahams, *Hawkwind*.

119 "the well-oiled Starship *Enterprise*": Abrahams, *Hawkwind*.

119 "seem to be moving away from the science fiction thing": Abrahams, *Hawkwind*.

120 "We grew tired of the record industry's": Moorcock, *London*, 170.

120 "We met Jodo several times": Allan McInnis, "Immersing Oneself in Magma: A Christian Vander Interview," *Big Takeover*, Mar. 2015.

123 "The moon had been visited, and was found wanting": Andrew M. Butler, *Solar Flares: Science Fiction in the 1970s* (Liverpool: Liverpool University, 2012), 6.

CHAPTER 8

125 "I carried [the typewriter]": Neil Peart, *Traveling Music: The Soundtrack to My Life and Times* (Toronto: ECW, 2004), 341.

127 especially one of them: a science-fiction epic: Peart, *Traveling*, 206.

127 *The Day of the Triffids* and *The Midwich Cuckoos*: Peart, *Traveling*, 206.

127 "To a struggling, twenty-year-old musician": Peart, *Traveling*, 206.

128 "In one of Wyndham's books": Peart, *Traveling*, 206.

128 "The idea for this track was suggested": John Woloschuk, "Klaatu Track Facts," www.klaatu.org/trackfacts/track_facts_12.html.

130 "I didn't want to be involved": Michael Watts, "David Bowie: From Brixton to Berlin," *Melody Maker*, Feb. 1978

130 "a strange and very different kind of human being": Doggett, *Man*, 281.

131 "My snapshot memory of that film": Pegg, *Complete*, 657.

131 "We listened a lot to the Kraftwerk albums": David Buckley, *Kraftwerk: Publikation* (New York: Overlook, 2015), Kindle edition.

131 "That was very important for us": Buckley, *Kraftwerk*.

131 "Much has been made of Kraftwerk's influence": Buckley, *Kraftwerk*.

132 "I don't have a great fascination for Bowie": Birch, *ZigZag*.

134 "In fact, the very words 'Childhood's End'": Birch, *ZigZag*.

134 "It was about dropping an earthman": Birch, *ZigZag*.

136 "The one thing I realized at PIR": "Philly 360° Masters Behind the Music: Dexter Wansel," Visit Philadelphia, Oct. 9, 2012, video, 3:50, www.youtube.com/watch?v=xFYROycuzmU.

136 "I sort of grew up with that": Russell Hall, "The Dark Humor of Donald Fagen," *Performing Songwriter*, Jan. 9, 2011, www.performingsongwriter.com/happy-birthday-donald-fagen/.

137 "The idea was escape": Larry Lange, "Boston's Scholz Engineers a Rock Dynasty," *Electronic Engineering Times*, Apr. 1998.

139 "Paul contacted him and was a *Star Trek* fan": Edward Gross and Mark A. Altman, *The Fifty-Year Mission: The Complete, Uncensored, Unauthorized Oral History of Star Trek: The First 25 Years* (New York: Thomas Dunne, 2016), 293.

139 He'd been reduced to accepting: Gross and Altman, *Fifty-Year*, 292.

139 "I have no idea what happened": Gross and Altman, *Fifty-Year*, 293.

CHAPTER 9

141 Domenico Monardo read those lines: Barry F. Seidman, "Interview with Meco Monardo," Equal Time for Free Thought, 2008, mp3, 44:40, www.equaltimefor freethought.org/wp-content/uploads/2008/06/080611_183001meco.mp3.

142 "I read every science fiction book there was": Seidman, "Interview."

143 "I had to convince the record company": Seidman, "Interview."

145 James Lipton pointed out: David Chute, "Spielberg Receives Usual 'Actors Studio' Reverence," *Los Angeles Times*, Mar. 13, 1999.

145 "In a couple years," he predicted: Nate Patrin, Mandré: A Tribute, *Red Bull Music Academy Daily*, Dec. 4, 2014, www.daily.redbullmusicacademy.com/2014/12/mandre-tribute-feature.

148 "I received a phone call from David": *David Bowie: Five Years*, directed by Francis Whately, featuring David Bowie, Brian Eno, Rick Wakeman, and Tony Visconti, premiered May 25, 2013, on the British Broadcasting Corporation.

148 "This is what I wanted to do": Pegg, *Complete*, 384.

151 "I did have a very pleasant call with Dr. Asimov": "Interview with Eric Woolfson

on Isaac Asimov relating to *I Robot*," TheOfficialAPP, Sep. 15, 2013, video, 2:24, www.youtube.com/watch?v=64eH6FqiKfU.

151 "It was basically," Parsons said: "Alan Parsons Project—*I Robot* 40th Anniversary," *In the Studio with Redbeard*, audio, 48:13, www.inthestudio.net/online-only -interviews/alan-parsons-project-irobot-40th-anniversary/.

152 "I'm a bit of a science fiction fan": Gary Graff, "Judas Priest's 'British Steel' Track by Track," *Billboard*, June 26, 2009, www.billboard.com/articles/news/268264/judas -priests-british-steel-track-by-track.

154 "We were both just into the same stuff": Dave Cantrell, "The Darkness and the Light Coexist—The Helios Creed Interview," *Stereo Embers*, www.stereoembers magazine.com/darkness-light-co-exist-helios-creed-interview/.

154 "People simply can't cope with the rate of change": Allan Jones, "Goodbye to Ziggy and All That," *Melody Maker*, Oct. 29, 1977.

155 "There are a lot of adolescents on the planet": Megan Gambino, "What Is on Voyager's Golden Record?," *Smithsonian*, Apr. 22, 2012, www.smithsonian mag.com/science-nature/what-is-on-voyagers-golden-record-73063839/?no-ist =&page=4.

155 "George Lucas has here constructed a universe": Butler, *Solar*, 63.

155 "When I saw the first *Star Wars* movie": Butler, *Solar*, 183.

155 "totally unoriginal, feebly plotted": J. G. Ballard, *A User's Guide to the Millennium: Essays and Reviews* (New York: St. Martin's, 1996), 14.

156 "It didn't hurt to smoke a joint": Crosby, *StarTalk*.

156 "It's like a comic book": Barbara Charone, "Alice Cooper: All Right, Son . . . Where's My Bog Boy With Extra Sauce?", *Creem*, Aug. 1977.

156 "Of course these days you can talk about": Howie Klein, "Case History No. 099: Bob Welch," *Creem*, Mar. 1978.

CHAPTER 10

158 "There's one band that I can mention": John Tobler, "Secret Secret Never Seen: An Interview With David Bowie," *ZigZag*, Jan. 1978.

159 "He had long hair down to his waist": Simon Reynolds, *Rip It Up and Start Again: Postpunk 1978-1984* (New York: Penguin, 2006), 77.

159 "It sounded really amazing": Reynolds, *Rip*, 78.

159 "You must use technology or else it uses you": Ian Birch, "We Are Devo, We Are the Next Thing," *Melody Maker*, Feb. 25, 1978.

159 "We wanted to make outer-space caveman music": Reynolds, *Rip*, 77.

159 William S. Burroughs and Philip K. Dick: Reynolds, *Rip*, 82.

160 "De-evolution was a combination": Jon Savage, "Devo: Are We Not Ready?", *Sounds*, Mar. 4, 1978.

160 "in the center of the most highly industrialized": Savage, *Sounds*.

160 But it was Devo who were chosen to open: George Gimarc, *Punk Diary: 1970-1979* (New York: St. Martin's, 1994), 21.

161 "An anti-capitalist science-fiction movie": Reynolds, *Rip*, 79.

161 "a sort of collage indoctrination": Birch, *Melody Maker*.

161 "the band of the future": Reynolds, *Rip*, 80.

161 "sort of like three Enos": Tobler, *ZigZag*.

162 "We were all basically aliens": Paul Rambali, "Hi! We're Devo and We've Come to Get Your Toilet Ready for the 1980s," *New Musical Express*, Mar. 18, 1978.

162 "Devo is like the science of music": Birch, *Melody Maker*.

163 Indeed, the band screened: Andy Gill, "Kraftwerk: Terminal Weirdness à Paris," *New Musical Express*, Apr. 29, 1978.

163 "Throughout the economically recessed '70s": Lisa Nocks, *The Robot: The Life Story of a Technology* (Westport: Greenwood, 2007), 69.

163 "Imagine yourself transported to a city": James Martin, *The Wired Society: A Challenge for Tomorrow* (Upper Saddle River: Prentice-Hall, 1978), dust jacket.

164 Her cheeks round and her teeth gleaming with braces: *Arena*, "Who Is Poly Styrene?", directed by Ted Clisby, featuring Poly Styrene, aired Jan. 20, 1979, on the British Broadcasting Corporation.

166 "My thing was more like consumerism": John Savage, *England's Dreaming: Anarchy, Sex Pistols, Punk Rock, and Beyond: Revised Edition* (New York: St. Martin's Griffin, 2002), Kindle edition.

166 "I wanted to write something using all kinds": Savage, *England's*.

167 "All of a sudden I looked out": Savage, *England's*.

168 "about this awful comic": Paul Rambali, "The Rezillos," *New Musical Express*, Feb. 25, 1978.

168 "There ain't that much I'd really be Interested in": Nick Tosches, "Patti Smith: Straight, No Chaser," *Creem*, Sept. 1978.

169 "It sounds like an electrical device": Peter Silverton, "Ultravox! New Music From A Doll's House," *Sounds*, Mar. 19, 1977.

169 "It sounds very programmed and computerized": Barry Miles, "Ultravox: Vee Hav Vays of Makink You Experiment," *New Musical Express*, Sept. 2, 1978.

171 she announced she was going to pay: Irene Klotz, "Singer Sarah Brightman Calls Off Flight to Space Station," *Reuters*, May 13, 2015.

172 "It has to get right to the top": John Abbey, "Jimmy Castor: Bertha Butt Meets Darth Vader," *Blues & Soul*, July 1978.

173 "After I'd seen *Star Wars* last year": Chris Salewicz, "Mick Farren: Is There Life After Dingwalls?", *New Musical Express*, Sept. 30, 1978.

173 "Like *Star Wars* but underwater": John Abbey, "Parliament Funkadelic: Watch Out, the Mothership Is Coming," *Blues & Soul*, Dec. 1978.

174 "The main German band I loved": Aug Stone, "Interview: Richard Pinhas Believes Music Can Fix the World," *Red Bull Music Academy Daily*, May 26, 2015, www.daily.redbullmusic academy.com/2015/05/richard-pinhas-interview

174 "I spent thirty-six hours with Philip K. Dick": Stone, *Red Bull Music Academy Daily*.

176 "Basically about people in an outlaw camp": Tamarkin, *Got*, 306.

177 "I was always fascinated with science fiction": Jeff Perlah, "Space Ace Frehley in a Groove Exploring Musical Origins," *Newsweek*, May 8, 2016, www.newsweek.com/space-ace-frehley-groove-exploring-musical-origins-456920.

177 "an avowed horror and science-fiction fan": Brett Weiss, *Encyclopedia of Kiss: Music, Personnel, Events, and Related Subjects* (Jefferson: McFarland, 2016), 208.

177 He counted everything from *Metropolis*: Susan Whitall, "Kiss: Bat Lizard Rocks the Boat," *Creem*, Apr. 1979.

178 "It's about a doctor who takes his people to a house of pain": "Van Halen—House of Pain—Live—Starwood," jonsilence, July 2, 2010, video, 3:42, www.youtube.com/watch?v=vAr4Q6fZFYk.

CHAPTER 11

179 "An oversized tram shed reeking of beer and glue": Dave Simpson, "Torn Apart: Joy Division and the Death of Ian Curtis," *Uncut*, Dec. 1997.

180 "This one's a love song . . . to Einstein": Andy Gill and Ian Penman, "Joy Division, Pil, et al.: Futurama '79 Festival—Set the Controls for the Squalor of Leeds," *New Musical Express*, Sept. 15, 1979.

180 Orchestral Manoeuvres in the Dark, a duo of electronic musicians: Dave Simp-

son, "Back to Futurama: The Gig That Changed My Life," *Guardian*, Oct. 25, 2006, www.theguardian.com/music/musicblog/2006/oct/25/themusicfestivalthat change1.

180 "other sci-fi attractions": Poster, www.joydiv.org/c080979.htm.

180 One of those attractions was people dressed: Gill and Penman, *New Musical Express*.

180 "grim," "bleak," and "with gray dust everywhere": Richard H. Kirk, "Futurama," *Mojo*, Sept. 2010.

180 "the Queens Hall venue floor came off": Simpson, *Guardian*.

181 They became acquainted after the singer: Wright, *Adventure*, 19.

181 "Ian Curtis and [Joy Division drummer] Stephen Morris": Simon Sellars, "Enthusiasm for the Mysterious Emissaries of Pulp: An Interview With David Britton," Ballardian, Feb. 22, 2010, www.ballardian.com/enthusiasm-for-mysterious-emissaries -britton-2b.

181 "There was some talk of us working together": Wright, *Adventure*, 19.

181 "hassling the Hawkwind fans": Paul D. Brazill, "Days of Futuramas Past," June 22, 2012, www.pauldbrazill.com/2012/06/22/days-of-futuramas-past-2/.

181 later admitted that he enjoyed the work of Philip K. Dick: Sean O'Hagan, "He's Still the Fall Guy," *Guardian*, Jan. 16. 2005, www.theguardian.com/film/2005/jan /16/bbc.

182 Said they drew inspiration from the sci-fi shows: *Synth Britannia*, directed by Ben Whalley, featuring Vince Clarke, Richard H. Kirk, and Gary Numan, aired Oct. 16, 2009, on the British Broadcasting Corporation.

183 He would later be diagnosed with Asperger's: "An Interview With Gary Numan," Post-Punk.com, Nov. 3, 2014, www.post-punk.com/an-interview-with-gary-numan -from-inside-film-score-work-21st-studio-begins-in-january/.

183 "was very loosely about what I thought London": "The Sci-Fi Films That Shaped Gary Numan," BFI, Nov. 12, 2014, video, 7:28, www.youtube.com/watch?v =thNCCjiemko.

183 "I read *Do Androids Dream of Electric Sheep?*": "The Sci-Fi Films That Shaped Gary Numan."

183 Became his most treasured tome: "An Interview With Gary Numan."

183 "Influences, when used wisely": "The Sci-Fi Films That Shaped Gary Numan."

184 But Numan insists he got the name: "An Interview With Gary Numan."

185 "I'm not particularly interested in Martians": "The Sci-Fi Films That Shaped Gary Numan."

186 "a row of little Daleks by the door": Giovanni Dadomo, "Human League: The Humour League Have Not Broken Up," *Sounds*, Dec. 8, 1979.

186 "had seen the future of pop music": Molly Lambert, "The Human League's Radical Future," MTV.com, Jan. 17, 2017, www.mtv.com/news/2972268/human -league-radical-future/.

186 "By frontman Philip Oakey's admission": Dadomo, *Sounds*.

186 "he considered Dick his favorite author": Lesley White, "Interview: Phil Oakey," *Face*, Dec. 1982.

186 "He had considered taking the writer's": Dadomo, *Sounds*.

186 "a crafted touch directly influenced by . . . Jerry Cornelius": Sharon Davis, *'80s Chart-Toppers: Every Chart-Topper Tells a Story* (Edinburgh: Mainstream, 1999), Kindle edition.

187 "Wasn't like science fiction in the sense": *Synth Britannia*.

195 "It had these bizarre lyrics": Hillary Crosley Coker, "Did Michael Jackson Reference *Star Wars* on 'Don't Stop 'Til You Get Enough?'", *Jezebel*, Jan. 14, 2016,

www.themuse.jezebel.com/did-michael-jackson-reference-star-wars-on-dont-stop-ti-1752911229.

CHAPTER 12

201 "When I originally wrote about Major Tom": Pegg, *Complete*, 29.

203 at the time, it was the most expensive: Pegg, *Complete*, 29.

203 "It was supposed to be the archetypal": Pegg, *Complete*, 29.

204 "some feeling of nostalgia for the future": Angus MacKinnon, "The Future Isn't What It Used to Be," *New Musical Express*, Sept. 13, 1980.

207 "We got that from *Rollerball*": Simon Reynolds, *Totally Wired: Postpunk Interviews and Overviews* (Berkeley: Soft Skull, 2010), Kindle edition.

207 "We call it futuristic science-fiction music": Stuart Coupe, "Buggles Sound In the New Decade," *Sydney Morning Herald*, Dec. 30, 1979.

207 "J. G. Ballard was a big inspiration at the time": Will Hodgkinson, "Horn of Plenty," *Guardian*, Nov. 5, 2004, www.theguardian.com/music/2004/nov/05/1.

209 "I had a class called Future Studies": Ben Beaumont-Thomas, "The Roland TR-808: The Drum Machine That Revolutionised Music," *Guardian*, Mar. 6, 2014, www.theguardian.com/music/2014/mar/06/roland-tr-808-drum-machine-revolutionised-music.

210 "Numan was doing that thing with 'Bombers'": JS Rafaeli, "We Spoke to Afrika Bambaataa About Hip-Hop, Afrofuturism, and *Bewitched*," *Vice*, Dec. 2, 2014, www.vice.com/en_us/article/5gkegn/afrika-bambaataa-interview-js-rafaeli-222.

214 adding that it was "the end of something": Pegg, *Complete*, 29.

DISCOGRAPHY

"(Gloryhallastoopid) Pin the Tail on the Funky," track 2 on Parliament, *Gloryhalla-stoopid (Pin the Tail on the Funky)*, released in 1979, Casablanca, NBLP 7195, 33 1/3 rpm.

"1983 . . . (A Merman I Should Turn to Be)," track 11 on the Jimi Hendrix Experience, *Electric Ladyland*, released in 1968, Reprise, RS 6307, 33 1/3 rpm.

"2000 AD," track 5 on the Rezillos, *Can't Stand the Rezillos*, released in 1978, SRK 6057, 33 1/3 rpm.

"21st Century Schizoid Man," track 1 on King Crimson, *In the Court of the Crimson King*, released in 1969, Atlantic, SD 8245, 33 1/3 rpm.

"After All," track 4 on David Bowie, *The Man Who Sold the World*, released in 1970, Mercury, SR-61325, 33 1/3 rpm.

"After the Gold Rush," track 2 on Neil Young, *After the Gold Rush*, released in 1970, Reprise, RS 6383, 33$\frac{1}{3}$ rpm.

"Alien Succumbs to the Macho Intergalactic Funkativity of the Funk Blasters, The," track 9 on George Duke, *Master of the Game*, released in 1979, JE Epic 36263, 33$\frac{1}{3}$ rpm.

"All Fly Away," track 7 on Jefferson Starship, *Dragon Fly*, released in 1974, Grunt BXL1-0717, 33$\frac{1}{3}$ rpm.

"Apocalyptic Bore," track 6 on Amon Düül II, *Vive la Trance*, released in 1973, United Artists, UA-LA198-F, 33$\frac{1}{3}$ rpm.

"Archy the Robot," track 9 on Amon Düül II, *Hijack*, released in 1974, Atco SD 36-108, 33$\frac{1}{3}$ rpm.

"Around the Universe in Eighty Days," track 3 on Klaatu, *Hope*, released in 1977, Capitol ST 11633, 33$\frac{1}{3}$ rpm.

"Art-I-Ficial," track 1 on X-Ray Spex, *Germfree Adolescents*, released in 1978, EMI International INS 3023, 33$\frac{1}{3}$ rpm.

"Ashes to Ashes," track 4 David Bowie, *Scary Monsters*, released in 1980, RCA Victor AQL1-3647, 33$\frac{1}{3}$ rpm.

"Astronomy Domine," track 1 on Pink Floyd, *Piper at the Gates of Dawn*, released in 1967, Tower ST 5093, 33$\frac{1}{3}$ rpm.

"Astronomy," track 8 on Blue Öyster Cult, *Secret Treaties*, released in 1974, Columbia, KC 32858, 33$\frac{1}{3}$ rpm.

"Automatic Lover," track 1 on Dee D. Jackson, *Cosmic Curves*, released in 1978, Jupiter 26 451 XOT, 33$\frac{1}{3}$ rpm.

"Backwater," track 2 on Brian Eno, *Before and After Science*, released in 1977, Island ILPS 9478, 33$\frac{1}{3}$ rpm.

"Ballrooms of Mars," track 11 on T. Rex, *The Slider*, released in 1972, Reprise MS 2095, 33$\frac{1}{3}$ rpm.

"Bicycle Race," track 4 on Queen, *Jazz*, released in 1978, Elektra 6E-166, 33$\frac{1}{3}$ rpm.

"Big Brother," track 10 on David Bowie, *Diamond Dogs*, released in 1974, RCA APL 0576, 33$\frac{1}{3}$ rpm.

"Bionic Unit," track 5 on Spirit, *Future Games*, released in 1977, Mercury SRM-1-1133, 33$\frac{1}{3}$ rpm.

"Birdland," track 4 on Patti Smith, *Horses*, released in 1975, Arista, AL 6066, 33$\frac{1}{3}$ rpm.

"Black Holes in the Sky," track 3 on Labelle, *Phoenix*, released in 1975, Epic PE 33579, 33$\frac{1}{3}$ rpm.

"C.T.A.-102," track 3 on The Byrds, *Younger Than Yesterday*, released in 1967, Columbia CS 9442, 33$\frac{1}{3}$ rpm.

"Come Sail Away," track 4 on Styx, *The Grand Illusion*, released in 1977, A&M SP-4637, 33$\frac{1}{3}$ rpm.

"Complete Control," track 1 on the Clash, "Complete Control" b/w "The City of the Dead," released in 1977, CBS 5664, 45 rpm.

"Crystal City," track 8 on Steve Hillage, *Green*, released in 1978, Virgin V 2098, $33^{1}/3$ rpm.

"Cygnet Committee," track 5 on David Bowie, *David Bowie*, released in 1969, Philips SBL 7912, $33^{1}/3$ rpm.

"Dan Dare (Pilot of the Future)," track 2 on Elton John, *Rock of the Westies*, released in 1975, MCA 2163, $33^{1}/3$ rpm.

"Dancing Machine," track 4 on the Jackson 5, *Dancing Machine*, released in 1974, Motown, M6-780S1, $33^{1}/3$ rpm.

"Dark Vader," track 6 on Instant Funk, *Instant Funk*, released in 1979, Salsoul SA 8513, $33^{1}/3$ rpm.

"Day the World Turned Day-Glo, The," track 12 on X-Ray Spex, *Germfree Adolescents*, released in 1978, EMI International INS 3023, $33^{1}/3$ rpm.

"Do the Robot," track 1 on The Family, "Do the Robot" b/w "Do the Robot (Instrumental)," released in 1972, North Bay NB-304, 45 rpm.

"Don't Stop 'Til You Get Enough," track 1 on Michael Jackson, *Off the Wall*, released in 1979, Epic FE 35745, $33^{1}/3$ rpm.

"E.T.I. (Extra Terrestrial Intelligence)," track 4 on Blue Öyster Cult, *Agents of Fortune*, released in 1976, Columbia PC 34164, $33^{1}/3$ rpm.

"Earth," track 1 on Smile, "Earth" b/w "Step on Me," released in 1969, Mercury 72977, 45 rpm.

"Electric Robot," track 2 on Harvey Scales, "(Leave It for the) Trashman" b/w "Electric Robot," released in 1974, Cadet Concept CC 7029, 45 rpm.

"Electron Romance," track 5 on Strontium 90, *Police Academy*, released in 1997, Ark 21 186 810 003 2, CD.

"Engineers," track 10 on Gary Numan, *The Pleasure Principle*, released in 1979, Atco SD 38-120, $33^{1}/3$ rpm.

"Escape from Planet Earth," track 4 on The Continental Four, *Dream World*, released in 1972, Jay-Walking JWL 1020, $33^{1}/3$ rpm.

"Fantastic Voyage," track 1 on David Bowie, *Lodger*, released in 1979, RCA Victor AQL1-3254, $33^{1}/3$ rpm.

"Five Years," track 1 on David Bowie, *The Rise and Fall of Ziggy Stardust and the Spiders from Mars*, released in 1972, RCA Victor LSP-4702, $33^{1}/3$ rpm.

"Flaming Telepaths," track 7 on Blue Öyster Cult, *Secret Treaties*, released in 1974, Columbia, KC 32858, $33^{1}/3$ rpm.

"Flying Saucer's Daughter," track 9 on Alex Harvey, *The Joker Is Wild*, released in 1972, Metronome MLP 15429, $33^{1}/3$ rpm.

"For the Dead in Space," track 2 on Tom Rapp, *Stardancer*, released in 1972, Blue Thumb BTS-44, $33^{1}/3$ rpm.

"Frequency 7," track 2 on Visage, "Tar" b/w "Frequency 7," released in 1979, Radar ADA 48, 45 rpm.

"From the Sun to the World," track 4 on Electric Light Orchestra, *ELO 2*, released in 1973, United Artists UA-LA040-F, $33^{1}/3$ rpm.

"Funky Space Reincarnation, A," track 11 on Marvin Gaye, *Here, My Dear*, released in 1978, Tamla T 364LP2, 33 1/3 rpm.

"Future City," track 2 on Eloy, *Inside*, released in 1973, Janus JLS 3062, 33 1/3 rpm.

"Future Legend," track 1 on David Bowie, *Diamond Dogs*, released in 1974, RCA APL 0576, 33 1/3 rpm.

"Future/Now," track 5 on the MC5, *High Times*, released in 1971, Atlantic SD 8285, 33 1/3 rpm.

"Genetic Engineering," track 7 on X-Ray Spex, *Germfree Adolescents*, released in 1978, EMI International INS 3023, 33 1/3 rpm.

"Hallo Spaceboy," track 6 on David Bowie, *Outside*, released in 1995, Virgin 7243 8 40711 2 7, CD.

"Here He Comes," track 6 on Brian Eno, *Before and After Science*, released in 1977, Island ILPS 9478, 33 1/3 rpm.

"Hijack," track 6 on Paul Kantner, *Blows Against the Empire*, released in 1970, RCA Victor LSP-4448, 33 1/3 rpm.

"Holding Together," track 12 on Paul Kantner and Grace Slick, *Sunfighter*, Grunt FTR-1002, 33 1/3 rpm.

"House Burning Down," track 14 on the Jimi Hendrix Experience, *Electric Ladyland*, released in 1968, Reprise, RS 6307, 33 1/3 rpm.

"How Much Longer," track 1 on Alternative TV, "How Much Longer" b/w "You Bastard," released in 1977, Deptford Fun City DFC 002, 45 rpm.

"Hyperdrive," track 8 on Jefferson Starship, *Dragon Fly*, released in 1974, Grunt BXL1-0717, 33 1/3 rpm.

"I Hear a New World," track 1 on Joe Meek, *I Hear a New World (Part 1)* EP, released in 1960, Triumph RGX ST5000, 45 rpm.

"Ice Age," track 2 on Joy Division, *Still*, released in 1981, Factory FACT 40, 33 1/3 rpm.

"In the Year 2525," track 1 on Zager and Evans, *2525 (Exordium and Terminus)*, released in 1969, RCA Victor LSP-4214, 33 1/3 rpm.

"It's the New Thing," track 1 on the Fall, "It's the New Thing" b/w "Various Times," released in 1978, Superior Viaduct SV108, 45 rpm.

"Jean Genie, The," track 9 on David Bowie, *Aladdin Sane*, released in 1973, RCA Victor LSP-4852, 33 1/3 rpm.

"Jet Silver and the Dolls of Venus," track 3 on Be-Bop Deluxe, *Axe Victim*, released in 1974, Harvest SM-11689, 33 1/3 rpm.

"Jupiter," track 3 on Earth, Wind & Fire, *All 'N All*, released in 1977, Columbia JC 34905, 33 1/3 rpm.

"Just for a Moment," track 10 on Ultravox, *Systems of Romance*, released in 1978, Antilles AN-7069, 33 1/3 rpm.

"Land of Nobody," track 1 on Eloy, *Inside*, released in 1973, Janus JLS 3062, 33 1/3 rpm.

"Life in the Air Age," track 7 on Be-Bop Deluxe, *Sunburst Finish*, released in 1976,

Harvest SPRO-8485, 33¹/3 rpm.

"Listen to the Sirens," track 1 on Tubeway Army, *Tubeway Army*, released in 1978, Beggars Banquet BEGA 4, 33¹/3 rpm.

"Machine Messiah," track 1 on Yes, *Drama*, released in 1980, Atlantic SD 16019, 33¹/3 rpm.

"Man-Machine, The," track 6 on Kraftwerk, *The Man-Machine*, released in 1978, Capitol SW-11728, 33¹/3 rpm.

"Master of the Universe," track 3 on Hawkwind, *X in Search of Space*, released in 1971, United Artists UAG 29202, 33¹/3 rpm.

"Mau Mau (Amerikon)," track 1 on Paul Kantner, *Blows Against the Empire*, released in 1970, RCA Victor LSP-4448, 33¹/3 rpm.

"Mechanical Man," track 1 on Devo, *Mechanical Man* EP, released in 1978, Elevator NICE 1, 45 rpm.

"Memory of a Free Festival," track 10 on David Bowie, *David Bowie*, released in 1969, Philips SBL 7912, 33¹/3 rpm.

"Metal Monster," track 4 on Arthur Brown's Kingdom Come, *Galactic Zoo Dossier*, Polydor 2310-130, 33¹/3 rpm.

"Mommy, What's a Funkadelic?," track 1 on Funkadelic, *Funkadelic*, released in 1970, Westbound WB 2000, 33¹/3 rpm.

"Moonage Daydream," track 3 on David Bowie, *The Rise and Fall of Ziggy Stardust and the Spiders from Mars*, released in 1972, RCA Victor LSP-4702, 33¹/3 rpm.

"Mothership Connection (Star Child)," track 2 on Parliament, *Mothership Connection*, released in 1975, Casablanca NBLP 7022, 33¹/3 rpm.

"Mr. Roboto," track 3 on Styx, *Kilroy Was Here*, released in 1983, A&M SP-3734, 33¹/3 rpm.

"Nightflight to Venus," track 1 on Boney M., *Nightflight to Venus*, released in 1978, Atlantic SD 361945, 33¹/3 rpm.

"Nightmare City," track 4 on the Sensational Alex Harvey Band, *Rock Drill*, released in 1978, Mountain TOPS 114, 33¹/3 rpm.

"Oh! You Pretty Things," track 2 on David Bowie, *Hunky Dory*, released in 1971, RCA Victor LSP-4623, 33¹/3 rpm.

"On Our Way to Hana," track 1 on Mu, "On Our Way to Hana" b/w "Too Naked for Demetrius," released in 1973, Mu MS-103-A, 45 rpm.

"P. Funk (Wants to Get Funked Up)," track 1 on Parliament, *Mothership Connection*, released in 1975, Casablanca, NBLP 7022, 33¹/3 rpm.

"Pioneers Over c.," track 5 on Van Der Graaf Generator, *H to He Who Am the Only One*, released in 1970, Dunhill DS 50097, 33¹/3 rpm.

"Planet Queen," track 7 on T. Rex, *Electric Warrior*, released in 1971, Reprise RS 6466, 33¹/3 rpm.

"Program Me," track 4 on Bruce Haack, *The Electric Lucifer*, released in 1970, Columbia CS 9991, 33¹/3 rpm.

"Prologue," track 1 on Parliament, *Gloryhallastoopid (Pin the Tail on the Funky)*, released in 1979, Casablanca NBLP 7195, 33¹/3 rpm.

"Radar Bug," track 6 on Punishment of Luxury, *Laughing Academy*, released in 1979, United Artists UAG 30258, 33¹/3 rpm.

"Rapture," track 8 on Blondie, *Autoamerican*, released in 1980, Chrysalis CHE 1290, 33¹/3 rpm.

"Red Shift," track 5 on Peter Hammill, *The Silent Corner and the Empty Stage*, released in 1974, Charisma CAS 1083, 33¹/3 rpm.

"Rock and Roll Island," track 7 on Jefferson Airplane, *Bark*, released in 1971, Grunt FTR-1001, 33¹/3 rpm.

"Rocket Man," track 5 on Elton John, *Honky Château*, released in 1972, Uni 93135, 33¹/3 rpm.

"Rocket Man," track 3 on Pearls Before Swine, *The Use of Ashes*, released in 1970, Reprise RS 6405, 33¹/3 rpm.

"Rocket Roll," track 1 on FM, *Surveillance*, released in 1979, Arista AB 4246, 33¹/3 rpm.

"Rok It to the Moon," track 2 on The Stranglers, "5 Minutes" b/w "Rok It to the Moon," released in 1978, United Artists UP 36350, 45 rpm.

"Saturn," track 18 on Stevie Wonder, *Songs in the Key of Life*, released in 1976, Tamla T13-340C2, 33¹/3 rpm.

"Saucer Surfing," track 6 on Steve Hillage, *Motivation Radio*, released in 1977, Atlantic SD 19144, 33¹/3 rpm.

"Saviour Machine," track 6 on David Bowie, *The Man Who Sold the World*, released in 1970, Mercury, SR-61325, 33¹/3 rpm.

"Sirens of Titan," track 2 on Al Stewart, *Modern Times*, released in 1975, Janus JXS 7012, 33¹/3 rpm.

"Smart Patrol/Mr. DNA," track 12 on Devo, *Duty Now for the Future*, released in 1979, Warner Bros. BSK 3337, 33¹/3 rpm.

"So Long Ago, So Clear," track 2 on Vangelis, *Heaven and Hell*, released in 1975, RCA Victor LPL1-5110, 33¹/3 rpm.

"Song of the Death Machine," track 11 on Bruce Haack, *The Electric Lucifer*, released in 1970, Columbia CS 9991, 33¹/3 rpm.

"Sonic Attack," track 14 on Hawkwind, *Space Ritual*, released in 1973, United Artists UA-LA120-H2, 33¹/3 rpm.

"Space Ace," track 2 on Brett Smiley, "Va Va Va Voom" b/w "Space Ace," released in 1974, Anchor ANC 1004, 45 rpm.

"Space Age," track 2 on the Jimmy Castor Bunch, *E-Man Groovin'*, released in 1976, Atlantic SD 18186, 33¹/3 rpm.

"Space Cowboy," track 7 on the Steve Miller Band, *Brave New World*, released in 1969, Capitol SKAO-184, 33¹/3 rpm.

"Space Flight," track 1 on I-Roy/Jerry Lewis, "Space Flight" b/w "Burning Wire," released in 1973, Attack ATT-8050, 45 rpm.

"Space Girl Blues," track 5 on Devo, *Mechanical Man* EP, released in 1978, Elevator NICE 1, 45 rpm.

"Space Junk," track 4 on Devo, *Q: Are We Not Men? A: We Are Devo!*, released in 1978, Warner Bros. BSK 3239, 33^1/3 rpm.

"Space Machine," track 5 on the Undisputed Truth, *Smokin'*, released in 1979, Whitfield WHK 3202, 33^1/3 rpm.

"Space Oddity," track 1 on David Bowie, *David Bowie*, released in 1969, Philips SBL 7912, 33^1/3 rpm.

"Space Plucks," track 2 on Arthur Brown's Kingdom Come, *Galactic Zoo Dossier*, Polydor 2310-130, 33^1/3 rpm.

"Space Talk," track 7 on Asha Puthli, *The Devil Is Loose*, released in 1976, CBS S 81443, 33^1/3 rpm.

"Space Truckin'," track 7 on Deep Purple, *Machine Head*, released in 1972, Warner Bros. BS 2607, 33^1/3 rpm.

"Spacer," track 1 on Sheila and B. Devotion, "Spacer" b/w "Don't Go," released in 1979, Carrere DM 4811, 45 rpm.

"St. Elmo's Fire," track 3 on Brian Eno, *Another Green World*, released in 1975, Island ILPS 9351, 33^1/3 rpm.

"Star," track 7 on David Bowie, *The Rise and Fall of Ziggy Stardust and the Spiders from Mars*, released in 1972, RCA Victor LSP-4702, 33^1/3 rpm.

"Stargazer," track 5 on Rainbow, *Rainbow Rising*, released in 1976, Polydor 2391 224, 33^1/3 rpm.

"Stargazers," track 5 on Khan, *Space Shanty*, released in 1972, Deram SDL-R 11, 33^1/3 rpm.

"Starman," track 4 on David Bowie, *The Rise and Fall of Ziggy Stardust and the Spiders from Mars*, released in 1972, RCA Victor LSP-4702, 33^1/3 rpm.

"Starsailor," track 7 on Tim Buckley, *Starsailor*, released in 1970, Warner Bros. WS 1881, 33^1/3 rpm.

"Starship," track 10 on Paul Kantner, *Blows Against the Empire*, released in 1970, RCA Victor LSP-4448, 33^1/3 rpm.

"Starship," track 8 on the MC5, *Kick Out the Jams*, released in 1969, Elektra EKS 74042, 33^1/3 rpm.

"Steel and You," track 7 on Tubeway Army, *Tubeway Army*, released in 1978, Beggars Banquet BEGA 4, 33^1/3 rpm.

"Strange World," track 6 on Iron Maiden, *Iron Maiden*, released in 1980, Harvest ST 12094, 33^{1}/3 rpm.

"Subhuman," track 2 on Blue Öyster Cult, *Secret Treaties*, released in 1974, Columbia, KC 32858, 33^{1}/3 rpm.

"Take Me to Your Disco," track 5 on Splendor, *Splendor*, released in 1979, Columbia JC 35798, 33^{1}/3 rpm.

"This Time Tomorrow," track 8 on the Kinks, *Lola Versus Powerman and the Moneygoround, Part One*, released in 1970, Reprise RS-6423, 33^{1}/3 rpm.

"Triad," track 3 on Jefferson Airplane, *Crown of Creation*, released in 1968, RCA Victor LSP-4058, 33^{1}/3 rpm.

"TVC15," track 4 on David Bowie, *Station to Station*, released in 1976, RCA Victor APL1-1327, 33^{1}/3 rpm.

"U.F.O.," track 1 on Curtis Knight, "U.F.O." b/w "U.F.O.," released in 1979, Golden Sphinx GSX 003, 45 rpm.

"UFO's," track 3 on the Undisputed Truth, *Cosmic Truth*, released in 1975, Gordy G6-970S1, 33^{1}/3 rpm.

"Unfunky UFO," track 3 on Parliament, *Mothership Connection*, released in 1975, Casablanca NBLP 7022, 33^{1}/3 rpm.

"Universe," track 3 on T. Rex, *Dandy in the Underworld*, released in 1977, T. Rex BLN 5005, 33^{1}/3 rpm.

"Video Killed the Radio Star," track 1 on the Buggles, "Video Killed the Radio Star" b/w "Kid Dynamo," released in 1979, Island IS 49114, 45 rpm.

"We Are Hungry Men," track 6 on David Bowie, *David Bowie*, released in 1967, Deram DES 18003, 33^{1}/3 rpm.

"What Is Soul," track 7 on Funkadelic, *Funkadelic*, released in 1970, Westbound WB 2000, 33^{1}/3 rpm.

"Which Way Do I Disco," track 6 on Fuzzy Haskins, *A Whole Nother Thang*, released in 1976, Westbound W-229, 33^{1}/3 rpm.

"White Car," track 2 on Yes, *Drama*, released in 1980, Atlantic SD 16019, 33^{1}/3 rpm.

"Workshop of the Telescopes," track 9 on Blue Öyster Cult, *Blue Öyster Cult*, released in 1972, Columbia KC 31063, 33^{1}/3 rpm.

INDEX